Farming to *Pharmacy*

Memories of a Sharecropper's Son

Farming to *Pharmacy*

Memories of a Sharecropper's Son

Truman Lastinger

Alpharetta, GA

The author has tried to recreate events, locations, and conversations from his memories of them. In some instances, names and identifying details have been changed to protect the privacy of individuals.

The opinions expressed in this book are those of Truman Lastinger and are based upon information and data obtained from his fifty years as a licensed pharmacist. Opinions in this book are provided for historical purposes only and are not intended as a substitute for the medical advice of a competent and knowledgeable physician. The reader should always consult a trusted physician in matters relating to his/her health and particularly with respect to any condition that may require immediate medical attention. The information provided in this book should not be construed as personal medical advice or instruction. Self-diagnosis and self-treatment are not recommended and may indeed be dangerous. Readers who fail to consult competent, trusted physicians assume the risk of any injuries or illness.

ISBN: 978-1-61005-545-1

10 9 8 7 6 5 4 3 2   1 2 2 3 1 4

Printed in the United States of America

∞This paper meets the requirements of ANSI/NISO Z39.48-1992 (Permanence of Paper)

This book is dedicated to my wife Rosalind; without her help and persistence it would not have been possible for me to achieve the degree of success that I have attained. She has been steadfast in believing in me and in what I could accomplish. I am forever grateful and am very proud to have her as a wife and helpmate.

A Sharecropper's Son

A tribute to Travis Hiram Lastinger in honor of Truman Lastinger

When Daddy was eight, Grandma said he was able
To work and put food on the dinner table.
His pa was still alive and at home
But he couldn't leave hard liquor alone.
Daddy was a farmer most of his life,
He started sharecropping when Mama became his wife.
When crops are bad we move away,
When the crops are good the boss lets us stay.
We have a small garden, which feeds us five,
That and Mama's biscuits keep us alive.
Collard greens and grits taste okay,
But a piece of fried chicken would sure make my day.
The President says that he'll pay
Road workers fifty cents a day.
A sharecropper don't get no pay,
Just a place to work and a place to stay.
Daddy turns the hot dirt with a plow,
I'm old enough to help him now.
The roadmen haul dirt with mules and sandpans;
Like Daddy, they sweat and have callused hands.

We crop the tobacco row by row,
Each day we watch the dirt road grow.
I marvel at the men on the W.P.A.
Getting rich off Mr. Roosevelt's fifty cents a day.
Daddy got mad at Jabo, our mule,
He hit him in the head with an iron tool.
Jabo can still pull the plow,
But he has only one eye now.
Daddy got saved in the woods one day,
He fell down on his knees to pray.
He prayed that God's healing hand
Would make him into a better man.
Daddy never learned how to read or write
So Mama takes down the Bible at night.
She reads Daddy's favorite stories
About Jesus and all his glories.
We sit and listen before we pray,
And thank God for our blessings this day.
Mama blows out the kerosene light
And Daddy tells us children goodnight.

By Rosalind Monk Lastinger

Table of Contents

Part IV: Truman's Drugs, Inc.

Part V: Life Around the Pharmacy

Memories of a Lastinger

always knew that my name was Truman. I don't remember getting here, I just was. It seemed right that I had a mother. I accepted the presence of my father and my sister immediately. I was what most people called a "yard young'un" when I found out that I had another name—Lastinger. That didn't mean a whole lot to me then, but it has become part of me and I would not change it for anything in the world. All of my early memories and most of my later ones seem to revolve around this name. Many of the people who had input into what I have become also wear this name.

I was born in rural South Georgia during the recovery stage of the Great Depression. I was privileged to witness rural South Georgia pull itself out of the throes of the Great Depression with the end of World War II and with the advent of the Rural Electrification Associations that electrified rural South Georgia. The changes that occurred during my generation probably have been the most astounding to occur to any one generation in history.

We were sharecroppers (tenant farmers). Sharecropping was a way of life that coexisted with and then replaced slave labor in the South. Will Rogers wrote in 1927 that the poorest class of people in this country is the sharecropper. He is in debt from one crop to the next to the storekeeper or the landowner. He never has a dollar that he can call his own.

1

Being born in 1937 to a sharecropper did not lend itself to getting a college education. Sharecroppers existed with and then replaced slavery after the Civil War. The only thing the sharecropper had was a mule and a little furniture. His family literally existed at the whim of the landowner.

Sharecropping was itself replaced by the advent of machinery. We made our living by the sweat of our brows. To say that cash money was scarce is an understatement. It was practically nonexistent. We lived and worked on farms throughout Colquitt County. At the end of each year, the farm owners would sell the crops, and they often didn't produce enough money to have any left over for the sharecropper. If the landowner liked your work, he would make you stay another year to get out of debt to him. Quite often, we would move to another farm and the process repeated itself.

We grew and raised just about everything we needed. What we couldn't raise or grow, we bartered for with the things that we could. Our social life consisted primarily of church meetings and was augmented by farm-oriented gatherings, which was work made into social gatherings. Just to name a few, we had hog killings, cane grindings, and peanut shellings whereby most of the adjoining families came together and worked jointly to make life a little more worth living.

We had no idea how poor we were because all our contemporaries were in the same condition. In order to realize you are a have-not, you have to be aware of the haves, and there were not any haves in our community.

At fifteen years of age, I got tired of working on farms and went to town, Moultrie, Georgia, to see if I could find a job. Most local folks called this "working for the public." I went almost all the way around the courthouse square going into every office and store. I got hired in the fourth drug store I went into. They needed a soda jerk so the owner told me to see his wife. She asked me to write down my name and the name of the store. When she saw she could read my writing, she told him to hire me.

There were six drug stores around that square, and they served about twenty-five thousand people. Every one of the stores seemed to be doing a good business and everyone had a lunch hour. After a week or so in the soda fountain, the boss told me to come into the back of the store and put me to pouring up and labeling wets and measuring and labeling drys.

It was here that I discovered some peculiar names for drugs. Acetylated salicylic acid (aspirin), phenylazodiamino pyridine (pyridium), acetylated para-aminophenol (APAP, which became Tylenol), to name some that caught my eye and I was hooked on pharmacy.

Memories are wonderful things. You cannot see them, touch them, or even count them. They all come together to form a basis for who you are. Memories of hearing an automobile coming and running to the road just to see it and see if you knew who was in it, hearing an airplane and looking for it and watching it in amazement, finding a bag of flour on the front porch one morning and being thankful and wondering who knew how badly you needed it, and awakening on Christmas morning to find some candy and clothes and maybe a toy. Many more memories are very special when you finally take the time to reflect on the past.

Memory is not necessarily my strong point, but I have to depend real heavily on it in trying to recall some of my earlier years. I am sure some of my kin and friends as well as my associates will remember some of these events somewhat differently than I do; however, I am going to try to portray them like I remember them.

Part I:
A Sharecropper's Life

Chapter 1:
My Family, Our World

My family unit consisted of Daddy (Travis), Mama (Susie), a sister (Altis), myself, and a brother (Roswell).

The first house I remember living in was the house on the hill on the Lower Meigs Road next to the Little Ochlocknee River just east of New Bethel Church. In most of these older houses, the kitchen was built separately from the main house and quite often was connected by a catwalk or porch. When we lived there, the kitchen was no longer used as a kitchen because Daddy put the wood stove in one of the back bedrooms and converted it to a kitchen.

In the old kitchen, Daddy was raising a bunch of young chickens. They were about four to five weeks old when a real bad storm came along. That storm rattled the windows and blew doors open and in general shook that house. When the wind died down and we could check, the kitchen and all the biddies were gone. We found tin from the roof and rafters scattered across the field and down in the woods by the river. We found about ten to fifteen of the biddies, losing the other 280.

Gone was the first cash crop for the year that I can remember. Sharecroppers always tried to increase their income by having something that was their own and would not have to be shared with the landowner. Sometimes it was a couple of acres of watermelons or cantaloupes or just about anything that could be converted to cash, like chickens.

While we were living here, Daddy had a mule named Jabo. Jabo was blind in the left eye and easily spooked. One Sunday, Mama hitched Jabo up to the wagon (the wagon was a farm wagon with a plank laid across the bodies for a seat). She loaded us up to go to church. Daddy couldn't go that day because he was running the heat on the tobacco barn (cooking a load of tobacco). As we were going down the hill towards the river, a rabbit ran across the road in front of old Jabo. Jabo spooked and ran hard to his right straight across the ditch and up the steep bank to the fence and then stopped. That bank was a good thirty feet high, and when stopped, the wagon was literally hanging down. Mama and us children slid out the back of the wagon, seat and all. We were a little dirty from the red clay. Mama couldn't climb the bank to get Jabo and the wagon down, so she had to bundle us up, go back to the house, and get Daddy to go get the wagon and old Jabo out of his mess. Jabo was like a member of the family.

One day Daddy decided maybe Altis and I could ride old Jabo. He put Altis on and led the mule around until I pitched enough of a fit to ride that he took Altis off and led the mule up to the side of the porch for me to get on. Remember I said that mule spooked easily? His knees happened to brush against the porch and he immediately began to buck and jump. To say I was scared is a terrible understatement. Daddy had the mule by the head and calmed him down fast, but I had had enough. He tried to convince me to stay on and have my ride, but once again, I pitched enough of a fit he relented and took me off. I never did get to ride that mule.

A short while later while Daddy was plowing, Jabo spooked at something and tore up a couple of rows of corn Daddy was plowing. Daddy didn't put up with stupidity, and he always kept a claw hammer on the plow stock to tighten or loosen or clean the plow point. He grabbed his hammer and the mule bridle and hit old Jabo right between the eyes with the hammer. He had done this before and managed to get the mule's attention, but this time he hit him a little too hard and old Jabo fell dead as a rock right there in the field.

A sharecropper with just a mule could make out but a sharecropper without a mule was in trouble. Daddy managed to borrow a mule to finish that crop with and it took the whole year's work just to replace Jabo.

While we lived there, I saw the WPA (one of President Roosevelt's public work programs to put people to work during the Depression) in action. One of the jobs created was building a new bridge over the Little Ochlocknee River. We lived at the top of the hill by the river. It is hard to describe; however, there must have been over 150 people working on that job. Men with picks and shovels and mules and sand pans worked from sunup to sundown. There was a big circle of men and mules going from the top of the hill to the approaches to the bridge moving dirt with the sand pans. They would scoop a pan full at the top of the hill, drag it to the bottom, dump it, and go back for another pan full. Men at the top were working with picks to loosen the clay and dirt so they could scrape it up, and men at the bottom were working with shovels, leveling it out for packing. Men were packing it with cross ties stood on end. They would pick up the cross tie and drop it on the dirt to pack it. Other crews were cutting timbers and dragging them to the river to build the trusses.

It was an experience that lives in my memory. The bridge had planks laid crossways the length of the bridge. Then there were three sets of planks laid endways across the bridge. The two outside runners were for the wheels of the wagons or cars to travel on and the middle one was for the mule or horse to walk on. When it was finished, it was over one hundred yards long. I was very proud of the new bridge.

When we lived on what I call the bank's place, Daddy was bathing in an old well across from the house that all my uncles enjoyed bathing in when he cut his foot real bad. The well was lined with an old stainless steel culvert, and when he jumped in, he landed on the edge thereby cutting his foot. That cut gaped open and just wouldn't heal properly. It was a terrible wound and the first time I had ever seen proud flesh. Grandma said that the moon was in the wrong phase was why the thing wouldn't heal properly. The injury was bad enough that he couldn't farm. Uncle Troy, Uncle Eulia, Uncle Elvah, and Uncle Andy, his brothers, pitched in and helped us that summer.

Grandma Maggie, Daddy's mother, lived in the big house at the end of the lane with Aunt Ouida, Uncle Elvah, and Uncle Andy. We lived in the house down the road halfway to the creek. Uncle Eulia and Aunt Theresa lived in the house nearer the creek. To my recollection, Uncle Troy and Aunt Evelyn lived in the big house with Grandma.

Grandma had a large farm bell outside her kitchen, and when dinnertime came, she rang it. If you have never heard a dinner bell, you have missed something. Aunt Zuleika and her sons, Weldon and Newell, lived with us at that time, for Uncle Maston was in service. Weldon and I were sure enough yard young'uns. We got into most everything that was not nailed down.

Daddy always had a yard full of chickens and ducks. He also had water and feed troughs sitting all over the yard. Mama had the customary wash pot in the yard with all the washtubs. Ice was a scarcity as I remember it, and we didn't have too much of this luxury. Sure enough it froze good one night, and Weldon and I found plenty of ice the next morning. Yep, it was in the chicken troughs, in the wash pot, and tubs where Mama had Roswell's diapers soaking. We are living proof that filth won't necessarily do you in and if everyone must ingest so much of it in a lifetime, we got our share.

As I mentioned, Daddy had some ducks. That spring when a new brood hatched, we had some of the prettiest little yellow ducklings you ever saw. As some of you know, a little duck or chicken is not the easiest thing in the world to catch. Weldon and I were up to it. We caught two apiece and headed to the creek. The creek ran across the road and was crossed by a low wooden bridge, a perfect place for a young'un to drop a small duck in and watch him swim to the side where he could be picked up and carried back for a return performance. We hadn't been in britches all that long. House young'uns wore a little shift or gown. So now in our britches we were expected to know that a little duck's feathers were different from a big duck's. After fifteen or twenty trips from the bridge to the bank, those little ducks were so waterlogged that we had trouble getting them out of the water. We were old enough to know that we were in trouble, so we carried them home and put them under the front doorstep.

To this day, I believe Newell or Altis told on us. How in the world someone could find out about the ducks under the doorstep within thirty minutes or so? Anyway, after a good switching we knew better than to try to teach little ducks to swim.

With chickens running loose in the yard, a young barefoot boy had to be careful where he stepped and quite often was not careful enough and wound up having to clean up a foot. Being inquisitive, I noticed that each pile of chicken doo had a white portion. I studied that phenomenon and one day asked Daddy what the white on chicken doo was. He said that he didn't know why it was white but that he knew that it was chicken doo too.

We always had a good time playing around the big house where Grandma lived. If we were lucky, we got to ring the dinner bell. Grandma Maggie had a big old prize Dominecker rooster. If you had chickens, you had to have a good rooster or you wouldn't have fertile eggs for new chickens. More than one rooster in a yard would lead to a good chicken fight. Daddy also had a prize rooster, a big old Rhode Island Red. No further apart than our houses were, it was inevitable that those roosters would wind up fighting. Sure enough, the big red won the fight or was winning when Grandma broke it up. His spurs left that old Dominecker with a gash on his chest about two inches long. Grandma grabbed up her rooster and ran through the house getting her sewing basket. She then ran to the back porch and laid that rooster on his back on her lap. She told me to hold his wings so she could fix him. She used a needle and some white thread and sewed him up.

That rooster lived and was still the cockiest rooster on the lane. He would in fact stroll down to our house and strut in front of big red because big red had been locked up in a pen for his indiscretion. You didn't pick on Grandma's rooster.

We had a flock of guineas and one of the first chores I had was to watch the guinea hens so we could find their nest to get the eggs. Guineas are a very wild type of chicken. They hide their nests in fencerows overgrown with weeds and in the edge of woods. They always roost high in a big old tree. When you find their nest you have to be careful in removing the eggs. You must use a long handled spoon because if they smell your scent they will abandon the nest. If you find a nest with a large number of eggs, you just leave it alone because they may be ready to hatch. I didn't find many of their nests because I was distracted by wanting to play rather than work.

One of the best times of any day was in the evening sitting on the porch, waiting for the house to cool off enough to go inside. We also had to wait for the bug spray or kerosene (used to kill or run off mosquitos) odor to die down enough to breathe inside the house. Most of the evenings, Uncle Elvah would sit on the porch of the big house and play on his banjo mandolin. We could hear him real good from our porch and to this day I can hear that mandolin ringing out clear as a bell. I think that is why I love that kind of music so much.

On Sundays after church Uncle Eulia always had a bunch of men in the community to come to his house to get a haircut on the front porch. When he was real busy, Daddy would help him and they would run two chairs. We always liked to hang around to hear the grown men talk and pass the time. We heard everything from why it was not going to rain to why President Roosevelt's New Deal was bound to fail because it didn't go far enough in helping the working class of people. It seemed to me that if Mr. Roosevelt would just listen to these men he could learn how to run the country in a hurry.

I always seemed to have a cold, and for a month or two in the fall and in the spring I always had what Uncle Eulia called a snotty nose. I never had a handkerchief handy so I tended to wipe my nose on my sleeve. Instead of having biscuits with syrup in the fall, Mama always had some baked sweet potatoes. You peeled them and walked around like it was an ice cream cone. They had a natural handle. I loved them things until one day Uncle Eulia made the comment "Truman—snot and tater is good ain't it?" For some reason, baked sweet potatoes have never tasted the same.

Uncle Eulia loved his pepper plants and always would trick me into eating some. I would wind up crying because my mouth was burning. Every time I would go to his house he would tell me that this pepper was not hot and it was cold and tasted like vanilla ice cream. He would then bite into one and smile and act like he was really enjoying it. I always seemed to cave in and bite into one and the burning would start all over again. I just didn't want to miss anything as good as ice cream.

Since Uncle Troy and his family were living in the big house with Grandma Maggie, I tended to envy Dewey, my cousin. He seemed to have an inside track to her attention. One night for some reason our family ate supper with Grandma. Dewey was sitting in Grandma's lap and that didn't help my feelings any until I noticed that she was chewing up food and putting it into his mouth. Suddenly I didn't envy him and her attention to him anymore. In fact, I figured I would rather have another one of Mama's baked sweet potatoes whether it bothered Uncle Eulia or not.

Hog killing time was something else. The weather had to be cold so the meat would not spoil before it could be processed. Most of the time, the men in community would start a fire under the scalding pot before daylight. As soon as the water got hot enough, they would begin killing the hogs and scalding them for scraping. The women would be through with breakfast clean up and would show up with their kitchen knives and pans that they would need as soon as the men had the hogs ready to cut up. Then the work started in earnest. The hams, shoulders, etc. were cut off and soaked in brine before being rubbed down good with borax. That kept the blowflies from ruining the meat. Then the meat was put in the smokehouse where a very low fire under green wood would produce the smoke. That meat stayed in there until it was cured. The women then cut up the other meat into the bacon and pieces that were used to produce the sausage, which was ground up and stuffed into the small intestines (cleaned and scraped for that purpose). The fatty part of the hog was cut up then boiled down (rendering) into lard. The result of rendering produced cracklins. One of the big treats was the cracklin bread Mama made. When butchering the hogs, Uncle Elvah and Uncle Troy always made sure to save the bladders and clean them so we children could play with them. That was my fist balloon. We always had liver for supper on hog killing day because the liver would spoil very quickly. The next morning Mama would cook the brains and scramble them in with the eggs. That was called eating high on the hog.

From the bank's place, we moved to the Autry place. This was my great grandmother's house. It was a big, old-style, unpainted house, and of all things, it had a parlor. This parlor was what we now call a living room. It was furnished with large overstuffed chairs and a sofa and she had an old Victrola in it. She kept the room locked until she had important visitors, like the preachers after church.

My great uncle Bud Autry farmed this place and he was pretty frugal. When he bought a mule that mule was his as long as he lived. He kept them in a mule pen attached to the barn. He primarily fed them fodder, which had very little nutritional value. As a consequence, those mules had eaten almost all the top boards around the pen. He had a pickup truck, and when there was a shortage of rubber for inner tubes, he packed the tires with broom straw. He kept a supply of the straw in the back of the truck because after riding on the straw for a while it would be packed down and he would have to put more into the tires.

While we lived here, it was decided that Altis needed to have her gums lanced so her teeth could grow in properly. So she made the trip to town with Daddy and Mama on Uncle Bud Autry's pickup truck. There were two roads leading to Moultrie. One was called the Upper Meigs Road and the other the Lower Post Road. When the county paved the Upper Meigs Road, Uncle Bud would not drive on the pavement because he said the pavement would wear out his tires, so he always used the Lower Post Road, which was not paved. The Autry place is a good twelve to thirteen miles from Moultrie, and Uncle Bud didn't drive very fast because he didn't want to wear out his tires.

Try to imagine my astonishment when they got home and there was Altis on the back of the truck with a nickel box of vanilla ice cream, you know the ones that come with a little wooden spoon.

Yes, there was a little of the ice cream left and she certainly enjoyed eating it in front of me. How can anyone nurse a nickel cup of ice cream for as long as she did just so I could see her eating it? She was gracious enough to allow me to lick her spoon and I can remember the vanilla taste to this day. Since I got big enough, I have tried to duplicate that feat, and to this day, I can't get ice cream to last that long even at modern day speeds in an air-conditioned auto. She did it on the back of a pickup truck going twenty to twenty-five miles an hour in the hot summertime. Of course, she always could make candy last so much longer than I could. It had to be one of the Seven Wonders of the World.

Our well was outside the kitchen across the yard, and during the summertime, Mama kept the milk jug and butter jug hanging down in the well water by strings. It was the coolest place on the farm and the iceman didn't come by but once a week. If we didn't have a nickel then we didn't get any ice that week. As I said earlier, ice was a luxury. One day, the wall in the kitchen caught fire from the hot stovepipe on the wood stove. Daddy was in the fields working when it happened. It was just lucky that the iceman pulled up right in the nick of time and helped draw water from the well and helped put out the fire. It burned a hole in the wall and scorched up that end of the house good. I often wonder that if the iceman had given up on us for not being regular customers and had quit coming, would the house have burned down? It probably would have.

At that time, I had a problem talking due to stuttering. Daddy quite often would swing by the house and draw a fresh drink of water from the well. When I saw him coming, I would run to the well asking for a drink of water. Most times it took me so long to say what I wanted he would be through drinking and ready to go back to work before he understood what I wanted. Few things tasted as good on a hot day as a fresh drawn bucket of water. Of course, the well—being a big hole in the ground—was in itself very enticing. I had been warned to stay away from the well at all times, but any growing kid couldn't resist playing around a big hole in the ground.

Sure enough, one day I got to playing with the strings holding the milk jar just swinging it back and forth. Suddenly the milk jar hit the butter jar and broke both of them. Daddy had to draw down the well a bucket full at a time to get rid of the milk and butter, and if you have never drawn down a well for cleaning, it will be hard to understand. Those things hold a lot of water. Even so, that water tasted funny from then on. I don't know if it was the butter or the switching I got, but it just wasn't the same.

That was the year my cousins Newell and Durell were helping Daddy on the farm and one day during the hot summer Newell made the statement that he could eat a whole gallon of ice cream. Durell agreed that he could too. Daddy assured them that they couldn't and they made a bargain. In order to prove they could do it they would drink a gallon of water. Daddy said if they could, he would buy them a gallon of ice cream each. Well they proceeded to try. You talk about sick. How could you have a better reason to try? I know Durell didn't finish his; however, Newell contends that he did. I don't know because when they threw up, I left. Newell may have but he made some more room for it, I guarantee you. Besides, that water probably still tasted like butter and milk.

Going to town was a real experience. It only happened once a month or every two months. Daddy would get up early, tend to the livestock, milk the cow, and then hitch the mule up to the wagon. Then we would all climb on board and head for town. It would take three to four hours to get there, so Mama had a jug of water for all to

17

have some if needed. When we got to town, we would tie the mule up as close to Holman Mule Company as we could get. They always had a watering trough out back so the mules and horses could drink. Then we would all go to the town square where on every corner and in between there were always lay preachers exhorting a crowd— mostly men because the women were off to do their shopping. Some of these preachers knew all about hellfire and brimstone, and when they got serious about it, a lot of the men would agree saying, "Amen, brother."

Most of the time, we kids would get lucky and get a Coca-Cola or an ice cream. We would pretty soon get tired and would be taken back to the wagon and rested or napped on some quilts brought along for this purpose. By mid-afternoon, we would all head back home so we could get there by dark and have time to feed the livestock and milk the cow while Mama cooked supper on the wood stove.

One afternoon, Altis and I were looking after Roswell while Mama worked in the field with Daddy. Lo and behold, we discovered that Daddy's prize rooster had wandered into the kitchen. We decided that we needed to run him outdoors so he wouldn't make a mess. We immediately closed the doors and windows. The windows in that kitchen were wooden and when we closed them and the doors it was fairly dark in there. Everybody knows that you have to catch a chicken to carry him outside and that was what we proceeded to do. That rooster proved to be very athletic and gave us a merry chase; however, we finally succeeded and carried him outside. The mess that rooster made in the kitchen was more than we could clean and straighten out before Mama came home. He had knocked down pots and pans, some bowls were on the floor, some broken, and worse of all, the chimney on the kerosene lamp was shattered. For some reason, Mama didn't believe us when we told her the rooster had done it all. She understood that the rooster was not the only one to blame, because we got a good switching and promised her that we wouldn't do that again.

If you have never seen a rolling store, you have missed a real experience. That thing was about the size of a school bus and was packed and filled with the most merchandise you can imagine. It rattled and made enough noise coming that he didn't even have to blow his horn to let you know he was there. He had practically anything in or on it that anybody might think that they wanted. From piece goods and oilcloth to plow points and well buckets, plus pots and pans. He had it all. Most of the time items were purchased by barter. That man would trade you merchandise for eggs, chickens, ham, and syrup or just about anything he felt like he could sell or trade later or possibly use himself. He even had chicken pens on top of the thing to put chickens in or to sell them out of. He had a supply of candy, and generally I could cry and carry on hard and long enough that Mama would buy or trade for a piece for me.

Farming at that time was a little different from now. In any eight to ten acre field there would be three or four men with mules turning land and getting ready for planting. Along here, I learned the difference in a doubletree and a singletree. A singletree connects the traces on one horse or mule to a wagon or plow. When you have two horses or mules, each horse or mule's singletree is in turn connected to the doubletree, which connects to the wagon or plow. I also found out what a coupling pin was for. One day while playing under the wagon hoping that Daddy would let me ride, I noticed a large pin in the front axle of the wagon. I thought it was interesting so I pulled it out to play with. When Daddy hitched the mule up to the wagon and said giddy up, the front axle went with the mule and the front end of the wagon fell to the ground. The coupling pin holds the wagon together and allows the front wheels to turn direction. Daddy had to unload the wagon in order to get it light enough to pick up so he could put the axle back under the front end.

I remember Uncle Bud Autry telling Daddy the land had been farmed out and needed fertilizer. That brought on a load of guano. Guano was a new word for me and I was very interested. It came in fifty-pound bags and had to be put in the guano distributer for application after the rows had been laid out. These bags had to be positioned in the field so that the distributer could be refilled as needed. One day, Daddy loaded the wagon and he allowed me to ride on the wagon while he threw bags off across the field. On these wagons was a little running board on the side so I stood on this and held onto the side. When the wagon started across the rows that had been laid off, it started bouncing up and down and sideways like crazy. I lost my grip on the wagon and fell down between the wheels. It was my lucky day because my head fell in between the rows and the wagon wheel ran over my head pushing me down further into the dirt. I had one heck of a headache but was all right. I never saw (before or since) Daddy so scared. Due to this accident, Altis and Roswell say I still don't act right. They are not sure, but they say that I have a permanent problem. I may be the only person in history that had their head run over by a two-horse wagon loaded with guano and lived to tell about it. When I found out guano was bird manure, it kind of let the air out of me. I had literally been run over by a wagonload of bird manure.

Aunt Zuleika, Newell, and Weldon lived there at the same time. Weldon and I spent hours just playing. There was no such thing as store-bought toys available to us so we had to make do with what was there. Our main toy was one-gallon syrup cans filled with dirt and a piece of haywire inserted through the middle of it just long enough to make a handle we could pull them with. We pulled those cans until we wore the cans out or our heels got too beat up to continue. Our other favorite was Grandma's empty milk of magnesia and swamp root bottles. We built little roads in the dirt and pushed those empty bottles for many miles calling them cars and trucks.

At that time, a postage stamp to mail a letter cost two cents and a post card only cost a penny. Our mailman was a Mr. Monk, and when Mama didn't have two cents for a letter she would leave an egg or two in the mailbox with the letter and Mr. Monk would put the stamp on. At the grocery store he would swap the eggs for cash. As it turned out, years later this Mr. Monk became Postmaster of Moultrie and my father-in-law.

Uncle Bud Autry's house was built up off the ground and we doodled for doodlebugs. We would actually fill up bottles with doodlebugs. If you don't know what a doodlebug is, I don't know if I could tell you. All I know is they are little bugs that burrow into the soft sandy dirt under a house. We used a piece of straw to stir their burrows with (usually to a chant something like "doodlebug, doodlebug, your house is on fire") until the bug came out so we could pick him up. Daddy said they ate spiders and other little bugs.

We spent hours climbing and playing in a big old tangerine tree on Uncle Bud's place. At cane grinding time, we had a ball playing on the pile of cane grindings and drinking cane juice. Everyone had an outhouse because a bathroom in the house was unheard of. In those days, we ate in the house and used the bathroom outside. How times change; now we eat outside and use the bathroom inside. One day, Uncle Bud decided to move the outhouse. Whenever the pit got full, he just dug another one and sat the outhouse over it. When he moved it, sure enough there was a hole in the ground. Remember how interesting a hole in the ground is? Weldon and I found it right away and were having a ball playing in the hole. That is until Mama found us. Talk about a bath! We got scrubbed good then scrubbed some more. Then we got a switching I didn't forget. We did learn better than to play in an old outhouse pit.

Chapter 2: School Life

I started school at Rock Hill while we lived there. I don't remember a lot about the school except that was the first time I had ever seen running water. We drew our water out of the well and had a bucket set on a bench on the back porch to keep the water in; when you wanted a drink of water you used the gourd dipper that Daddy kept hanging on a nail by the bucket. There was also a wash pan by the bucket so that you could wash your hands. At this school, if you wanted a drink of water you just squeezed the handles of a faucet and the water spouted up out of it and into a trough. You had to drink from the stream. I almost got waterlogged because that was a very amazing thing. There was a rack of faucets set on a water pipe coming up at an angle so there was one for any size kid. I had to try all of them, and sure enough, they worked.

Aunt Viola, Uncle Bud's wife, always seemed to have a big crowd for Sunday dinner. The kitchen and dining room was built separate from the house but was connected by a runway. It didn't have glass windows, only wooden shutters. In the summertime, it could get mighty hot in there and somehow the houseflies always knew when food was on the table. The shutters (windows) would be propped open and they were able to congregate freely inside. Uncle Bud had rigged up a pulley system whereby someone could stand off in one corner and pull a length of heavy twine that in turn would cause some boards to swing back and forth over the table. These boards had sheets of paper fastened to them and hung down and would effectively keep the flies from lighting on the food.

On most Sundays, there would be at least two tables full of people and sometimes three. The grown folks and visiting preachers always got to eat at the first table. That table would hold eighteen grown people. The children in those times were to be seen and not heard; therefore we were relegated to the second or third table. Aunt Viola always seemed to know that we children were very hungry and to have to wait until the second or third table to eat with the smell of all that food was almost unbearable. She would quite often fix us a syrup biscuit or give us a sweet potato to nibble on. Most of the time when we children got to the table, the best pieces of chicken were gone.

My cousins John Ed and Willy Autry and sometimes Newell Lastinger were the ones chosen to run Uncle Bud's fly flapper. I sure did envy them. I kept on pestering Willy until he finally arranged for me to run the fly flapper. That Sunday, I couldn't wait and was in position before any food was put on the table. As soon as the table began to be loaded, I started swishing flies. When all was ready, the men folk began filing in and took their places. The preacher asked for quiet and began asking the blessing. That blessing turned into a full-blown sermon or so it seemed to me. I thought that he had preached himself out at church that morning and was surprised that he still had that much left to say. They finally began eating and passing food back and forth. Here I am standing in the corner pulling that fly flapper back and forth and it was beginning to get tiresome. As I began slowing down swishing flies, Uncle Bud made it a point to catch my eye, thereby reminding me to keep going.

Those men just ate and ate and ate. I thought they would never get full. The women continued bringing food in and refilling the bowls and I began to get concerned that there would not be enough left for the second table, which most times included us children. When they finally quit eating they just sat there and carried on a conversation that I felt could have been carried on out on the front porch. I was tired of that fly flap and didn't care who knew it. When they finally got up and left, I quit and found Willy and told him that I was through. I didn't want any more to do with that thing. He got on to me and told me that I wouldn't hear any more of their gossip if I didn't run the fly flap. I told him that was all right because I hadn't heard anything that I wanted to remember anyway. He said he would see to it that I would be sure to have a regular turn with that thing. I assured him that I was through and he could do what he wanted to. I learned right then to be careful what you want, you might get it.

We moved and I went to school at Funston for the first grade. That was a big building all made of brick. That was the first brick building I remember seeing. It had a tall set of steps that I had to climb just to get inside. When I went back years later those steps were not as intimidating as I remembered. We moved again up on Doerun Road and I finished the first grade there.

Doerun Road was not paved while we lived there; in fact, as I remember it, Sylvester Highway was the only paved road going into Moultrie. It was only fourteen feet wide, not graded, and very twisted, but it was paved. Thomasville Road was paved to just outside the city limits. The county began paving Doerun Road while we lived on it. I remember Uncle Elvah having a black Ford Coupe auto, not a Model A like Uncle Troy's, but sure enough a late model auto. While they had the road torn up and prepared for grading, we had a natural mess when it rained. The clay made it very slippery. Uncle Elvah was dating our future Aunt Julia, and one day, he allowed me to ride with him on the wet road. We had a ball, especially me. I know now that he was cutting donuts and making the car spin around. At the time, I was just enjoying the ride.

While at Doerun School, I made a new friend and I'm sorry I don't recall his name, but he lived in downtown Doerun and was allowed to go home for lunch. Mama always packed our lunches, generally wrapped in brown paper from the store or old newspaper that Mama's Aunt Jody saved for her. My new friend asked me to go to his house for lunch one day and boy was I amazed. They had a white kerosene stove in the kitchen, not a wood stove, and a genuine refrigerator that made its own ice, not an icebox. We had a good dinner, but the crowning item was Jell-O for dessert. I had never even heard of Jell-O much less eaten any. At our house, meals consisted of mostly vegetables with some meat occasionally. Quite often, there was only tomato gravy with flour in it to thicken it. There were many suppers with Clabber milk and corn bread. If we had chicken, it meant that we had to catch one out of the yard, clean it, and prepare it for cooking. I always thought we had a lot of collard greens and turnips because Mama liked them. I had now been introduced to Jell-O and still like it—even though it still shakes like it is nervous when I eat it.

I discovered coal at Doerun School. They had a big coal bin behind the school and my new friend and I played in the bin all during recess. Naturally, we had to start throwing the small pieces at little girls. Sure enough, we got a spanking when one piece of coal hit its mark. We were black as smut and when the teacher's paddle hit us a cloud of black dust boiled up. As soon as I got home, Mama whipped me again and worse than the teacher did. I got scrubbed good in the number two washtub full of cold water, but then Mama got to thinking about it and, when I got out, she whipped me again. So much for playing in a coal bin and throwing coal at girls.

Little boys and trains just naturally have an affinity for each other. I had never been close enough to a train to examine the thing much less ride on one. I had heard them at night from way off and they seemed both mournful and powerful. The Georgia Northern Railroad came by Sigsbee about a half mile in front of the house, and I could see the train as it went by. It had to cross the road about a mile down between us and town, and when it approached the crossing that engineer laid hard on that whistle. What a wonderful sound! An amazing thing was also on that track—a single car passenger train. It was a passenger car with an engine built in and could be driven from either end so that it didn't have to turn around at the end of the line. It ran from Albany through Moultrie to Thomasville, and you could get on there at Sigsbee, go to Moultrie, and then catch the thing on the return trip back home. I am sure that the thing had a proper name, but I only ever heard it called "the dummy." I remember riding the dummy only one time and enjoyed it thoroughly, but they charged money to ride and money was scarce in our family.

At the crossroad was a grocery story operated by a Mr. Smith. That was where Mama and Daddy got their staples during the year. They would charge them to the landowner who would pay the bill; at the end of the year, when the crops were sold, he would settle up with Daddy. We had to walk from the house to the store to catch the school bus and would get off there in the evening to walk back home. One evening when I got off the bus, one of my friends talked me into going into the store and getting an ice cream cone and charging it to Daddy. I surely enjoyed that ice cream, but when Daddy found out what I had done, he tore me up. Most of the time when it was time to check up at the end of the year, there was not enough money to pay all the bills for the year and Daddy had to stay another year to try to get out of debt.

I had been in three schools so far in the first grade and had learned a lot. At least I had heard a lot, such as there is no Santa Claus; so, I was having my doubts. Altis would not comment on the situation. We had our tree up and decorated. We brought some colored construction paper and glue home from school and made garland for the tree and cut out stars. Mama popped some popcorn and we sewed the kernels together into a strand for roping. We put these and some ornaments Mama had on the tree. When we got through, we had what I thought was a real pretty tree.

It so happened we had a Christmas program at Rose of Sharon Church on Christmas Eve. The church was half a mile from the house, so we walked instead of hitching up the mule and wagon. On the way back from church, about two hundred yards from home, Daddy stopped suddenly and yelled that somebody was at the house and broke out running real hard. Altis, Roswell, and I took out right on his heels. Mama couldn't run but she walked fast. We all got to the house and everything seemed all right to Daddy so we went in. Right there under the tree was some peppermint candy, apples and oranges, and assorted nuts. Daddy said what he heard must have been Santa Claus and he must have left when we surprised him. He said he sure hoped he would have time to come back and finish his job. He was awful busy and might not make it. That was one of the most awful nights I have ever spent. He might not come back! I don't know about Altis, but I sure exercised my Christian upbringing that night. I even promised myself I would never doubt his existence ever again and would not even listen to anybody who said or believed otherwise. Imagine my relief when the next morning there was the rest of Christmas. I was true to my promises and did not question that incident until I was grown. I found out many years later that Daddy had Uncle Troy come by and set the stage. Talk about child abuse, I think I am still scarred.

Chapter 3: Mama's Family

Our rooster got killed that year, so Daddy rounded up some fertile eggs and borrowed an incubator to hatch them with. If he had had some money, he could have ordered baby chicks through the post office. We needed some new chickens and that was a good way to get a new rooster. Daddy put a lot of importance in his eggs and was very particular to rotate them when they should be rotated. One day he had to be away and he left very strict instructions for Mama to turn those eggs. When he got home that night, he checked the eggs and decided that Mama hadn't turned them properly. I had never seen an argument between Mama and Daddy, and before that night was over, I never wanted to experience another one. I already knew that Daddy had a temper—I learned that Mama also had one. In fact, if Mama was threatened or scared, she was a tiger. She could and did use language that would embarrass a longshoreman. I had no idea where she learned some of the words that she used that night because I had never heard anything like that before in my life. I think she blistered the corn crop in a five-acre area right around the house. Can you imagine what might have happened if that corn had been popcorn? It had boiled down to her bundling me, Altis, and Roswell up to leave and her telling Daddy exactly what he could do with those eggs. To my great relief, everything settled down and nobody got killed. I found out later where she learned some of the words she used that night.

Grandpa Holland (Mama's daddy) lived in Lakeland, Florida, and wanted Mama to come down to visit him so he sent her tickets on the Trailways bus. She packed us kids up and we were off on quite an adventure. The Japanese had bombed Pearl Harbor (wherever that was) and killed a lot of American servicemen and President Roosevelt had declared war on Japan. The Trailways bus was loaded with servicemen of all branches, so we were crowded on the trip. Most of the time one of the servicemen held Roswell for Mama. Altis and I had to share a seat most of the way. That bus would stop at any little crossroad, pick up passengers, and let some off anywhere they wanted off. When we would get into the bus terminals quite often we would have to change busses and the loudspeaker blared out the bus numbers and their routes. I had never been outside of Colquitt County, Georgia, and when they announced the names of the towns we were going to, I was impressed. Names like Jacksonville, Cross City, Old Town, Ocala, Gainesville, Tampa, St. Petersburg, and Lakeland blaring out over those speakers made me feel very much like I imagine young children feel on their first trip to Disneyland now.

We arrived in Lakeland and were met at the station by Grandpa Holland. He carried us out into the county to a little town called Kathleen where he lived and operated a barbershop. When she was two years old, Mama's mama died in the great flu epidemic, and so mama was raised by her Grandma Autry in Colquitt County, Georgia. Grandpa Holland's wife was my step-grandmother. Her name was Grandma Vera, and she was a very jolly person— optimistic and quick to laugh. They had indoor plumbing, the first indoor bathroom I had ever seen—complete with commode, lavatory, and bathtub. Roswell and I were put into the bathtub that night for our bath with hot running water. We had a ball for a while. My stomach was upset and when I had the urge to relieve myself I didn't know that I could get out and use the commode so I just yelled for Mama. She didn't hear me and before anybody got to me I had to go. Grandma Vera got there first and looked and yelled "g-- d--- Susie (Mama's name), don't you teach your children anything? One of them just s--- in the bath tub." Right then, I made the connection as to where Mama had learned some of the language she had used earlier. I also discovered that Grandpa had a good command of that kind of language too.

Around then was the first time I remember hearing a radio. One of our neighbors had a large floor model that ran off a tray of flashlight batteries and had a long strand of haywire running out across the yard on poles for an antenna. Batteries cost money so they didn't play that radio very often, mostly on Saturday nights to hear the Grand Ole Opry. When I first heard that thing it blew my mind. How in the world could little bitty people fit in that thing and sound so loud and so good? I looked in the little window by the dial trying to peek inside to see them. Daddy and Altis explained to me that they were not inside but were in Nashville, Tennessee. How could anybody believe that? Anyway, one night the batteries went dead so they pulled the neighbor's Model A Ford up close to the house and played the radio off the car battery.

Early that spring, our neighbor across the road got a tractor to farm with—the first one I had ever seen. It was awesome, having metal wheels with cleats on them. We had about two weeks of rain, and sure enough, one Sunday morning he bogged that thing down in the field across the road. He came over and asked Daddy to hitch up the mules and help him drag it out, but Daddy told him he would on Monday but not on a Sunday. He told him that was probably why it bogged down in the first place, he just didn't have any business working on Sunday.

That summer we moved again, about half a mile down the side road that connected the Doerun Road to the Arrow-S Club Road. Believe it or not, we had electricity. There were no outlets to plug anything into, but that didn't bother us. We didn't have anything to plug in anyway. We had electric lights hanging down from the ceiling in every room in the house. We had it made. No more cleaning globes for the kerosene lamps and we could actually see. The biggest problem I remember was trying to find the string hanging down in the middle of the room at night to switch them on.

Grandpa Tom Holland, Mama's daddy, came to see us and, lo and behold, he brought along a small radio for Altis. It was about ten inches square and made of celluloid, but it made just as much noise as that large floor model the neighbor had. We had just joined the now generation.

That summer Great-grandpa Simpson, Grandma Maggie's daddy, spent a couple of weeks with us. I don't remember a lot about him, but I liked him. He always wore his long-sleeved white shirt, buttoned to the collar, and a hat. He spent most of his time in the backyard under a shade tree sitting in a straight chair. He told us tales of when he was a boy and what he had done and where he had been in the Civil War. I sure wish I had written them down. Shucks, I couldn't write anyway. I had only finished the first grade, though I could print *Truman*.

Chapter 4:
The Yearly Toil of a Sharecropper's Family

Newell spent that summer with us helping Daddy farm. That was quite a summer. Everybody in the family had to help, and we all had chores that we were expected to do. Being rather young, I wanted to do the things that I was not old enough to do. I remember Daddy letting me weed peanuts. The mule did all the work and all I had to do was guide the weeder. It didn't take me long to figure out it was easier to ride the weeder than to walk and guide it. Daddy got all over me about that. It took me a while to figure out how he knew I was riding. Obviously, when you ride you don't leave footprints; also you manage to kill a few peanut plants when the weeder got off-center.

Daddy got through with his chores and came to relieve me from the peanut weeder. I looked around for a good tree to climb. I had always liked to climb and had a few accidents in the chinaberry tree in our backyard when the limbs would break. Nothing serious, just bumped up pretty good. I learned not to cry because Mama would get onto me for climbing in trees. That day I saw, at the end of the field, a big tree just made for climbing. If I climbed the fence and stood on the post, I could reach the bottom limb. I immediately climbed right on up to the top of that tree. I sat up there and enjoyed the view, swaying back and forth until I got tired and decided to climb down and do something else for a while. When I got back down to the limb that I had originally climbed up on, I discovered I couldn't reach the top of the fence. I tried and tried and finally realized I was trapped up that tree. I looked around and realized that Daddy was still out in the field plowing so I started yelling for him.

Daddy just kept plowing and I thought he couldn't hear me. I could see myself left up that tree all night and I knew Mama insisted I be home by dark no matter what I was doing. I kept trying to reach that fence post so I could get down but I just couldn't do it. I began to cry because I knew that I was destined to sit in that tree until I got too weak and fell out. The fall would surely kill me.

Finally, Daddy came back to this side of the field working and hollered at me that he would be over in just a few minutes. I couldn't believe my good fortune. When he got close he told me to just walk out onto the limb, it would gradually bend down to the ground, and I could then get off. I assured him that if I did that the limb would break and I would then fall. He laughed and said that the tree was a black gum and it would bend a lot further before it would break. Even so, I couldn't get up the nerve to crawl out. He walked over and pulled the limb down to the ground and told me to come on down. I sure was relieved to be out of that tree and I have never been stuck up a tree since.

A typical year for us started in January. We always had our routine chores. We had to feed and water the livestock in the mornings. These consisted of the mules, cows, hogs, and chickens. It always amazed me how much water this took. We had to draw the water from the well by hand using a bucket and tekle. A tekle is a pulley the rope was on to help draw up a bucket of water. The cows had to be milked and the eggs had to be collected. This normally was done early, usually before daylight, so we would be ready for work as soon as we ate breakfast. By daylight, we were ready to go to the fields. In the evening before dark, we had to do this all over again plus get enough wood in the house for Mama's cookstove and for the fireplace.

We had to pull up all last year's cotton stalks and burn them. We didn't just cut them down because they would sprout and grow next year, but these plants would not produce enough new cotton The ashes produced would help nourish the land for next year's crops. Our next job was to clean out the fencerows by removing the weeds that grow up during the summer. Some of those rail fences were hard to clean. We had to use axes as well as hoes.

Then we would head to the woods with the crosscut saw and cut wood for the summer. We cut pine into stovewood lengths and split it for Mama. I wasn't nearly as big as Daddy; however, it took two people to use a crosscut saw. Daddy would pull the saw, and with his arms longer than mine, I had to walk back and forth as we pulled the thing. I would get a little tired and bear down on the handle and he would get onto me for riding the saw. He said all I had to do was pull it and it would do the work. When the saw began to stick and get hard to pull, he would take the saw out and sprinkle kerosene on it. I thought that he was greasing it, now I know that the kerosene would dissolve the pine tar on the blade so it would slide again. This woodcutting had to be done early enough for the stovewood to dry out good because Mama didn't like to cook with green wood.

We then cut oak or hardwood for use in the fireplace and heating the wash pot. This wood went to replenish the woodpile. Then we cut enough wood to cook the flue-cured tobacco during the summer. This work would really heat you up and Daddy said we cut wood in the winter so it would warm you up twice: once when you cut it and again when you burned it.

Then, still in January, we would begin breaking land. This was done with mules and turning plows. The dirt was literally turned over to a depth of about six inches. As soon as we finished that we would level the land with harrows, which would break the clods into a good workable layer of dirt on top. Now was time to plant tobacco. The seed was planted in a bed of finely worked ground by broadcasting them by hand, then the bed was covered with thin cotton sheets to keep them from freezing. The little plants would sprout and grow under these sheets until time to transplant them into the fields.

Next, Daddy would begin laying off rows for the corn crop. By February, we were ready to plant corn. It was planted two kernels to the hill and eighteen to twenty inches apart. The seed was dropped by hand because Daddy didn't own a corn planter. He did have a guano distributor though and that saved a lot of time. That thing dropped about a tablespoonful of guano at every place he wanted a plant then we would drop the seed with the guano. He would then cover the seed with a scrape using the mule. We planted about twenty to thirty acres like this every year.

In March as soon as the corn was in the ground, and usually in April we began planting peanuts. The peanut seeds were dropped every four to six inches because the seed was not as predictable as corn and he had to be sure to get a good stand. Later on, we would take the hoes and thin the plants out enough so that the remaining plants had room to produce all they could.

As soon as the peanuts were in the ground, we began planting cotton. The cottonseed was planted two to three inches apart in rows because these seeds were also not as predictable as corn. And once again they later had to be thinned out with a hoe to get a good stand with room to grow.

Then we began transplanting tobacco. Usually by now, we were just about past having a hard frost. We spent the evening in the tobacco bed pulling up plants about six inches tall and bundling them in twenty-five to forty plant bundles. The next morning after chores, we headed to the tobacco patch. Daddy already had the rows laid off, filled up fifty-gallon drums with water, and placed them along the rows so that we could have plenty of water for the plants. The water was drawn from the well by hand and moved to the field on sleds using the mule. Daddy had informed me that my job this year was to be the water boy. I was excited and could hardly wait. After about one hour I began to realize that this was work too but I couldn't quit until the planting was done. The tobacco transplanter was a tube of metal about as big around as a stovepipe and two- to two-and-one-half-feet high. It had a chamber down front to drop the plants in. The plants would go to the bottom and, when the trigger was pulled, the tip opened up and the plant fell into the hole that it had made in the row. The trigger also released a little less than a cup full of water from the gallon-sized reservoir in the planter. My job was to keep the reservoir filled with water so the planting could move right along. That thing needed a gallon of water about every twenty-five plants, so it was obvious to me that I would be running for a while. It took lots of plants to plant four acres. Daddy ran the planter and Mama and Altis swapped off dropping the plants for him. Roswell's job was to keep them supplied with plenty of plants. By the time we got through transplanting that tobacco patch, I sure didn't want to be a water boy again. That gallon bucket I was using got heavier every time I filled it with water.

As soon as the tobacco was in the ground, Daddy began sharpening hoes. Each one of us had his own personal hoe, and we got to be good friends with it before the summer was over. The corn, cotton, and peanuts were up by now and the primary weeding job was done with the hoe. The corn had to be hoed until it got big enough to be plowed with the mule and scrape. The cotton had to be chopped.

Right here I learned the difference between chopping and hoeing cotton. When chopping cotton, you thin the hills out leaving enough room for the remaining plants to grow, when you hoe cotton you remove the weeds. The peanuts had to be chopped and weeded with the hoe also. In addition to all this hoeing, Mama made sure that the yard at the house was always hoed. If a sprig of grass showed up in the yard she would have us hoe the whole yard then sweep the yard with a yard broom. Usually during the winter Daddy and I would hitch up the mule and wagon and go to the river and haul in a load of river sand to spread in the front yard so that we wouldn't have a mud hole at the front steps during the winter.

In early spring, we had put in our vegetable garden near the house and it was beginning to produce. We had peas, beans, squash, potatoes, and okra coming in now and our dinner table had a bigger variety. We had laid the corn by late April into May, and the corn was coming in. Now we had fresh corn also.

It didn't take long for the corn to get too hard to eat as fresh corn so then we had roasting ears for a while. As soon as the leaves on the corn stalks began to turn yellow, Daddy began pulling fodder. We would pull the leaves off the corn stalk and tie them in armload bundles then stack them into the attic at the mule barn for mule feed during the winter. When the corn dried out, we had to pull it and store it in a corncrib. As soon as we got a break from work we then shelled a good bit of corn and went to the gristmill to have it ground into meal. This ensured that we could have cornbread for a long while. After a while, the cornmeal began having beetles hatch in it, so Mama had to sift the meal to get rid of them. I enjoyed going to the grist mills because they were built on a creek or small river that had been dammed up. The water then went over a spillway and turned a water wheel, which powered the grinding stones. The ponds created were a natural place for a young boy to play in or skip rocks on— even do some fishing.

One of my chores was feeding the mule. You cannot feed a mule only corn for long before he founders. He must have some roughage. The only pasture we had was the wooded areas around the fields and the cows and hogs pretty well kept the grass ate up. Since we didn't have a way to cut hay and bale it, we used fodder. The only hay we had was peanut hay when the peanuts were picked and that was not usually enough to go through the winter. I know now that fodder is not very good food for a mule because in remembering those times, the top of the boards around the mule pen were always chewed up pretty good. I know those mules had to be hungry to eat wood.

In May, the tobacco was up pretty high and had to be suckered regularly to ensure that the leaves on the stalks received all the available nutrients to grow well. When it began to bloom, we had to break the blooms off to keep the plants growing as much as they could.

One summer, I remember seeing POWs working in the fields with us. All the ones I remember were Germans. I had been hearing about those bad Germans for quite a while and was quite anxious for our safety. As it turned out, they were very much like us except they couldn't speak English very well. As I remember, they worked hard and didn't cause any trouble. One of them really took a liking to Roswell and gave him candy and spoiled him in general. At the time, I felt that Roswell was already spoiled enough and didn't need any help from the Germans.

When the peanuts matured, we had a grand time. We had to split poles and build frames to stack the peanuts on so they could dry. Then the peanuts were plowed up with a turning plow so the roots with the peanuts were above ground. We then had to come along after the dirt dried and pick them up and shake the dirt off the peanuts. Then they were transferred to the frames for stacking. They had to be stacked just so with the nuts inside and the plants tilted down on the outside so that when it rained the water could run off without wetting the peanuts.

The peanuts stayed there on the stacks to dry until the peanut thrasher came to the neighborhood. Then the peanuts were thrashed and the plants were bailed into peanut hay to supplement the mules and cows over the winter.

As I said, Newell spent that summer with us and brought along his bicycle. I had a heck of a time of it, but I learned to ride a bicycle that summer. Newell made it look so easy I could hardly stand it. I would stand on the pedal and push with the other foot like riding a scooter but I couldn't get the hang of it until Weldon spent a weekend with us and he could ride it. He didn't ride it conventionally because he wasn't tall enough to reach the pedals over the crossbar. He stuck one leg across to the other side under the crossbar and rode the thing anywhere he wanted to go. As I said, he looked peculiar but he was riding it. That was all I needed. If Weldon could do it, I could. After a bunch of scrapes and bruises, I mastered that thing. Boy was I proud of me. Lot of good it did me, I didn't have a bicycle and was not to have one for a while.

That spring Altis got a new Sunday dress, a pretty pink frilly thing. She was really proud of that dress until we went to Uncle Troy's house. He lived up the road around the corner past Grandma Lastinger. As soon as he saw her in her new dress, her name became "Panky," Uncle Troy for Pinky. Her new name tickled me and I teased her, but it wasn't long before I forgot her new name.

Uncle Troy had some goats. He had also built a little cart and used the goats to pull it. Alda and Dewey (my first cousins) suddenly had the equivalent to a Cadillac. I could hardly wait until it was my turn to be pulled up the road toward Grandma's house. Finally, my turn came and boy was I in high cotton. Then the goat decided he had gone far enough and would just eat grass. I got out of the cart and tried to turn him around to go back to Uncle Troy's house. That goat got aggravated with me and butted me down into the ditch and continued butting. I figured he was trying to kill me and I ought to let somebody know. When you are in a fix like that you yell. I apparently did a good job because Uncle Troy came running and pulled the goat off me. Needless to say, I lost all interest in riding in the goat cart and haven't cared too much for goats since.

As I remember, it was about that time when Mama got her first driving lesson. Uncle Troy had his Model A Ford and I think that it was the one Mama learned to drive in. Anyway, we wound up at Smith's store where Mama had to pick up some stuff and when she got back into the car she put it into reverse and hit the gas. Up to now, she only had to go forward and had done a fairly good job. When she hit the gas in reverse, she apparently forgot all her lessons because she couldn't stop that thing. She made a great big circle in front of Mr. Smith's store and would have kept going except that she dead centered the outhouse—and that stopped her. There was no damage to Uncle Troy's car because of the spring steel bumpers and there was very little damage to the outhouse, but Mama's nerves were damaged pretty good. She got out of that thing and would not get back in it to drive and Uncle Troy had to come get his car and drive it home.

Everybody who has ever been a young one knows that nothing beats going swimming in the summertime. That is the only time you can get a small one in the water without threatening him with his life. I still don't like bathing on the back porch in a number two washtub with the whole world watching, even if it has sat in the evening sun so that the chill is off. We didn't know what a swimming pool was; however, everybody knew what a swimming hole was. It was just a wide spot in a creek or river usually with a sandbar on one side that made a natural beach. Just such a place was on the creek where the Arrow-S Club was, about a mile from where we lived. Bathing suits were about as scarce as swimming pools, and if Mama allowed it, we could go swimming in our overalls. If overalls were out then we had to go down the creek to the next wide area where we could swim and play without the benefit of clothes, also known as the jaybird hole.

I remember well one Sunday when Uncle Maston (Daddy's brother who married Mama's Aunt Zuleika) came to visit us with Newell and Weldon. We all got to go to the swimming hole. We even got to wear our overalls. I couldn't swim any more than I could ride that bicycle I was telling about earlier. I wasn't the least bit afraid of the water as long as it wasn't above knee high. If it got up to my heinie then I began to get nervous. Anything deeper than that was just too much. Uncle Maston had brought along an inner tube and decided that all us young'uns needed to learn how to dive. Newell did real well. He would just dive right through that thing. Weldon didn't much want to so Uncle Maston threw him through a couple of times before he began to get the hang of it.

Diving through that inner tube was just not my cup of tea. That meant your head had to go underwater and I already knew what a nose full of water could do to you. I just couldn't breathe underwater and I knew it. Yes, I wanted to swim, but I sure didn't want to dive. I sneaked away, went down to the jaybird hole, and proceeded to play and swim my way with the fellows down there. I thought I had it made until Uncle Maston had me by the leg and arm. Yep, it was my time. He carried me back up that creek to the swimming hole not even minding me yelling at the top of my voice. I thought that maybe he had gone deaf. That experience put off my learning to swim by at least three years, but that is a different story. He threw me at that inner tube at least three times before he finally decided I really didn't want to learn how to dive.

Fishing is every boy's dream come true. Daddy sure liked it and he would let me go with him every time Mama said it was all right. Mama always liked fresh fish. We would go to the creek or the river late in the evening after chores were done and use set hooks and fishing poles and striking irons just like everybody else did. Daddy never used a fish trap. He just wouldn't allow it. I remember he built one and used it in the river behind Uncle Bud's place, but he said it wasn't very sporting and he destroyed it. He used a striking iron. That is a long flat piece of metal kind of like a sword. He also made one for Roswell and me. In the summertime, fish will sleep (he called it) in the shallow water close to the edge of the bank. When the moon is right, you can use a lantern to see them and walk right up to them and strike them across the back and pick them up.

Weldon, Roswell, and I used to sneak off and go fishing. We would cut our own poles and use tobacco twine for line and, quite often, we made our own hooks out of Mama's safety pins. Sinkers were something else. That twine just would not sink into the water without sinkers. Weldon and I solved that problem. We climbed up on the barn and took the lead off the nail heads on the roof. While we were up there we got enough to last so we wouldn't have to climb right back up. We had it made, that is, until the first good rain. Daddy climbed up to find out why the roof was leaking. He had to go to town and get new nails with lead on them, climb up, pull the old nails out and replace them. It is not true that a whipping loosens a kid's skin so he will grow. I would be at least eighteen feet tall, but I did learn not to strip lead off the nails on the roof.

We were in the middle of World War II and there were shortages of a lot of items that people depended on. You couldn't get tires or tubes for automobiles, and while that didn't affect us too much, it sure did Uncle Bud Autry. He couldn't get tubes for his truck tires so one day he had all us children go to the broom sage field and cut him up a supply of broom straw to pack in his tires. It is amazing how much straw you can pack in one tire. This worked pretty good, but every fifteen to twenty miles he had to take off the tires and stuff some more straw in them. Gasoline was in short supply and rationed for five gallons each auto. Some people were using kerosene mixed in with gasoline in their cars instead of just gasoline. They didn't run very well on kerosene, but if you got one going it did the job. You could not even buy sugar at all for a while and when some became available, Mama got a ration book somewhere and took us kids to town to get some. We went to the A & P store in downtown Moultrie and got in line. Altis and I were big enough so we were handed a ration stamp and enough money to buy a five-pound bag of sugar. We got in line behind Mama and each bought a bag of sugar. I had never spent a nickel in a store in my life and here I was in the big time. Boy did I feel important. Daddy needed some shoes and found that the only ones available were some cloth shoes. They didn't last very long but everything was being used in the war effort. Everybody was encouraged to buy war bonds. These bonds started at ten cents, and the stamp issued was kept in a small book, like S & H green stamps were later.

I think, while we lived at Sigsbee, Daddy got his notice from the draft board to report for induction. We were in a terrible fix. I have never seen Mama so worried. The government was scraping the bottom of the barrel and all able-bodied men were called up. I know it was a mixed blessing, but Daddy was sent home because he didn't pass the physical. Right then Daddy quit sharecropping. After finishing that crop, he got a job at Potts Dairy Farm so that's where we moved next.

Part II:
Moving Up in the World

Chapter 5:
Our Daily Life

That was the first house that I remember us living in that had paint on it. In fact, a lot of the houses we lived in didn't have glass windows, just wooden shutters. Some didn't have ceilings in them. Quite often, there was no doorknob. The latch on the front doors was a board latch on the inside. When you went outside you let the drawstring hang on the outside through a hole. At night, you used the latch and kept the drawstring inside to prevent someone from coming in. This was a neat little white house set back off the road at Potts Dairy. The only thing wrong with it was that the people who had lived there before us had a bunch of cats and they had a bunch of kittens that were allowed to run wild. You just can't live in a house with eight or nine wild half-grown cats. It became my job to catch them. I won't go into it but it took a while and a bunch of scratches to get rid of those cats.

While we lived there we had to walk down to the highway to meet the school bus. A boy who lived there on the highway, I think his name was Mashburn, had a little dog that he had trained to do tricks. It sure made waiting on the bus more tolerable. That dog would wear a pair of sunglasses and hold a pipe in his mouth while walking on his hind legs. I had never seen anything like it. Uncle Troy had trained his dogs to catch hogs and Uncle Maston had trained his to round up the cows but neither one could wear sunglasses and smoke a pipe.

While we lived at Potts dairy, we went to school at Okapilco. I don't remember much about that place. The main thing I remember was that we could pick up pecans during recess to pay for our lunch. I didn't necessarily like picking up the pecans but I sure did enjoy eating in the lunchroom. This was the first school where each child had an individual desk. They were metal and wood and had an inkwell on the top. Apparently, many kids had used them in the past because initials were carved in some of them.

Daddy agreed to work for Mr. Duncan Sinclair on his dairy. This led to three movings while waiting for the big house on Mr. Sinclair's dairy to be available. First, we moved to a house behind Minissee Railroad Station out in the middle of nowhere. It was off the Shade Murphy Road and we were back to no electricity, wooden shutters instead of glass windows, and no ceilings again. We didn't live here long before we moved down on the Quitman Highway to run Sinclair's dairy farm. So off we moved again. This time into a small wooden two-story camp house next to the dairy until the people who had been running the place could find a job and move out of the big house. This little camp house was built next to a pond and we had a water supply straight from the pond. A water pipe ran out into the pond and we had a hand pump in the kitchen to pump water with. That was well and good; however, the pump was a little old and the water would leak back down and would not pump water unless you poured some water into it to prime the pump. Even so, this beat having to draw water from a well with a bucket and tekle. This was the first two-story house I had ever been in and I sure enjoyed it. The little narrow stairwell was very steep and I didn't like it as much after I fell down it one morning. I also might add this house also had no electricity. We were back to the kerosene lamps again.

The big day finally came and we moved into the big house on the dairy. It was a mansion with three bedrooms, a living room, a dining room, and a kitchen with large front and back porch, but still no indoor bathroom. I should add it had the most marvelous contraption I could imagine—a telephone. It was a wall type with a crank on it. Our number was one long ring and two short ones. We were on a party line and everybody had different ring types. If it was for someone else you could pick up and listen to their conversation. It didn't take long for me to discover that was not the thing to do; just two spankings. We turned the crank to get the operator and told her who we wanted to call and she would ring them up for us. I didn't know anybody who had a phone so I would sneak in and ring it to hear the operator say number please. I enjoyed that until she called Mama and told her to keep me away from the telephone. One good tearing up and I didn't like that telephone nearly as much as I thought I did.

That dairy farm was quite a place for a young'un in the third grade. It had the milk barn where we milked the cows, a large feed barn to store feed in, and a large tin barn to store hay for mixing into cow feed. It also had a large pond on it. We lived there for seven years and I guess I will always think of it as home.

We moved there after the school year started and that was quite traumatic. The first morning the teacher had me come to the front of the room and write my full name on the blackboard in front of the whole class. I proceeded to print my name and she stopped me and told me to write it. Bingo, I was introduced to cursive writing. I had no idea how to do that. She said she would have to remedy that but to print my name so I printed Clarence Truman Lastinger. I was immediately branded Clarence and it took me three or four years to get most of those kids to call me Truman. It helped some when Harry S. Truman became president after Roosevelt died. But some still call me Clarence. That was when I learned that I was named after Daddy's brother,

Clarence Lastinger, and Mama's brother, Truman Holland. Both these people died in childhood, and when I found that out I was a little worried, I was still a child.

That school was Culbertson School and it was brand-new. In fact, it was not finished yet and some workmen still were working on it. That in itself got me into some trouble. We had to walk about a half mile to catch the bus to school. Our bus got to school first and then the bus went back out for another load. We were the last load to be picked up for the ride home. That meant we had some time to play and entertain ourselves while waiting on the bus. One afternoon I discovered a vat of cement the workmen had been using that was still wet and was in need of using. It didn't take me long to find a good use for it. I gathered up a supply of it and went completely around the school packing it into the door locks. The principal lived on the backside of the schoolyard about two hundred yards away. Every morning he walked over swinging his keys on his key chain. That next morning I was certainly watching him. He marched up to the door and tried to put his key in and it wouldn't go. He bent down and looked but the key still wouldn't work. He went completely around that school trying all the doors and none of the locks worked. There were six main doors not counting the big auditorium doors. He finally busted out a window and sent a kid in to open the doors from the inside. They still wouldn't work. He finally had to get a crowbar and break into school that morning. Needless to say, because of this we had chapel that morning. He eliminated the girls right off and sent them to class. Then he started eliminating boys one by one. When he got to me I had to confess. I won't go into detail but I thought I had been detailed before he was through with me. Then he carried me home to Mama. That was worse. The bad thing was Daddy had to pay for all new locks and repairs on the building, and I had to work and pay Daddy back. Do you have any idea how long it takes to pay that kind of bill out of an allowance of twenty-five cents a week? I obviously had more chores assigned to me.

Around every dairy farm there is always a bunch of cats. What with the spilled milk and mice and rats after the cow feed—it is what could be called cat heaven. We always had plenty of them. One day I caught two yearling cats and tied their tails together. They fought and scratched some then just sat down so I draped them over Mamas clothesline. A clothesline was a necessity and every time you moved you had to take it down and set it back up at your new house. Those cats hung on the clothesline for a short while then began to howl and fight—boy was fur flying. Mama got an earful and came on the run. When she saw what was causing the racket, she broke a peach tree limb and went to work on me. I don't know which was loudest me or the cats. She was so mad she made me take the cats down and untie them the hard way. Nope, I couldn't take down the clothesline; I had to take those cats off the line by hand. I'm not sure which looked or felt worse—my hands and arms or my behind, all were raw.

As far back as I can remember Mama had suffered from asthma. When she had an attack we all had to suffer the consequences. She smoked Asthmador cigarettes and inhaled burning green mountain asthma powders. That odor could and did permeate the house. There is no way I can describe the odor, but it was a lot worse than rutabagas being cooked inside. When I was small, I had had diphtheria and subsequently wheezed a lot. Mama decided that I also had asthma and accordingly treated me quite vigorously for it. In the past, I sneaked some of Daddy's tobacco and tried to smoke like he did and got torn up for it. Now she decided that I had to smoke her Asthmador cigarettes. If you have ever been sick off tobacco, just imagine how sick you can get from that asthma mixture. She would pour out a little pile of the green mountain asthma powders in a dish and light it with a match. When it began smoking good, I had to hold my head over it and inhale the smoke. To make sure I got a good dose she would drape a sheet over my head to form a tent so that none of the good stuff could escape. When we used up all her powders, she carried me out to the back of the garden next to the branch head and found some jimson weed plants. We would pick up the dead leaves and mix in some green ones, which she ground up into a powder. From this powder, she rolled us some cigarettes. After trying to smoke that stuff I assured her that she had cured my asthma completely and I made sure that I didn't wheeze in front of her anymore.

There always seemed to be a home remedy for most any ailment. At times, we were made to wear an asafoetida bag around our necks to ward off measles, mumps, pneumonia, etc. I don't think it worked very well but most of my friends tended to stay away from me. When we did get sick we quite often wound up with a pine tar poultice applied to our chest. This was supposed to draw out the poisons and help with our breathing. During the polio epidemic, everyone was advised not to go to the pool. I didn't have to worry because we couldn't go anyway. The pool was in town and we had no way to get there. We were also advised to avoid crowds. That made me a little leery because there was always a crowd at church. Mama always made us go to church. I didn't get polio, but I later met some schoolmates who had.

One summer Uncle Maston visited with Newell and Weldon and brought along a bunch of firecrackers. That was a new experience. We had a real good time. We also got in trouble again. Weldon, Roswell, and I got inside the feed barn and proceeded to burst some. They made a lot more noise inside the building and the smoke kind of hung heavier inside. It was a lot more exciting until we noticed we had set some of the feedbags on fire. Yep, the feedbags set the barn on fire. The water hose in the milk barn just was not long enough to put the fire out so we went to carrying water in the feed buckets. We managed to put the fire out but not before it had burned a big hole in the floor of the barn and alerted the neighbors who alerted Daddy. Then he and Uncle Maston proceeded to put our fire out. Somehow lighting firecrackers never was as much fun anymore.

We quite often would choose sides and play baseball. The ball we used was homemade out of tobacco twine wound up real tight, and we used broomsticks or boards for bats. The only one who had a baseball glove was Newell and we thought that was great. One evening Uncle Eulia told us we could play at night as easy as we could in the daytime. All we had to do was soak the ball in kerosene and strike a match to it and we could see it in the dark. It's amazing how well that worked. You had to catch and throw the thing fast to keep it from burning yourself. We managed real well until either Roswell or Dewey held it too long and burned himself. Mama put a stop to our nighttime baseball game quickly, but not quick enough to keep us from setting the front yard on fire. It's amazing how much water and work it takes to put out a one-acre yard fire. We managed to avoid a spanking that time because it was Uncle Eulia's idea.

We kids always had a slingshot and almost always had a pocket full of rocks for ammunition. Some of us got pretty good with them. We stalked birds, rabbits, and rats all the time. Birds and squirrels were easy targets. When we had shooting contests, Uncle Troy and Daddy could always outshoot us, so we were always trying to improve our aim. I remember bagging a rabbit one Sunday. That made me feel like the great white hunter. At that time, no one in our community ate rabbits. There had been cases of rabbit fever and most people just quit taking a chance, I found out later that rabbit fever is better known as tularemia.

Quite often, when Uncle Maston would visit us Mama would let Roswell and me go home with them to spend a few days. He had a Model A Ford that he cut down into a truck and we got to ride on the back. One Sunday, Weldon, Roswell, and I were riding on the back of the truck on the way to Uncle Maston's. We were going out the Thomasville Road when we began to practice with our slingshots. Now there is no better target than a car coming toward you because the rock and the target met so much faster than if the target was sitting still. Everything was going pretty good until one car turned around and caught up to us and stopped Uncle Maston and told him what I was doing. If you ever had Uncle Maston get mad at you, you know what we were up against. I will say that I have never shot another rock or anything else at a moving car.

Spending a few days at Uncle Maston's was always fun. He was the only man I knew who wore short britches most of the time. He had a pet crow. He had catfish in his shallow well. He said it was to keep wiggle tails (mosquito larvae) out of the drinking water. He had a bunch of martin gourds right by his outhouse by the garden and it was always busy with martins. They would chirp at you when you went to the outhouse. He said they were talking to you and made up rhymes that sounded just like the birds. Our all-time favorite was "Shitty britches, shitty britches, poor old boy." I don't think that was what they were saying but it sounded like it.

When Uncle Maston was working in his fields, he always kept his water jug in the sun. He said warm or hot water was better for you when you were working than cool water was. He had built a nice barn close behind his outhouse for his mules and had a nice big corncrib in one end. We always liked to play in the corncrib because there was always a nice big pile of corn in there to climb on. One day, I was playing in there when the urge to use the outhouse struck. The outhouse was right outside the corncrib, but I thought it would be neat to just go ahead right there and proceeded. As soon as it was time to feed up that night, he stormed up to the house and demanded to know who used the corncrib for the outhouse. I knew right then that my number was up and confessed. Yep, I had to empty that corncrib completely that night and clean it up all by myself.

Across the road from his house was a patch of young pine trees all of them about fourteen to eighteen feet high. Weldon, Roswell, and I discovered that you could climb them and play Tarzan by swinging in the tops. In fact, you could make them bend over and ride them like a rocking horse. The only problem was, after you had ridden them down they would not stand back up straight. After we had rode about half of them down, Uncle Maston discovered us again. We didn't understand why everybody was so upset; however, we stopped riding his neighbor's pine trees.

During winter, time was made for cutting wood for the fireplace, wood stove, and firing the tobacco barns. Any tree struck by lightning or otherwise in distress was cut down and sawn up into appropriate lengths. This job called for a crosscut saw. Daddy and I did a lot of work with the crosscut. Once again, I would begin to bear down on my end and Daddy would tell me to quit riding the saw. He said the saw would do the work, This wood was then hauled to the backyard and piled up for the winter for year round use as stovewood. At the woodpile, the axe was the primary tool for splitting the logs into useable sizes.

Mama generally claimed Monday for washday. One Monday as usual, it was my job to fill up the wash pot for boiling the clothes and three washtubs for rinsing with fresh water. I had to make sure Mama's scrub board was clean and ready in one of the tubs, and then build a fire under the wash pot. Before you can build a fire you have to get wood. We used wood for the fireplace, cookstove, and the wash pot, so I had a good bit of experience at the woodpile.

One particular Monday, it was my good fortune to find a small green snake in the woodpile. I was in hog heaven until Altis came out with a load of clothes and fussed at me for not having the fire going good. Not liking being fussed at, especially by Altis, I chased her with the snake and managed to catch her and dropped it down the back of her dress. If you know Altis, you know she doesn't like snakes, especially down her dress. She proceeded to wake up the whole east side of Moultrie, which was five miles away. Mama finally figured out something was wrong and came on the run. It took the rest of that day for Altis to calm down and me a good switching to calm Mama down. I didn't really see what all the fuss was about and was downright put out that I was the scapegoat because a little old green snake never hurt anybody. Besides the switch, Mama used was a gallberry switch lifted right out of the yard broom and had left me in a terrible state.

I proceeded to finish building the fire and slamming things around in general. I slammed the wrong thing. A necessary part of using the wash pot was the battling block and battling stick. The battling stick was an oak pole about four feet long that we stirred the clothes in the wash pot with and dipped them out with. We used it to beat the clothes on the battling block. About the time the water got hot, I slammed the battling stick into the wash pot a little too hard and burst the bottom out of the wash pot. All that water hitting a good hot fire creates quite a lot of steam. In fact, it looked like a locomotive had exploded in the backyard. Right then I didn't want to have to tell Mama I had done that to her wash pot. That wash pot was a necessity for our living. Mama not only washed clothes in it she made lye soap in it and, at hog killing time, it was used to render the lard. With all the steam and smoke in the yard, she checked it out immediately. By the time she got through with me that yard broom had seen its better days, and I was sure I would have to eat standing up the rest of my life—that is, if I were ever to be allowed to eat again.

Church was always a big part of Mama's life, and you can bet I found a way to get in trouble there too. Early on when we had dinner on the grounds it was usually after three or four preachers dwelling on hellfire and brimstone and it seemed they were always looking at me. I had a pretty good idea of what hellfire was, but I had absolutely no concept of what brimstone was. I was sure it must be pretty bad. When we had dinner on the grounds most of the women spent Saturday and early Sunday morning cooking and preparing food to carry. Mama made real good deviled eggs and I loved them dearly. She had some that Sunday. After all the preaching the meal was put out on the makeshift tables under the shade trees outside. Then the preachers had to bless the food and did so almost as long as they had preached.

That table of food was very impressive to me because I remembered well the many times when there was not enough on our table to feed our family properly. Mama had cooked the chicken heads and feet and we ate everything but the feathers and innards. I had seen Daddy crack the long bones from the chicken with his teeth to get to the marrow so he could eat it also. Our family got in line like everybody else, but we were right behind one of the visiting preachers. Mama was filling mine and Roswell's plates with the stuff we asked for. When we got to her deviled eggs, I knew I wanted some but I couldn't remember what to call them. The only thing I could remember was that the name was bad like in devil, but that wouldn't come to mind so I told Mama very loudly that I wanted some of the damned eggs. Bingo, I found out what brimstone was. Yep, it was bad.

Chapter 6:
Moving Up in the World

When Daddy started working for twenty-five dollars a week at the dairy farm, our family had moved a step up from sharecropping to a steady income type work. It was still a seven-day-a-week job. I knew we were better off though because Daddy bought a 1931 Model A Ford. Man, how excited can a young boy get? It sure beat riding around on a one-horse wagon. It was black and had two doors with a self-starter. The only problem with the starter was the thing would not work, so Daddy had to crank it with a hand crank. Right then I thought I was as good as anybody in the world. It didn't bother me one bit that it was already fifteen years old. Daddy also bought Mama a new stove, a kerosene stove. If you have never had to split and tote wood for a wood stove, you just don't realize what a step up that was. I still had to keep the kerosene replenished for her but that was lots better than splitting and toting stovewood. Mama never did like green stovewood or wet stovewood so the kerosene eliminated a lot of my problems. About once a week I had to walk up to Bennett's grocery store and get a nickel's worth of kerosene. Bennett's was about a mile from the house and if it was raining or cold Daddy would pick up the kerosene for me.

Now that we were up in the world, we could go places at the drop of a hat. One Halloween we had a program at the school auditorium and Daddy carried us. One part was a local magician. I thought he was real good so when he asked for volunteers for part of his program I was the first one up on the stage. When he looked at me he asked me where my shoes were. I told him they were at home because I could only wear them on Sunday. He said he couldn't use me as one of his volunteers because I didn't have shoes on but he would do something else. He took me by the hand and led me to the center of the stage and announced to the audience that he was going to show them something that they would never see again. He held up a peanut for them all to see, then told me to eat it. I have never wanted to be center stage in front of an audience since.

On the way home that night, when we came to the creek, the car broke down. That creek didn't have a bridge over it, so the cars and wagons going across had to ford it. Sometimes after a big rain, Daddy would stop and walk through the creek to make sure the car could get through. I loved going through all that water. Daddy thought the car had drowned out. We had to get out and push the car out of the creek onto dry ground so Daddy could work on the car. He discovered that the car had not drowned out at all, but that the points in the distributor box had broken. Ten o'clock at night and seven miles from town is not a good place to find replacement parts for an automobile. Daddy was up to the challenge. He borrowed one of Mama's bobby pins and managed to use it get the car to run. It always seemed to me that Daddy could do anything because anytime a challenge came up, he would always rise to the occasion.

Tires and tubes were still in short supply or at least too expensive to just buy new ones any time we needed them. Whenever we went on a trip in our car, we had to have plenty of patches for the tubes. We didn't have a jack to lift the car with, so when we had a flat tire Daddy would go to any nearby fence and borrow a wooden rail off of it to use as a tire jack. He kept a block of wood in the car and would use it and the rail to lift the car. He would have Mama and us kids to sit on the rail to hold the car up while he took the tire off and patched the tube. Then he would replace the rail on the fence. I know we presented quite a picture for the people who passed us, but it just didn't seem unusual at all at the time.

Daddy was a kind and just man. He put up with me many times when I would push his patience, but when he had had enough, I always knew it. He allowed our corncob wars, our slingshot wars, and even Altis and me teasing Roswell about being a little Jap, but when I built up enough points he could untie a plow line or take off his belt as quick as anybody I have ever seen. There was only one time in my life that he tore me up when I did not deserve it. We had a family living on the dairy with two boys mine and Roswell's age. The one my age was sickly and puny, and the one Roswell's age was tough as a brick and strong as an ox. These boys had a penchant for picking on Roswell and one day they pushed him too far and he fought back. Seeing him being beat up, I joined the fray and we had a free for all. I know that Roswell and I were getting the better of them when their Mama discovered us fighting. She called their daddy and my daddy to come help her stop the fight. Their daddy grabbed his belt and proceeded to tear them up. My daddy seeing this took off his belt and gave Roswell and me what for also. That was the only time I ever felt he was unfair to me in any way and later on he apologized for it. This was a lesson I didn't want to learn. There are times when you feel you have to do something even though your heart and head tells you it is wrong.

I enjoyed going to school at Culbertson, not necessarily for the classes, some of which I liked, but the recesses and lunch period were special. Mama still prepared our lunch. We didn't eat in the lunchroom because it cost a nickel and Mama didn't have fifteen cents every morning. The teacher always sold lunch tickets during the first period. I soon discovered that if I looked a little sad, sometimes she would slip me a ticket and I could eat in the lunchroom free that day. One day I had eaten in the lunchroom and was carrying my plate back to the kitchen area when a boy stuck his foot out and tripped me. I fell on a bench with the plate between the bench and my head. The plate I was carrying shattered and cut my head, leaving small pieces of china under the skin. Those small pieces of china worked their way out of my head over the next few years. When I got home, I had to explain to Mama why I was bandaged and she was mortified. From then on, she saw to it we had lunch money. I guess that since we had an automobile and a kerosene stove and Daddy was bringing home twenty-five dollars a week we were no longer poor folks.

During the recesses and lunch period, some of us boys discovered that the field next to the school was grown up in broom sage (pretty brown straw that people used to make house brooms with). There was plenty of it so we decided we could build ourselves a straw house. We cut broom sage and wove it into a neat little fort or house that four or five us could actually get into. The next logical step was for some of us to snitch some of our Daddy's smoking tobacco and stash it in the house so we could practice smoking. Everything went real well for a while because the straw roof would dissipate the smoke and nobody could tell we were smoking. One day, the boy next to the door decided to have some fun and set the house on fire. The straw was nice and dry and it went up in a hurry. There was panic for a few minutes but we all got out all right. The only problem was our singed hair and eyebrows. I still don't know why the principal was so upset because nobody was hurt but he lined us up and whipped us anyway.

We kind of missed our fort, so we decided we would build us a shebang. This time we dug a pit out in the middle of the field and covered it with boards then scattered dirt over it. Now we had a fort nobody could burn down and we were back in business. We were doing real good until somebody's milk cow happened to stroll right over our house and fell in. We were lucky nobody was in it when that happened, but the principal didn't let us off so lightly. After he got through with us that time, none of us wanted any more forts or houses, and besides, the principal explained to me that since I was president of my class that I should be setting a good example for the other students. Yes, I had been elected president the first of the year simply because my name was Truman. President Roosevelt had died and we now had a president named Truman so my class felt it was patriotic that we could do the same. For the rest of the year I tried to stay out of trouble and be a good example. Being president of my class was no problem because I had no duties. I think I did as good a job as anyone could have. I was not impeached.

The war was finally over in Europe when Hiroshima and Nagasaki became the subject of conversation. Apparently, we had some kind of bomb that had stopped the war. All of our family was very happy because that meant that Uncle Maston, Uncle Elvah, and Uncle Andy would get to come home safe. They were all overseas and, at that time, that was a very bad place to be.

One day, with all the men home from the war, they all came to our house to spend the day. Grandma Maggie, Aunt Ouida, Uncle Maston, Uncle Troy, Uncle Eulia, Uncle Elvah, Uncle Andrew, Aunt Florence, and their families were there. Uncle Preston had moved to Thomaston and that was too far for them to travel.

All the men went for a stroll behind the dairy barn all the way to Okapilco Creek. The women stayed at the house to prepare dinner (lunch). My cousins and I were allowed to tag along behind or with the men. It was amazing to me how the men knew all the names of the trees, shrubs, plants, and animals that we saw. All of them seemed to have a reverence for the world around them and were very interested in it.

We passed one bush and Daddy said this is a pop gun elder bush. He cut off a foot-long piece and showed us that the center was soft and could be pushed out and then we would have a pop gun to shoot chinaberries with. Uncle Elvah then cut a shorter piece and proceeded to carve out a flute and played a short tune on it. He gave it to me and I tried to play a tune but failed. I did get a whistling sound out of it.

They all had good information to share with us younger ones. Such as, if your second toe is shorter that your big toe you will be henpecked. You nose is exactly as long as your forefinger is past the end of your thumb. If your nose, lips, and chin form a straight line in profile, you are dependable and can be trusted. A three-colored cat or calico cat is always female. If your dog has dew claws, he won't die from a rattlesnake bite. A male dog won't fight a female dog. A brown thrasher's nest is always four to five feet above the ground. You don't allow a hen to set her eggs if they will hatch in May. Biddies that hatch in May are stupid and wouldn't learn to go to roost at night. And if it rains they just look straight up with their mouths open and drown. You should plant your garden on Good Friday because that is a rising moon and the above ground crops will be more plentiful. You plant your underground crops on a receding moon and the crop will be more plentiful. Dig a hole in the ground on a full moon saving the dirt and you can't get all the dirt back into the hole. Dig a hole on a new moon saving the dirt and you won't have enough dirt to fill the hole. If that kind of stuff isn't important, I don't know what is.

These brothers all had a good feeling of camaraderie and were happy being together. They also seemed to be very competitive because of the lively conversation and friendly arguments they enjoyed. When we returned to the house, they got into athletic competitions. They each held a broomstick in both hands and jumped over it forwards and backwards. They did broad jumps, high jumps, threw balls, etc.—just about anything they could think of to demonstrate their abilities. My cousins and I tried to emulate them and discovered that we could not compete.

We were called to dinner. All the women were good cooks and we had a feast. Afterwards everyone had to take a nap for a short while. When we woke up the men decided we should play baseball and chose sides. The men allowed us cousins to participate, and we had a grand time.

Soon it was time for Daddy and me to begin our milking chores so all the families began leaving. That started us children having a ball, running and chasing each other in order to get the last tag before they left. That was the first time I remember all the family being together after the war.

The year the school system introduced me to geography was quite an occurrence in my life. I had studied the Dick and Jane books and enjoyed the stories, but the geography book they gave me one Friday at school was an eye opener. I read the whole book over the weekend and have enjoyed reading ever since. I had heard about elephants, giraffes, and monkeys and had always assumed they were not real—a figment of somebody's imagination, like all the ghost stories I heard. That book had real pictures of all the places in the world. I knew there was a Europe and a Germany and a Japan, but I had no idea until then what the world was really like. There really were such things as lions and tigers. I have been learning ever since.

That was the year the library system started sending the bookmobile to Culbertson School and my teacher made arrangements for it to stop at our house that summer. I was in hog heaven and checked out all the books that the lady would let me have. For the next few days after the bookmobile came it was very hard for Mama to get me to do my chores because I was immersed in the books. Then it was an awful long wait for the bookmobile to get back because it only came every two weeks.

This was the year some of us boys discovered that we could ask to go to the bathroom and be able to spend some time out of class. It got to be such a problem the teacher announced one day that no one would be allowed to go to the bathroom during class. We would have to use the bathroom before or after class and that was it.

Not too long afterwards, we were sitting in class one day when a girl in the class who sat up front of the room raised her hand and asked to be allowed to go to the bathroom. The teacher told her no, that she would have to wait. In a few minutes, the girl jumped up and began running down the aisle for the door. As it turned out, she had a case of diarrhea. She could not hold herself, and suddenly she was making a mess as she ran. This situation was what was normally known as the trots. Most people we knew did not have a bathroom in their house and the outhouse was a good distance from the house. If you saw someone trotting to the outhouse, you knew what was going on. Me and Jackie Dozier were sitting in the back row and began laughing. The teacher ordered me and Jackie to clean up the mess, and she went to the principal's office and didn't come back to class that day. The principal came to finish the class and made sure that Jackie and I finished the cleanup job and told us we shouldn't have laughed.

During the year, I had joined the 4-H Club at school and had the opportunity to go to summer camp. All it cost was ten dollars and I got to stay for one week. It took me most of the early half of the year doing chores and farm work to raise that ten dollars and I was really looking forward to it.

Mama arranged to borrow me a bathing suit from somewhere and that meant that I was going in style. She also bought me a toothbrush and some toothpaste. That was the first toothbrush I remember owning. We had always used a sweet gum twig and baking soda. How uptown can you get? The big day came and I got on the bus along with the other children carrying my suitcase (an old one Mama had used on our trip to Florida). When I got on the bus, I was delighted to see that we had a trailer loaded with canoes. I felt like I was really going somewhere now. That was as close as I ever got to one of those canoes. If they were ever taken off the trailer, I didn't see it. Every morning we got up and did calisthenics in front of our cabins then were taken on a nature hike. On these hikes we had someone who pointed out the wildlife around us, primarily the birds and squirrels. I had been hunting birds and squirrels with my slingshot most of my life, so I didn't really need somebody pointing them out to me. In fact, squirrel had been very prominent in my diet for quite some time.

Then we would go back to the cabins and get ready for lunch (normally a sandwich), then we had a class in crafts all afternoon. The only craft we had was weaving little strands of flat plastic into a lanyard that would hold keys or a whistle like the counselors used. I didn't have any keys and certainly didn't have a whistle like that. After craft class we were allowed to go swimming in the pond for forty-five minutes. In the evenings, we had supper then got to sit around a campfire and listen to one of the counselors sing songs while playing his guitar. That was all right, but that boy couldn't sing like Roy Acuff or Ernest Tubb, so I wasn't all that impressed with that either. Anyway, his songs weren't hillbilly and I didn't know the stuff he was singing, so I couldn't sing along. I was very glad when my week was up and I could go home. The only thing I had to show for the experience was a lanyard and nothing to tie onto it.

Chapter 7: Health Problems

I had always been healthy and had an appetite accordingly. I could and would eat anything. One day on the backside of the dairy, I found a fencerow plumb full of juicy ripe blackberries. I ate my fill of the biggest, juiciest ones you can imagine. By the time I got to the house I just didn't feel good and assumed I had eaten too many berries. I started throwing up and just laid myself down on the porch and let her fly. I was too sick to hold my head up. I couldn't even answer Mama when she wanted to know what was wrong. I felt so bad I was afraid I would live. Anything would have been an improvement. I was sick all night, felt a little better the next morning, and could answer questions. Mama discovered I had eaten blackberries right next to a tobacco field that had just been sprayed with poison. Right then I lost my appetite for blackberries and anything that even looks like blackberries. I can't even eat blackberry pie, which had been one of my favorites.

We had some neighbors one time who spent a great deal of their time arguing and throwing the dinner dishes at each other. That was something we had never been exposed to and we thought they were bad people. The house they lived in was next to one of the pastures. One day I was gathering the cows up for milking and had to chase one of them right by the neighbor's house. In doing so, I stepped on a broken tea glass they had thrown out and cut my foot pretty bad. I cut the leader under my big toe and an artery. Every time I picked my foot up blood would spurt out with every heartbeat. I made it back to the house and Mama made me put my foot in a pan of kerosene. Kerosene fixed anything we had wrong with us from a cold to a scratch or pneumonia. Kerosene didn't stop my foot from bleeding. Every time my heart beat, blood would spurt out. About this time, Mr. Sinclair, who owned the farm, pulled up in his late model car and decided he better carry me to town to the doctor. That was my first ride in a new car and my first trip to a doctor. By the time we got to town and into the doctor's office, I was feeling a little peaked and don't remember too much. I know the doctor had to put some stitches in my foot and said he couldn't do anything about the leader to my toe. So to this day, I can't pull that toe down. It has always felt a little weird. He told Mama to let me take it easy for a few days and to stay off of it. When we left the doctor's office, we went into the drug store next door—the first time I had ever been in one. We got a nickel ice cream cone and Mama let me buy a comic book. It was the first comic book that I had ever seen. I thought maybe I ought to cut my foot more often.

In my early years, I always knew that Mama had a physical problem because she was incontinent and had to use homemade incontinence pads, which were usually ragged clothes that she rewashed and reused all the time. I knew that I had two sisters who died shortly after birth. Their names were Cherry Jane and Gwendolyn. Later on Mama had another child who was stillborn. His name was Anthony. Two years later she had another stillborn baby whose name was Alana Gail. I helped Daddy bury these last two. We didn't have a cemetery plot, so Uncle Maston told Daddy that he could use his burial plot down at New Bethel Church. We took those babies out to the cemetery and he had them wrapped in a receiving blanket. We dug the graves and he would unwrap the babies and let me see them, then we put them in the ground and covered them up. We mixed up some concrete and poured markers for them, and Daddy scratched their names and date in the concrete. That was when I learned that when Altis was born the doctor used some brass clamps in Mama's uterus. This was accepted medical practice at the time. Like many other medical theories and practices, this one also turned out not to be true or helpful after much usage. It was later discovered that the human body would not accept brass and that the brass caused problems. I was born with few complications; however, Roswell almost didn't make it. Shortly after he was born, he apparently died and they laid him out for burial. He started breathing again and they warmed bricks by the fire, wrapped them in blankets, and put them in bed with him to keep his body temperature up. The subsequent children were not so lucky. The lack of prenatal care, abject poverty, and subsequent malnutrition all took their toll.

The brass continued to cause Mama problems, and in the fifties, she was almost down. The doctors in Moultrie couldn't help her and recommended that she go to Georgia Baptist Hospital for help. The Baptist Association was helpful in getting her into the hospital and helped to pay her bills for the required surgery. She had a close call and almost died shortly after the surgery, but she pulled through and lived a normal life for quite a few years. For the first time since Altis was born, she didn't need any incontinence pads.

One day the well pump at the end of the milk barn quit working, so Daddy decided we would have to pull the pipes out of the ground to get to the valve on the end of them. He didn't have a block and tackle, so he rigged up a well tekle so he could pull the pipe up about two feet at the time. When he pulled the pipe up, he would have me clamp off the pipe so he could get another grip and pull some more.

When we got the pipe about one-third out of the ground, on one pull the rope he was using slipped and the pipe fell back to my clamp. He said, "Consarn it, I mashed my finger," and proceeded to pull the pipe back up. I reached to prepare the clamp and when I looked down there was Daddy's finger lying on the ground next to my foot. I told him he had cut his finger off and he couldn't believe it, but when he looked he agreed it was gone. That incident wound up the repair on the well right then. He and Mama took off to the doctor to get fixed up and called Mr. Sinclair to tell him what had happened. Mr. Sinclair sent someone out to repair the well but I didn't offer to help that time. I got Roswell and we put Daddy's finger in a matchbox and had a funeral for it. Mr. Sinclair sent a man out to work the dairy until Daddy got able to do it again, and it was left up to me to teach him what to do and when as to running the dairy.

Roswell started having trouble with a boy at school. It seems the rascal started making his life miserable and would chase him all during recess and after school until the bus came. We got our heads together and decided we would have to put a stop to it. We made an arrangement whereby I would have a stout oak limb and would wait around the corner of the school, and Roswell would run by while the boy chased him. Sure enough I hadn't been in position long when here came Roswell. He zoomed around the corner and stopped right by me. Here came his tormenter hell-bent for leather hot on his heels. I won't go into detail about what happened, but that boy decided he didn't want to pick on Roswell anymore. Roswell and I could pick on one another all we wanted to, but when somebody else picked on either of us we just wouldn't put up with it. When we got through with that boy, he didn't even want to tell the principal on us so we dodged a switching that time.

Going to spend some time at Newell and Weldon's house was always something I looked forward to. Newell could make the neatest cars and trucks to play with. In fact they looked real and had wheels that turned. I was still pushing empty milk of magnesia bottles around and calling them trucks. In his backyard, he even created a small village complete with houses, fences, roads, and power lines. The only problem was that I was not allowed to even touch any of it so we had to make do with other things.

Wonder of wonders, I discovered that one of our neighbors was a boy a little younger than me and we got to be friends. The wonder was that his dad worked for the Lifesaver candy company. He had one whole bedroom of their house filled with lifesaver candies and promotional material. There was literally hundreds of plastic trucks filled with candy. My friend gave Roswell and me some still filled with candy. We no longer had to push empty bottles for toys anymore.

When we moved onto the dairy, the pond had a broken dam and was not much of a pond. Mr. Sinclair had the dam repaired, and boy, did we have a pretty pond of water. The only problem we had was we didn't have a boat. So Roswell and I proceeded to fix that situation. We took a sheet of tin off one of the sheds and discovered if we put a board in one end and folded the other end in half we had what looked like a boat. The main problem was it wouldn't float but about four or five minutes so we went to one of the turpentine trees and got some pine tar to patch the holes with. It would float pretty good, but we did have a mess with the pine tar. It would stick to our bodies and clothes and we had to use kerosene to get it off. That boat would float for about fifteen minutes before it would sink. In fact, right there was where I learned to swim.

I didn't plan to learn to swim but when you are out in the middle of a five-acre pond and have your boat sink, and you can't walk on water, you start swimming. Planning ahead never had been one of my strong points and sure enough it still wasn't, but I managed to get out of that pond and have never been afraid of water again. If Mama had known what we were doing, it is possible that I may have never learned to swim.

When we visited Uncle Maston's home we used to all sleep in one bed, but we had gotten too big for one bed and some of us had to sleep on a pallet on the floor. One morning, we were still on the pallet when Roswell began picking at Old Shep. That was Newell and Weldon's big old German shepherd dog. Old Shep was a good dog. He was not afraid of anything except lightning and thunder and Roswell didn't qualify for either of those. Roswell would hide under the quilt and reach out and pull Shep's tail. He would turn and snap at Roswell, but Roswell would jerk the quilt over himself and Shep couldn't hurt him. After a few minutes of this either Shep got faster or Roswell got slower. Old Shep managed to catch Roswell right in the face. I felt like we should shoot the dog but they said it was Roswell's fault, so Old Shep got to live and Roswell still has the scars.

Weldon and I always enjoyed going hunting. We were getting big enough to use guns. We hunted robins, doves, and most anything that moved and some things that didn't. One day we tried to shoot some doves and did not have much luck. We came back to the house and were going to eat dinner when Weldon shouted that some doves had just landed in the field next to the house. I grabbed up Uncle Maston's old double-barreled shotgun and whirled around to go outside and that thing went off as I was turning. Have you ever heard a shotgun go off inside a room? Man, what a noise. Then the little birdshot pellets just seemed to keep bouncing around. When the smoke and noise settled, I discovered that I had shot a hole in Aunt Zuleika's bed. There was the smallest hole in the top about the size of a nickel but when you picked up the mattress you could have put a watermelon in the hole where it came out. Nobody had to tell me what could have happened if it had been pointed at somebody. Well that stopped my dove hunting at Uncle Maston's house. It also took a while to clean up all the cotton and birdshot that was scattered all over the place.

One summer, Mrs. Sinclair, whose husband owned the dairy farm, bought her son, Duncan Jr., a boy scout outfit. As it turned out, the pants for the outfit was too big for Duncan Jr., so she gave the pants to me. They were a perfect fit. They were the color of army dress pants and had a gold stripe down the outside of each leg. When I had those pants on, I just knew that I looked like a soldier. Those pants became my official dress when I was at home. In those days, we had clothes that we wore to school, and when we got home, we put on work clothes so we would not mess up our good ones. Those pants were my pride and joy.

Imagine my surprise one evening when I got off the school bus to discover that some girl was in my yard wearing my pants. Altis was going to high school and that evening she had brought one of her friends home with her to play. The high school bus always got to our house before my bus did. Coming straight from school like they did, her friend did not have any play clothes, so Altis just offered her my clothes to play in. Upon seeing the situation, I dropped my books on the spot and took off after Altis's friend. I caught her and proceeded to liberate my pants and almost did so, but Altis called Mama and Mama took care of the situation. Obviously, Mama's opinion of what was proper and my opinion of the same were at odds, so with the help of a switch from the yard broom, Mama convinced me that my way was not acceptable. That was when I learned for sure that you were not supposed to tear the clothes off any girl.

Off to high school, and boy, was I a big shot. Mama had bought me some dungarees and a belt. Oh boy, no more overalls. I opened the year with an accident, though. While waiting on the bus that morning, E. J. Graham and me were playing tag and running up and down the road when I fell on a dead dog fennel bush and drove one of the stems through my jaw. I bit the stem off and pulled the rest back out of my jaw and went back to the house where Mama doctored me with the turpentine. I missed the first day, but I went the next day even with a bandage on my cheek. My first year was uneventful except that I discovered I could work in the lunchroom and receive my lunch free.

Early in my second year of high school, one morning while waiting for the school bus, I discovered a free sample of railroad snuff in the mailbox. I had tried to dip some snuff in the past and was not interested in trying again, but I discovered if I punched a hole in the top of the can and shook it would produce a nice little cloud of dust. I entered the bus and shook it in everybody's face I met saying good morning. I had no problems. So when I got to school I marched down the corridor shaking that can and greeting everybody I met and still no problems. I had been sitting in my first class about twenty minutes when our principal came to the room, asked for me, and told me to bring along my snuff. It seemed one of the students had complained, so he marched me to his office and talked to me rather strongly about what I had done then he introduced me to the high school coal pile.

Every fall the school system bought a year's supply of coal for the boiler and it was placed at the back corner of the gymnasium. That coal pile was ten times larger than any woodpile I had ever seen. He informed me that for my punishment I had to shovel that coal onto a wheelbarrow and move it to the other back corner of the gym. I had two months to complete the job working each recess and lunch period. I felt that this might be payback for hitting that little girl with a piece of coal in second grade at Doerun. It wasn't long before some other miscreants were assigned to basically the same job. I don't have to tell you that I would rather have been playing and passing time with the other students, but fate works in mysterious ways.

About the time I finished my tour of duty, I was in a science class one morning with the assistant football coach as the teacher. He had a habit of cracking and eating pecans during class, and when some of us boys got a little unruly, he would throw a pecan at us. When you were least expecting it one of those pecans would bounce off your head and the whole class would laugh at you. After about the third time I managed to catch the next one and threw it back at him as hard as I could. My aim just was not as good as his was and I hit one of the girls on the front row. We both knew we were in trouble immediately because we were summoned to the office together for a little chitchat. I don't know what his punishment was, but I got sent back to the coal pile and told to move it back to where it was originally.

Mr. Sinclair built an underground silo to keep feed in for the dairy cattle. It was just a large ditch, twenty-four feet wide and fifteen feet deep cut into the side of a hill and lined with roofing felt. We grew corn and millet, which we cut green and filled the silo with it. That summer Daddy was working in the silo getting the feed out and got too hot. The doctor said he had a heat stroke. He was not able to work at all for a couple of weeks, leaving Roswell and me to milk and tend to the dairy cattle. We had always helped as part of our chores, but now the whole process was on our shoulders. Milking, feeding, cleaning up, and cooling the milk twice daily was quite a chore and was a seven day a week job. Daddy never did quite get over his heat stroke, and in a short while, told Mr. Sinclair that he could not continue to run the dairy.

Chapter 8:
The New Used Cars

D addy went to work at Baell Mercantile in Moultrie and so we moved again. This time we moved to a small house down the dirt road behind Bennett's Grocery Store, still five miles from town. While living there I worked in tobacco for J. A. Norman and made enough money to buy a bicycle. It was not a Schwinn or anything fancy like that, just a pretty rebuilt used bicycle. My next step was to try to get myself a job. I went to the *Moultrie Observer* and asked for a paper route, but they told me that since I lived five miles out in the country there was no way I could deliver papers for them. A boy I had met in high school told me to go to Waits' Newsstand and ask him for a job because they distributed the Atlanta papers, both the *Atlanta Journal* and the *Atlanta Constitution*, in the mornings. Mr. Waits asked me if I could be at his newsstand every morning at four. I assured him that I could, so he told me to be there the next morning. When I got there the next morning, there were four or five boys already working. The truck from Atlanta had come in and unloaded the morning papers and it looked like a small mountain of newspapers in bundles stacked on the sidewalk. The boys all had routes and were counting out their papers and folding them for delivery. Mr. Waits told me that my route had five hundred and ninety three papers, about half *Journals* and half *Constitutions*, and for me to count them and put them on his truck. He had to carry me on the route so that I could learn it. My route started almost at the newsstand and worked southwest and southeast Moultrie out South Main on both sides of the street, including the area around the high school and Colonial Heights, which was outside the city limits at the time.

He carried me for two mornings and told me I was on my own. Obviously, nobody can carry that many papers on a bicycle at one time. I had to bundle papers according to how many I could carry and then he would drop them off the truck at spots I designated so I could reload without having to go back to the newsstand. My route ended about two and one-half to three miles south of the newsstand. Every morning I had a five-mile ride into town, worked my route, rode the two and one-half to three miles back to town, and then the five miles back to the house in time to get on the school bus and go to school. I never did measure the mileage for my morning excursions. However, I definitely got my exercise, because I continued this job for two-and-one-half years.

Later, we did move to town and cut off a good portion of my miles. I still had a seven-day-a-week job, and it had to be done rain or shine, hot or cold—I had plenty of all situations. The mornings that it was pretty weather it was not bad at all, and at times I enjoyed it. All I had to do was deliver the papers, not collect for them as Mr. Waits handled all that. He paid me a half cent per paper. All of a sudden, I felt rich. I was making almost three dollars every morning. He had snacks and cold drinks at the newsstand. It didn't take me long to find out that I could eat up my salary, so I began to make sure I had my breakfast when I got home instead of spending my money at his place.

That fall, with Daddy working at the hardware store and me with my newspaper route, I didn't have as many chores at home, so I went out for the football squad. I made the "b" team and played that whole year. That was quite an experience. I stood a little under six feet tall and weighed one hundred and thirty-five pounds. It was pretty easy for some of those guys to run all over me, which they did at every opportunity. The only problem I had was the ride home in afternoons. While doing all this I still had my paper route. I did not ride the bus to school but rode my bicycle back to school in the mornings so I would have it handy to ride home after football practice. I don't know exactly how many miles I rode that bicycle every day but it was in the vicinity of sixty miles or more. I know that I wore out four sets of tires on that thing before I quit my paper route. I probably would have continued to play football, but the next year I had to find a job in the afternoons.

We moved again, this time down to Autreyville across the road from Newell and Weldon. At least now when I finished my paper route I was halfway home. For some reason, we didn't stay there for very long and moved up on the Sylvester Highway just inside the city limits. While we lived there, Daddy began to make plans to buy a lot and build a house. With the help of James Baell, he borrowed enough money to buy the lot for five hundred dollars and enough to build a house on it. While we were building the house we moved again over on West Boulevard right by Uncle Andy and Grandma Lastinger.

The spring we were building our house was when I first met my future wife. A girl named Shirley had been a friend of some our neighbors while we lived on the dairy and I had gotten to know her. Shirley was a cheerleader for the football team, and one day I met her coming down the steps at the end of the hall at Moultrie High School. With her was the prettiest girl I had ever seen and it was love at first sight. I have never since met anyone like her or that I liked better. She eventually became my best friend and my helpmate and at times my driving force. Her name was Rosalind Monk. Her daddy had been the postmaster in Moultrie. I found out later that Mr. Monk had been our rural mailman while we lived at the Autry place. He had been real good to take eggs in exchange for postage on letters and postcards.

We moved into our new house in June of 1953 and, wonder of wonders, we had an indoor bathroom including a bathtub with hot water and all. We had become part of the landed gentry. We were no longer have-nots. I suppose you could have called us might-haves then.

That summer Roswell and I worked on a farm in Pavo. The man who owned the farm had an old 1936 Ford two-door automobile sitting under a shed, and when we asked about it he said he would give us the car if we would tear down an old house on the farm on our own time. I knew that I was getting old enough to want to drive and have an automobile, and if I ever could get enough courage to ask Rosalind for a date, then I must have a way to go. By the end of the summer, Roswell and I were the proud owners of that automobile. Every tire on that thing was flat and worn out. We had to go to a service station and search through their stack of used tires and got four of the best we could find for two dollars each. Tubes were a different story. We could not afford new ones so we got a tire patch kit and proceeded to get that car rolling. We had two flat tires that we had to fix on the way home, and I reckon that was a blessing because it had mechanical brakes and they were not working. If we had gotten moving very fast, we may not have been able to stop the thing. It seemed that every time we wanted to go somewhere we had to patch the tires. Even so, we enjoyed having that car.

Uncle J. D. Holland, who lived in Fort Myers, Florida, bought a car dealership and told Mama that if she and Daddy would come down he would fix them up with a good used car. So the week of Thanksgiving we rode a bus to Florida. The plan was for Roswell and me to stay in Lakeland with Grandpa while Mama and Daddy went on down to Fort Meyers to get the car. They would pick us up in Lakeland and spend Thanksgiving Day with Grandpa before coming home.

That week was a busy one because Grandma Vera expected a large crowd for Thanksgiving dinner. On Wednesday before Thanksgiving, we all got dressed up real good and went in to Lakeland to purchase all the needed last minute groceries. Then we hurried home to kill and dress the turkey. Grandpa Holland had put on his best suit of clothes and cut quite a picture while in town. When we got home, he proceeded to do his chores and had Roswell and me help him catch the turkey. When we had rounded up and caught the turkey he cut off his head and dressed him. When he carried the dressed turkey in the house to Grandma Vera, you could have heard her in Lakeland. She had just realized that he hadn't changed out of his best suit of clothes into his work clothes. He shrugged off her fussing and went right back outside and continued doing his chores.

Late that evening Mama and Daddy came rolling in in the new car. It was a 1940 four-door Chevrolet and white as snow. We finally had a car that looked like a car. The Model A was twenty-two years old. Roswell and I were all over and in that thing for at least an hour until Daddy told us to get out and leave it alone because we had seen enough.

Thanksgiving morning lots of kinfolk began to arrive. There were people I had never seen before and some that I had not even heard of. One was a boy my age and we took a liking to one another right off. He was a distant cousin on Mama's side of the family. While the women were busy preparing the Thanksgiving feast, we decided to go walking around a big patch of scrub oaks across from the house. It was about twelve to fifteen acres, and being boys, we thoroughly checked it out. We discovered terrapins, gophers, and all kinds of birds in there. We were having a good time until we heard his mother calling him at the top of her voice. She was almost hysterical so we ran back to the house. It seemed that he was an only child and she was very protective. In her mind, he had already been bitten then swallowed by a rattlesnake. I couldn't imagine anybody being that worried about us. That broke up a good, budding friendship. I got blamed for leading him astray and told to keep myself in the yard for the rest of the visit.

That was all right because I got to meet Uncle Charlie. That was one of Granddaddy's brothers. He was apparently the black sheep of the family. The menfolk were sitting in the backyard talking and I began to get interested in what they were talking about. Uncle Charlie had a piece of adhesive tape on his ear and the men were ragging him about it. He told them not to worry about it. He had been in a fight and his opponent had bitten the bottom half of his ear off. The adhesive tape was not as hard to explain to people as having only half an ear showing.

He talked a lot about what he had learned in college. I found out later that the college he was referring to was Raiford Prison. It seemed that a friend of his wanted to open a tavern or bar, and the county wouldn't allow it because there was a church close by. He told his friend not to worry that he would take care of the situation, and sure enough, within a short while the church caught fire and burned down and was no longer a problem. The upshot was that Uncle Charlie went to college.

For the last few years, he had been living with a woman down somewhere near Lake Okeechobee. One of the men asked him where she was and he answered, "I fed her to the gators." Nobody asked about her anymore, and in later years, some of us would ask each other if we reckon he actually did feed her to the gators. I don't think we really wanted to know. At any rate no one ever heard from her again.

Finally, Thanksgiving dinner was on the table and the call went out to come and get it. Everybody traipsed in and Grandma Vera asked Granddaddy to say the blessing. Then she looked at him and started cussing like a sailor. He had come to the table with his old dirty work clothes on. That was the last straw. She told him off good in front of all of us and sent him to bathe and change clothes. We all ate as quietly as we could because we didn't want any attention from Grandma Vera.

The year I entered the eleventh grade at Moultrie High School, everything went smoothly for me until February. I had been assigned a period called study hall under a math teacher named Mr. Slaton. This was supposed to be a time when we could get all our homework done so we wouldn't be up all night. One afternoon I finished my work and was sitting in my seat bored, so I raised my hand and asked the teacher if I could go to the side blackboard and play ticktacktoe. He listened to my request and elected to ignore me. I raised my hand and asked again and he ignored me again. I announced to my friends Joe and Carl that apparently it was all right if we did so because the teacher didn't say no. So we got up and proceeded to play ticktacktoe. Suddenly, I heard a loud whap followed by another whap. I turned just in time to see that teacher with a paddle drawn back fixing to hit me. He had already hit Joe and Carl. I grabbed his arm, took the paddle away from him, spun him around, and hit him twice just as hard as I could across the seat of his pants. He immediately left the room in tears. About that time the bell rang for us to go to our last period, which I did even though I knew I was in trouble.

I had been sitting in my last class for about five minutes when Mr. MacDonald, the principal, came in and asked me to follow him. When we got to his office, he asked me if I had hit the teacher. I told him that I had and why. He told me it didn't make any difference why, he just could not tolerate that type of behavior and that I was expelled from school for two weeks.

Getting expelled happened on Friday afternoon and I had to go home and tell Mama what happened. Mama got all over me just like I knew she would. She said we both were going to school on Monday morning. I had a long weekend. Monday morning, sure enough, Mama took me to school. She marched me into Mr. MacDonald's office and told his secretary that she wanted to see him. When he admitted us into his office Mama told him she knew what happened and that she had punished me for it. She told him I would apologize to the teacher and that Mr. MacDonald could punish me in any way he considered appropriate, but that being expelled was not acceptable. I was going to go to school and graduate or she would whip his a-- and mine every day until it happened if she had to.

He apparently understood her because he called the teacher into his office where I apologized profoundly to him. He accepted my apology and they assigned me to another teacher for study hall. He dismissed the teacher and proceeded to give me a whipping in front of Mama. Then he sent me back to the coal pile. I probably would not have finished school at all if it had not been for Mama. I'm not sure how much education I received, but I sure learned how to shovel coal at Moultrie High School.

Late that spring a tornado hit Warner Robins and just devastated the town. From all reports there was hardly anything left standing. Newell and Lucille had just gotten married and they decided that we would ride up and see the damage. Early Saturday morning we took off. The roads at that time were all just small, two-lane highways and I thought that we would never get there, and in fact, we didn't. There was so much traffic when we got close that we would sit awhile then inch up awhile. After what seemed an eternity, we decided that we should turn around and go home so we could get back by dark.

During all that sitting and waiting nature called upon us for relief, and there being no bathroom around, Newell, Weldon, and I got out, jumped the ditch, and went into the nearby woods to relieve ourselves. There was an old cat face stump right where we stopped, and being a boy and having discovered that I could aim pretty good, I proceeded to paint that stump. Have you ever seen a mad swarm of yellow jackets? There was no way I could have known I was desecrating their home; however, they proceeded to convince me to stop. I got stung at least four times—and possibly more—however, one sting in particular was very personal. I don't think Newell or Weldon got stung at all, but I know they beat me back across that deep ditch. All that excitement led to a miserable ride home. I have never been inclined to go rubbernecking at any natural or accidental disaster since.

As I remember, that was the summer that a trustee at the county jail managed to kill the warden and his wife by slashing their throats and escaped. The next morning my brother—who was working on a bread truck—stopped by a small grocery store to deliver some bread and saw the early morning clerk lying on the floor with his throat slashed also. Three people were now dead and the whole county was in turmoil all day. A lot of people were riding around armed to the hilt with whatever weapon they could find searching for the escaped convict.

My friend Pete came to the house and picked me up. He had a '46 Ford Coupe convertible. The top had rotted off so there was no cover. A little earlier, he had asked me to help him install a rebuilt motor in it. We joined the mass of people out looking for the convict. We both had a household butcher knife and I don't know what we would have done if the convict had found us, but we were doing our civic duty. The convict was discovered the next day hiding in some woods near the jail. The sheriff convinced him to come out and give himself up, which he did. It was the talk of the town for a while. Things like this just shouldn't happen in a small town.

That summer I kept my paper route and worked in tobacco for J. A. Norman. Gathering tobacco all day after running that paper route turned into a chore, but I was making good money. I was making a total of seven dollars a day as long as it lasted.

During that summer, my friend Pete Williams asked me if I would like to go to Canada with him and work in tobacco. He said they paid ten dollars a day and the season started in Canada after we got through with tobacco in South Georgia; we would be through for the summer in time to return to school for our senior year. I told him I would like to, so he arranged for his Canadian contact to send me a visa. We were to be gone for about six weeks, so I arranged with Mr. Waits for me to be off my paper route while I was gone and still get it back when I returned.

Pete borrowed his daddy's 1951 Ford automobile for the trip. Pete, Gene Carter, Charlie Parker, and I piled into that auto and took off for Canada. The first time in my life I saw a four-lane highway was on that trip. Going into Cincinnati, Ohio, there it was: a sure enough expressway, two lanes in both directions. There were still red lights at intersections and driveways into and out of service stations, but it qualified in my mind for a super highway. The highways in Georgia, Tennessee, and Kentucky were all only two lanes.

Going through Tennessee was quite an experience. There we were, young people in a late model automobile flying through Tennessee. Traveling the steep grades and hairpin turns was like being on a rollercoaster that lasted for five to six hours with only brief intermissions while we were down in the valleys. On some of those hairpin turns on the downgrades, we could see wrecks of autos and trucks that had not successfully navigated the turns and were still in the places that they landed. It apparently would have cost more to winch them out of those canyons than they would have been worth, so they were left there to rust away. Pete's daddy had put new white sidewall tires on the car before we left. Whitewalls on tires were wider then than they are now, and when we got onto level ground in Kentucky, we realized that Pete had worn off some of the white on the sides of the tires going through Tennessee.

Pete had been warned that Canadians ate meals a little different from South Georgians and none of them knew what grits (a staple breakfast food in South Georgia) were. Before we left Moultrie we purchased a case of grits and made sure they were in the trunk. When we got to the Canadian border in Detroit, the customs agents made us open our luggage and the trunk of the car. I am sure they were apprehensive because we were four teenagers in a late model auto crossing the border. When an agent spied the case of grits he said, "Grits? What is grits?" Charlie Parker stood up tall and said, "Hey man, grits is groceries." The agent said, "Oh," closed the trunk, and told us we could proceed. I didn't realize it at the time, but I had just become a migrant farm worker.

We were actually in Canada in the official capacity of teaching the Canadians how to grow and cure golden leaf tobacco, but in reality, we were there to supply them with a good work force. When the temperature reached the middle eighties the French, Dutch, and German Canadians would begin to suffer from the heat. Being from South Georgia and having left the same job with temperatures in the upper nineties, we were very comfortable and could turn out a lot more work than they could.

In South Georgia, a tobacco field usually would not be over eight to ten acres and cropping the ripe leaves would just about fill one of our tobacco barns. When we got to Drumbo, Ontario, where we were to work, we went out to see the field. What a shock! That field must have been eighty acres. Their barns would hold five to six times as much as a tobacco barn in South Georgia. It meant we would be in the same field for the entire gathering season. By the time we cropped the ripe tobacco leaves it would be time to start over. When you were in South Georgia cropping tobacco, you could see the end in sight and had something to look forward to. You knew when you finished cropping that you had to hang the tobacco in the barn to finish the day's work, but at least it was a different job. In Canada, they had a crew at the barn hanging the tobacco as fast as we could send it in. Our job was the same day in and day out. The only thing that helped was knowing we were being paid ten dollars a day.

The man we worked for was named Otto Swiggum. I had never heard of anybody named Otto in South Georgia, let alone Swiggum. He was a good man and fixed up a room in his barn as a makeshift bunkhouse for us. His wife cooked and we ate in the farmhouse that they lived in. Sure enough, the first morning we were served something they called cream of wheat. I thought, surely this was what people meant when they spoke of mush. We talked her into fixing us our grits for breakfast. From then on she was gracious enough to comply, but the first serving didn't even look like grits were supposed to look. It took some doing but we finally taught her how to cook grits properly. A workingman needs the proper groceries and that probably is why we could work rings around those Canadians.

In South Georgia, we never saw or heard of interracial couples nor could we believe it could happen. When we were going across the border into Canada, the car next to us had a white woman and a black man in it and they were both in the front seat. We all almost got whiplash because we just couldn't believe our eyes. One Sunday afternoon we went into a city named Ayre and cruised around. We went to a roller skating rink where Gene Carter managed to talk a girl into riding around town with us. While we were riding down the street, we saw a young black man walking down the sidewalk. When Gene's girlfriend saw him she leaned way out the window and yelled hello to him. Gene slammed on the brakes and asked her what did she think she was doing. She said the boy was in her class at high school and played football. Gene told her to get out of the car and go play with him because he just couldn't understand a girl being that friendly with a black, and if she was he didn't want anything to do with her. He drove off and left that girl standing on the sidewalk.

One day when we had caught up with our work, one of Mr. Swiggum's neighbors asked us to help him in tobacco. We gladly agreed and went to help him. When it came lunchtime we were invited into their house for dinner. The table was set up real nice with plates, plenty of utensils, and a large glass of water. I had never been to a dinner table that had two forks and two spoons as well as a cloth napkin. I didn't quite know what to expect. I knew these people were French Canadians and supposed that they were more different from us than I had expected. I did know what to do with the water though because I was thirsty. I picked up that glass and took a big swig and liked to have choked to death and actually sprayed it all over the table. That water wasn't water, it was wine. I had never had a sip of wine in my life, and the last place I expected to find some was on the dinner table. After an apology and cleaning up, I was allowed to eat with them, and they explained that it was their custom to have wine with their meals and assumed that we did too.

Part III:
Our New Future

Chapter 9: Life Changes

When we finished the summer's work and got back home, I immediately went car shopping. I bought a 1940 Chevrolet four-door sedan that was just as black as that Model A Ford I mentioned earlier. The only problem was that it took every bit of the money I had made that summer and left me so broke that I couldn't afford the gasoline to operate it. The only solution was to find a job in the evenings to supplement my paper route money. That was my senior year in high school and we had moved into the brand-new Moultrie High School building. As soon as school started, I went on my first job hunt.

I started asking for work at Holman Mule Company, which was one block off the Moultrie town square. I began working my way to the square, then proceeded around the square going into every business and office asking for a job. I asked at the production credit association, Bird's Eye Feed Store, the fish market, loan companies, shoe stores, Belk-Hudson Company, the bank, two drug stores, McClelland's five and ten cents store, and two jewelry stores.

When I walked into Crystal Pharmacy, there was Gene Carter behind the soda fountain. I asked him for a job and he carried me to the back of the store and told Mr. Ben Daniels that I needed a job. Mr. Ben told me to go over to his wife and ask her. When I asked her for a job she gave me a pencil and some paper and told me to write down my name and the name of the store I was in. Thank goodness I remembered what store I was in and didn't have to ask.

When she saw that she could read my writing, she told Mr. Ben to hire me. Mr. Ben called Gene back and told him to carry me into the back room and comb my hair and put an apron on, then to teach me how to make cokes and sodas. We made cokes by adding carbonated water to the coke syrup. I learned how to make banana splits and chocolate sundaes. We had people wanting a milk shake with a raw egg mixed in it. Some wanted an ammonia coke, said to relieve headache and used as a stimulant. We prepared doses of castor oil. Hooray, I had a job.

We had not discussed pay or hours, and I suppose it was because I didn't ask. I knew that the store closed at ten o'clock at night and supposed that I would get off then. When ten o'clock came around, nobody told me I was off and Mr. Ben kept working and talking. He sat down on the floor and began dusting shelves and merchandise and kept talking. I got a dust towel and sat down across from him. We dusted and cleaned merchandise until I realized that it was getting daylight outside. When he realized it was morning, he got up and said we had better get home.

When I got home Mama was frantic. All she knew was that I had gone to town to look for a job. It took a little talking but I assured her that I had one at Crystal Pharmacy and had been working all night. I couldn't call her because we didn't have a telephone. I had my bath, ate breakfast, and ran my paper route and still got to school on time. I am happy to say that was the latest that we ever worked; however, quite often it wasn't until two to three o'clock in the morning before we quit. I later learned the reason we worked so late. About six o'clock every day he would send me down the street to the pool hall to get him a six-pack of beer. Then he would take a Dexedrine tablet and drink beer. By closing time he was wired and in no mood to go home.

Dr. Ben moved me to the back where the pharmacy was so I became his helper. I fell in love with pharmacy, and to this day, I still love it. I discovered words like acetylated salicylic acid or aspirin, acetylated para-aminophenol, or APAP, which became Tylenol, and phenylazodiaminopyridine or pyridium. I was permanently intrigued. I learned a lot working for that man. He would listen to his customers and sell them something he felt would help them with their complaints, and if he felt that the customer needed something that was not commercially available, he would compound or make them whatever he thought would help.

At that time about forty to fifty percent of prescriptions were compounded by the pharmacists. They made charts, ointments, liniments, douche powders, gargles, eye drops, eardrops, tonics, gums, lozenges, etc. My job was delivering prescriptions and measuring out drys (Epsom salts, alum, lime, soda, etc.) and pouring up wets (spirits of ammonia, spirits of turpentine, tr. Merthiolate, tr. Iodine, tr. Mercurochrome, benzoin compound, castor oil, liniments, etc.). The drys were packaged in boxes and the wets in bottles with cork stoppers. These wets and drys were purchased in bulk quantities and repackaged for retail sale.

All parcels were wrapped in paper using what was called the druggist's wrap with no string or tape. Large packages were wrapped with paper and tied with string. We used an old Remington mechanical typewriter to write prescription labels. A druggist around the square was still writing labels with a number two lead pencil, so I knew that Crystal Pharmacy was up to date.

Dr. Ben apparently thought a lot of me and suggested I submit an application to college to study to become a druggist. Until then it had never crossed my mind that I could go to college. I knew that wealthy people went, but it was, in my mind, something beyond my capability. He assured me that he would pay for my tuition in college if I would come back and work with him. Wonder of wonders, I was accepted at the University of Georgia and at Southern College of Pharmacy. Suddenly, my senior year in school I was working toward something besides graduation.

I would like to report that I had no more disciplinary problems in high school, but that was not to be. A good friend named Romeo and I were horsing around before history class one day, and when we had been seated and brought to attention by the teacher, he reached up and thumped my ear. When he did, I jumped up and hit him over the head with my biggest geography book. From that we went to it. We managed to disrupt that class pretty good before the teacher could stop us. We were sent to Mr. MacDonald's office and were sentenced to walk the flagpole during recesses for the rest of the year. When we moved into the new high school, we did not have a coal-fired boiler and therefore no coal to shovel, so during recesses we had to continually walk from the main office out and around the flagpole back and forth for our punishment.

The fall of my senior year was when I had my first date with Rosalind. I had arranged to get off early one Saturday night to go to the Colquitt Theater with Pete; when we got to the ticket office there was Rosalind sitting up there selling tickets. Apparently, Pete knew Rosalind because they began talking and Rosalind invited us to go out to the Arrow-S Club on a church social. They were having a wiener roast. Pete asked me if I would rather go to the social or to the movie. I happened to have a silver dollar in my pocket and I told him I would flip it for him to call heads or tails for what we would do. I flipped the coin and told him that the social had won, so we went with Rosalind.

He never did ask to see the coin when I flipped it, and I hadn't bothered to look because I wanted to get to know her. I kept that coin in my pocket for a keepsake until 1976 when we were robbed.

In April of that school year, Mr. Ben was spending a week at his place in Daytona Beach when he drowned in the surf. There went my chance to go to college, but I had already told Rosalind and she expected me to go. We had been dating since the wiener roast and we went to the senior prom together. I had to go to Friedlander's Department Store and buy a suit for that. That was the first suit of clothes that I ever bought—and boy, did I think I looked great.

The night of the senior prom, we wound up in Norman Park for some reason and pushing the clock to get Rosalind home in time for her curfew. About halfway home I heard my motor start knocking and realized that one of the rods in the engine had come loose. The only thing I could do was drive it as far as it would go before the engine froze up to try to make it to her house. It finally quit about a mile from her house, and we had to walk the rest of the way in. While we were standing on her front porch saying good night, the porch light came on and Mr. Monk opened the door and told Rosalind that it was time for her to come in. I took that to mean that I should go home and did so immediately.

Daddy helped me pull my car into town the next morning to Parker's machine shop where they rebuilt the engine for me for one hundred and twenty dollars. I only had one hundred dollars so Mr. Parker accepted that amount and allowed me to finish paying him on time.

Graduation day finally came. Probably the best part of the whole thing was seeing Mama and Daddy sitting out there very proud. Daddy had gotten to the third grade when he had been forced to quit school and work on the farm. Mama had a good deal more schooling than Daddy did; however, neither had been able to finish school. I kept expecting to feel grown up, but the only thing I felt was that I didn't have to go to school anymore. What a relief.

I took off a few days and drove down to Lakeland, Florida, to visit Grandpa Holland. I had always gotten along real well with him because he made me feel special. He always had a knack for making me feel grown, and I felt like I needed some more of that. Mama informed him I had been accepted to college and he was real proud. He told me that I only had one chance to go through this life so to try to make the best of it, that the days of a "jack of all trades" doing well in this country was over, and if I ever expected to do well, I had to specialize.

He had been a barber as long as I had known him and he was beginning to get old. He had gotten to where he couldn't sleep well all night and would get up at two or three o'clock in the morning and make himself a pot of coffee. He also had an old fiddle that he loved to play even though he was not good at it. He could play just well enough to please himself. I suppose he learned because his brother-in-law, Uncle Bud Autry, could play. Uncle Bud, Mr. Ernest Watson, a neighbor, and my Uncle Maston (also his brother-in-law) would get together when they were younger and make music for the peanut shellings and neighborhood get-togethers. Quite often when Grandpa made his pot of coffee in the early mornings he would take out that old fiddle and play his favorite tune "Red River Valley." After a couple renditions, Grandma Vera would yell "Tom, quit making so damn much racket in there and put that g-- d--- fiddle up or I'm going to come in there and shove it up your a--." He generally would put it up and go back to bed, but usually would do it all over again the next night.

I went back to Moultrie and continued my paper route, worked in tobacco again that summer, and kept my job at the drug store during the evenings. I was seeing Rosalind as much as I could and she kept telling me I could go to college. Around July 1, I asked Rosalind to marry me and go to college together. She agreed, so we arranged another trip to Canada so we could both work in tobacco and raise enough money to pay for my first quarter tuition. I was bringing home eighteen dollars and thirty-six cents a week at the drug store so obviously we needed more money.

Mr. Swiggum had already made arrangements for that summer's help, but he arranged for his neighbor, Mr. Bob Tillotson, to use our services. We talked two young men from Moultrie into going with us and working for that good money. We charged them thirty dollars apiece for the round trip and that paid for our gasoline.

I traded my 1940 Chevrolet four-door that had been rebuilt for a 1946 Chevrolet two-door business coupe hoping to feel safer on the trip. We told Mama, Daddy, Rosalind's sister, Rachel, and her husband, Lester, that we were getting married and they were the only ones who knew. On the night of July 25, I told my bossman that I would not be back, and he gave me my week's pay of $18.36. We met Mama, Daddy, Rachel, and Lester in Sylvester and found Judge Paul who performed our marriage ceremony. After our wedding, Rosalind called her mother and told her we had gotten married and that we would spend the night in Americus with Rachel and be back in Moultrie the next day.

We loaded our possessions in our Chevy, picked up our passengers, and took off for Canada. We had a fairly uneventful trip except for flat tires. Not being able to afford new tires, every time we gassed up at service stations I would go through their stack of used tires and buy the best wore out tire they had for two or three dollars and tie it on the luggage rack on top of the car. The trip lasted a little over thirty hours and we were proud to get there. Upon arrival,

Rosalind and I were assigned a bedroom in the attic of the main house and the boys were housed in the bunkhouse.

One of our neighbors in Canada was a man named Rolley. He was an elderly gentleman and found our southern accents very entertaining. He invited us boys up to his house where he had a basement, and in that basement, he had a thousand gallon keg. Every year when the apples got ripe, he would make home brew and fill up that keg. During the long winter months, that keg helped keep him warm. He naturally was proud of his home brew and insisted we help him drink some. It didn't take long for me to begin to feel peculiar. I didn't know what was wrong, but I felt real good. That stuff tasted pretty good and I did a good number on it. By the time we got back to our place Rosalind had to help me climb that little ladder up into our attic bedroom and pour me into bed.

The Tillotsons were of German descent and enjoyed their beer. In fact, even the children were allowed to drink it. One evening after supper and before bedtime, Rosalind and I were sitting in their living room talking with them when their youngest, a little over two years old, came into the room with his beer bottle. As he came through the door he tripped over the doorsill and fell on the floor. Before he hit the floor he managed to jam his thumb into the mouth of that beer bottle and even though he sprawled out on the floor, he never spilled a drop of his beer. He got up off the floor and continued drinking from his bottle.

Mr. Tillotson had a good 22-caliber bolt-action rifle and, on slow days and in the evenings, we would take that thing and do some target shooting. It shot very true and I enjoyed shooting it—in fact, I discovered that Rosalind was as good a shot as I was. When we got tired of shooting cans at fifty paces, we began to laying coke bottles down with the neck facing us and would shoot out the bottoms from fifty paces.

The Canadians had huge barns and Mr. Tillotson's was at least one hundred yards long. It was built on the side of a hill and the upper level was at ground level in front. They had to have large barns because all the livestock had to be penned up and kept inside during the winter, because quite often, the snow was ten to fifteen feet deep. In the back end of the barn on the bottom floor was where he kept his livestock including his chickens. Every now and then some of the chickens would fly up to the top floor and make a mess and he spent a lot of time shooing the chickens back down to their level. I suggested that I could run the chickens back down by splitting the cones on their heads with the rifle. It is amazing because it worked. Not one of the chickens that had been run down with the rifle came back up, but every one of them had to have a dose to cure them. After a while I got to thinking about fried chicken and dropped my sights down and killed a good fat one. I just knew we could have chicken for supper. That put a stop to my running his chickens back downstairs right then. His wife cleaned that chicken and put it up or did something with it. We never did get any fried chicken while we were in Canada.

While we were there, we had one weekend with some time off so we decided we would go to Niagara Falls and see the sights. We drove over to Hamilton, about ninety miles, and picked up the Queen's Highway direct to Niagara Falls. From where we entered the Queen's Highway to Niagara Falls was about sixty miles and it was a four-lane highway right through the farmland. It had streetlights every quarter to half mile. Compared to what I had seen in Cincinnati, Ohio, this was really something. It was literally a super highway.

At the time, Niagara Falls was the most awesome natural sight that I had ever seen. You just cannot imagine how much water goes over that fall in twenty-four hours and consider that it has been going on since before it was first discovered. Standing on the Canadian side of the gorge and looking down the boats that were carrying tourists to see the falls from that level looked like little toy boats. When we went down the elevator to that level and looked at the boats up close, I was surprised to see that they were huge. In fact, they could carry over one hundred people at one time. We went over Rainbow Bridge to the American side and enjoyed the view from over there also. We later enjoyed telling people that we went to Niagara Falls on our honeymoon.

Working in tobacco in Canada was generally much easier than in Georgia because of the cooler weather. However, early in the season we would quite often have to sucker and crop that tobacco with ice on the leaves. Rosalind was a real trooper. She had never suckered tobacco before, and it was a new experience for her. By the end of the day's work, I knew she was tired. She handed tobacco to the stringer to be tied on the sticks all day long. There was one lavatory inside the house and no indoor shower or bathroom where we were, so we rigged up a fifty-gallon drum in the greenhouse to use as a shower. We would fill it with water in the morning and hope that the sun would warm it enough to be able to stand it at night. Sometimes it was just lukewarm but that was lots better than ice cold. The work was hard and long, but between us we were making fifteen dollars a day. We were going to need it when we got home.

Our trip home was fairly uneventful. We had the usual amount of flat tires and had accumulated four or five tires. Somewhere close to Cincinnati, Ohio, I was pulled over by an Ohio State Patrol car. The patrolman checked my license and asked me where we were from. I told him Moultrie, Georgia. Then he asked me where I got all those tires on top of the car. I explained to him that I always checked and bought the best wore out tires I could find because we went through them pretty quick. The explanation seemed to satisfy him, especially after he examined them and realized that if we were stealing tires we would surely steal better tires than what we had.

We got back to Moultrie on a Wednesday and were due in Atlanta on the next Monday to start college. We packed everything we owned and everything our parents could give us into the car and on a trailer we borrowed from Altis and her husband, Bill. We left on Friday morning. We arrived in Atlanta late Friday evening and checked into a hotel to spend the night. We knew that we had to find an apartment and get settled on Saturday. The hotel we stayed in was an old one and we had to use the bathroom down the hall, but we were only going to be there one night so it wasn't too bad. We picked up a newspaper and checked it for the rent section. We knew we couldn't afford much rent so we started looking at the lower priced efficiency apartments.

We started looking up Peachtree Road and were amazed because the only things available were in some of the old houses. The owners had divided some of the rooms by hanging sheets of canvas down the middle, putting in a small table with a hot plate, and calling them efficiency apartments. All of those apartments shared a common bathroom. The amazing thing to me was that they were renting them to people to live in and were successful in doing so. We made our way up to Buckhead and worked our way east looking at everything advertised for rent that we thought we might afford. Finally, we found a furnished duplex about five miles east of Buckhead on a little road called Lookout Avenue. We should have known from the name that we were in for a rough time, but after seeing some of the aforementioned apartments, this one seemed great.

The man who owned the place was a self-styled brick mason, built it himself as a single dwelling, and added on the duplex side to increase his income. The windows were drafty, which was all right in the summertime, but in wintertime, it was impossible to heat. The one thing that he was so proud of was the bathroom. We had one indoors that both families utilized. He had made the bathtub himself out of concrete. It looked all right; however, when you bathed in it you scratched your skin on the rough concrete and when you got out of the bath you felt gritty from the sand and concrete that continually washed out of the tub. There was just no way you could get clean in that tub. Our side also was blessed with an icebox for a refrigerator. The iceman came once a week, and on weeks we didn't have any money, there was no way we could keep things cold. Even that would have been all right except that occasionally slugs would climb up into the thing through the drainpipe. Rosalind had never seen a slug before and some of these were three to four inches long and as big around as your finger.

We found our place late Saturday afternoon and had Saturday night and Sunday to get settled in. I had to be at Oglethorpe University Monday morning because the first year of pharmacy school was there, at eight a.m. for my first day. We had hit the big time—I was in college.

Chapter 10:
The College Years

I paid my tuition for the quarter and attended orientation. We went through a short schedule of our classes and listened to our professors give us an overview of our college courses. In our chemistry class, the professor told us to take a good look at the people seated on either side of us because in four years both of those people would not be here to graduate. I hoped right then that I was the one in the middle because I wanted to graduate.

I had just spent most of the money Rosalind and I had earned during the summer and was in school, so now I needed a job. When I left Oglethorpe University that afternoon at three, I began looking for a job. I found one right there in Brookhaven at Brookhaven Pharmacy just about one mile from the university. They hired me to begin work at three-thirty p.m. and work till closing at ten p.m. I was to work eight hours each Saturday and six hours on Sunday. My weekly take home pay was about thirty-eight dollars. I was making the grand sum of eighty-five cents per hour. This more or less set the tone for the next eight years of our lives. We always needed about fifty dollars more than we earned just to pay rent, utilities, and tuition.

Oglethorpe was good enough to allow us to pay our tuition weekly after the first quarter. That helped a lot because there was no way we could raise enough money to pay the whole quarter at the beginning of each one. Notice I didn't include groceries in the necessities. When we went to Moultrie, Rosalind's parents always sent foodstuff home with us, thank goodness. We stayed slim and trim all the time we were in school, but without her parents' help we may still be in school. We didn't have enough sense to realize that we couldn't do it.

During high school, I had taken no college preparatory courses and the first day in chemistry class the chemistry professor asked everyone who had taken high school chemistry to raise their hands. All but about four or five of us raised their hands and he said for everyone to pay attention because he was going to cover high school chemistry that day. I had mixed emotions at that announcement. I didn't know whether to be glad I hadn't wasted a year in high school chemistry or be sad that I was going to have to do a year's work in one day. All in all that first year of college went pretty well as far as schooling was concerned.

Rosalind found a job in a dime store on Peachtree Road close to Piedmont Road. We were both working now and as the weather began to get cold it was obvious to Rosalind that we would probably freeze to death in our modern apartment. We discovered that we were going to be parents in the spring, and we didn't want a little one to be in this place. Rosalind kept working until she had to quit. One of our neighbors told her about Techwood apartments. Techwood apartments were one of the original Atlanta housing projects and the rent was based on our income. Rosalind checked them out and we decided we should move. We were on the third floor but the place was warm as toast. They were heated with steam radiators, and quite often, we had to open the windows just to cool down some. This apartment was unfurnished so we had a warm place with no furniture. Rosalind's mother gave her the bedroom suite that she had used at home and ordered us a dinette set from Sears. It was a neat red table and six chairs with chrome legs. Next, she ordered us an overstuffed sofa and matching chair to use in the living room. She realized that with a baby coming, and with what we were making, there was no way that we could afford furniture. Rosalind's sister donated us her old wringer type washing machine.

Until then Rosalind had to carry the laundry down three flights of stairs and into the basement where there were some coin-operated washing machines. She would maneuver the laundry down, then have to go back upstairs to wait while the clothes washed. Then she had to go back down and take them out and hang them up on the lines out back to dry then go back upstairs to wait till they were dry then go back down and gather them up to carry back upstairs to fold and iron. The addition of the washing machine helped very much. The only problem was that the transmission on the thing was leaking oil on the kitchen floor. I took it apart and made a new gasket and put it back together, and wonder of wonders, no more oil. The location helped also. We were in the block next to Grant Field at Georgia Tech and had access to Peachtree Street. We could get to work and home more easily.

I enjoyed working at Brookhaven Pharmacy. It was owned by two men who were as opposite as Mutt and Jeff in the comic strips. One was short and stocky, the other tall and slim. We had a soda fountain that occupied the whole left side of the store. At that time, we wrapped most everything that was sold and didn't use many bags at all. We always prewrapped the Kotex so that the ladies would not be too embarrassed when they purchased them. One day, a lady came in and when I asked if I could help her she said she was just looking so I let her shop by herself. Because of the problem of shoplifters, we always kept our eyes on people, so it was normal that I did so. She went up and down all the aisles until she came to the Kotex. When she found them, she picked up a package and placed it under the flap of her coat.

Then I definitely kept an eye on her. She went up to the front cash register and got into line to pay for her purchase. When it became her time to pay, she eased the package onto the counter as inconspicuously as she could. The cashier took the package, looked it over, and could not find the price on it. She held it up over her head waving it around and yelled to the back of the store for the price. The lady was mortified. She took two quick steps to her left and studiously began picking out some chewing gum. I yelled out thirty-nine cents and immediately went to make sure all the rest of the packages had the price on them. I don't think that lady ever came back in that store. If she did, I didn't see her. We also explained to the cashier to be a little more considerate of what she was doing in order not to embarrass anybody else.

The tall, slim owner had a copy of a check framed and hanging on the back wall from Gillette Company. The druggist who worked there told me that he had submitted the idea for adjusting the angles on safety razors so that you could get a closer shave. This idea led to the adjustable safety razor that became Gillette's trademark. I don't know if the story was true, but it made a good conversation piece.

One day while I was working with the short one—the tall one was off—a salesman came in selling Camay soap. We had a good business and moved a lot of merchandise. That salesman put a job on my boss and sold him a railroad boxcar load of Camay personal size soap. Do you have any idea how much soap a boxcar will hold? I didn't either until it came in. There literally was not enough room in the stockroom to hold it all even if there had been nothing else in there. We had a problem because the deliverymen began to stack the soap outside on the drive. My tall bossman came in about the time they had unloaded the soap and were driving off. He couldn't believe what he was seeing. He got so mad I thought he was going to explode and went immediately to the prescription department where he confronted the short one.

They got into the loudest argument I had ever witnessed (and I had seen some good ones) right there in the store. I thought they were going to kill each other. No blows were passed but I couldn't understand why not. If anybody had talked to me like that I would have had to fight. They finally settled down and sent me to find a storage place to put the soap. I found a room in the back of a dime store there in Brookhaven that we could rent. They assigned me the job of hauling and storing the soap. Before I got through I was just about as mad as the tall bossman. Any price concessions he had gotten on the purchase price was eaten up by the rent. I bet there is still some boxes of that Camay soap somewhere in Brookhaven, Georgia.

The tall bossman had a friend who came in to see him and visit with him quite often. His friend had been a salesman for Nunnally Candy Company for a long time and had just recently retired. They and their wives apparently socialized together and were all very good friends. One day when the man was leaving the store, I happened to see him take something off one of the shelves and put it in his pocket. I told my bossman what I had seen but he couldn't believe it. From then on, anytime he came in we would watch him. After the man had picked up some item or other over a three-week period and with some of the other clerks agreeing that they had seen him do it too, my bossman agreed to watch also. Sure enough, the man picked up something on his way out. My boss man accosted him in the parking lot and they had a long discussion. He came back in with a bottle of shaving lotion, put it back on the shelf, and told us he had asked the man not to come into the store anymore. I never saw that man in there again and I believe that it ruined a good friendship. That was my introduction to kleptomania. That man was in good shape financially and had no reason to steal anything.

There was one professor at Oglethorpe that I will always remember. He was an Englishman and had quite an accent. The first day of class he walked into the room as the bell signaled the start of class. He had a stack of papers in his hand, the top of which was a list of the students in the class. There were about thirty of us in the class and he asked us to raise our hand when he called our name. He told us that he would not call the roll anymore that quarter, however, that didn't mean that any of us who didn't show up would be marked as present. He would remember each of us and if we didn't show up he would certainly mark us absent.

He said calling the roll each class just took up a lot of time that we could be spending in studies. He then passed out the stack of papers he had brought into the room with him. He told us that these papers were an outline of the course that he would teach and for us to study and be prepared because he would give four pop quizzes during the quarter and the final would be comprehensive. He said that the bell's ringing signaled the start of class and the end of class. We were to be in our seats and have our pencils and paper ready at the sound of the bell and we were not to put anything up until after the bell at the end of the class.

The rest of the quarter, he would walk through the door at the sound of the bell and would be talking as he entered. He would continue talking for the hour, and just as the bell rang at the end of class, he would be going out through the door still talking. He was always the last one in class and the first to leave. Some of the students tried him on his ability to remember us and he always responded to the students by their name. Sure enough, four times during the quarter he would walk in talking and suddenly tell us to put up our books and then give us a pop test that usually took about fifteen minutes. He would take up the papers and finish the class with his talking. He would leave on schedule. The next morning he would hand our papers to us with the grades on them. I had heard of the English and their punctuality. This man must have been whom they were talking about.

On March 17, 1956, the miracle we had been expecting appeared—a beautiful baby girl that we named Laura Sue. She was born at Georgia Baptist Hospital and was just gorgeous. What an experience! I was a father. I was strutting around in the drug store for a few days when the druggist told me that any man could do what I had done up to that point. It was what I would do from now on that would decide whether I would be a daddy or not.

I finished my first year of pharmacy school at Oglethorpe University in June that year and was all set to continue my education in the fall at Southern College of Pharmacy in downtown Atlanta. It became obvious to me and to Rosalind that we were not making enough money for me to continue my schooling on a full time basis. When I asked my bossman for a raise, he said that he couldn't afford to pay more than he was paying for the job I was doing. Shortly thereafter, I went next door to the Shell service station and asked for a job pumping gas and greasing and washing cars. The man hired me on the spot and began paying me fifty dollars a week. This was a twelve dollar a week increase above my pay at the drug store.

Even though I had a larger income, we still couldn't afford for me to go to school full time at Southern College of Pharmacy. We talked to them and made arrangements for me to go to what used to be the Atlanta division of the University of Georgia (Georgia State College now) and take some courses at night that would count when I could go back to Southern College of Pharmacy full time.

We were selling gasoline for twenty-six cents a gallon and a lube job cost seventy-five cents. A wash job was one dollar. Most of the time, a complete service job on a car, including gasoline, was less than ten dollars. I worked at that service station for around six months before I found another job in a drug store.

On March 12, 1957, we were blessed with another little girl. Her name was Karen Lee and she was just as beautiful as her older sister Laura. She was born at St. Joseph's Infirmary in Atlanta. I was proud as could be and realized that I could not feed my family and go to school on fifty dollars a week, so I began looking for a better paying job.

I found a job at Mimms Pharmacy at the corner of Ponce de Leon Avenue and Boulevard Drive in Atlanta. The boss agreed to pay me seventy-five dollars a week. Now I was in high cotton. We still were not making enough to pay all of our bills, but we started whittling them down slowly. I was still going to night school at Georgia State College three nights a week, but I had to drop out of school for two quarters in order to pay bills. In the meantime, somehow, I got my hands on an old guitar, and since Weldon was playing and singing, I decided that I wanted to do the same thing. My biggest problem was that I was totally tone deaf. I could not carry a tune in a bucket and knew absolutely nothing about music. We had a neighbor named Donald Peace who could play a guitar, and he agreed to show me how to tune it and how to form three basic chords—C, G, and D. He assured me that was all I had to know in order to actually play the thing. Believing him completely, I proceeded to play the stew out of it. As tone deaf as I was, I knew that I didn't sound like he did.

Through my perseverance, and Rosalind's help and tolerance, I finally got a recognizable tune out of that guitar. Rosalind had a good ear and knew music as well and could sing good. She has to be a saint to have put up with my framming and bellowing. She helped me by telling me when I was off-key or had the wrong note. For a while there, I thought I was going to be as good as Merle Travis. I finally realized I would never be in that category and contented myself by trying to play some of the songs I thought I knew.

We had a neighbor downstairs who was a whiz at electronics, and he helped me to build an amplifier for the guitar using an old radio. He disconnected the tuner and put a plug into the amplifier part. We used a needle from a high-fi record player for the pickup by taping it onto the body of the guitar with the needle embedded. We plugged it into the amplifier and bingo! I had an electric guitar. He then took a small speaker out of another radio and put a transformer in the line and we used this for a microphone. Now I could really get loud. It was a wonder Rosalind didn't kick me out, but I had a ball.

We needed more room for all of us to live in, so Rosalind talked the Techwood housing authority into giving us a two-bedroom apartment to move into. We were living on the third floor and the move would be one block down the street and back up three flights of stairs. We were told that we could move immediately, and not having time to gather up boxes, we moved using the drawers out of our chest of drawers. We would carry a load in the drawers, unpack, and go back for another drawer full. My sister Altis and her husband Bill came up to Atlanta to help us with our move. We didn't have all that much, but by the time we got through my disposition was not at its best. Before we went to bed I said too much too loud to Rosalind about one thing in particular. When we awoke the next morning, we discovered that Altis and Bill had left during the night and returned to Moultrie. I didn't even get to thank them for helping us move.

After being out of school for two quarters, Rosalind assured me that it was time for me to get back in school. I went back down to Georgia State to enroll for night school for the next quarter and was told that I could not go. It seemed that the school had instituted a policy whereby if you were not continuously in school, you had to take an entrance exam and wait a quarter to go to school. I was told by friends that this had been adopted in order to prevent some colored factions from disrupting school in order to push integration. I was crushed at this news and told Rosalind that I might as well find another job and go to work. She reassured me that we were here to get a pharmacy degree and that is what we will do.

I was told to take the exam anyway so that I could go the next quarter. The exam was to be given on Thursday evening before classes started on the following Monday. I went on down and took the exam then begged the admissions lady to allow me to get back into school. She informed me that it was not possible. On Monday, Mr. Noah Langdale called the house and told me to be in school that evening without fail. He inferred that I had made a good grade on the examination. Obviously, I was not intending to disrupt school. What a relief, I was back in school. After that episode, I was very careful to stay in school.

My boss at Mimms Pharmacy asked me if I had any classmates in school who may want to work. I recommended a high school classmate and a friend of his, Gerald and Malcolm. He hired both of them. The peculiar thing about Malcolm was that he went by the first name of Mac. His last name was Forte. When he received his telephone and was listed in the Atlanta telephone directory, of course, it was under Forte, Mac. In any town except Atlanta, that would have been okay, but Atlanta was the home of Fort McPherson army base and was commonly referred to as Fort Mac. For the first week or so, he said that it was fun receiving calls at all times of day and night by people trying to call Fort Mac.

But then it got very annoying.

An antihistamine called Benadryl (diphenhydramine) was on the market and was heavily promoted for allergies. Many people used it to treat cold symptoms; however, it produced so much drowsiness it wasn't accepted well for colds. Mac had a problem with hay fever and used it regularly. This was the year Schering Drug Company came out with an antihistamine called chlor-trimeton. It was hailed as a drug that would eliminate colds. Benadryl, another antihistamine, had already been on the market and was used to combat allergies. Mac came down with a cold and began taking Benadryl when Gerald recommended chlor-trimeton. He began taking it and immediately got better and hailed chlor-trimeton as a cure for the common cold. Suddenly, I came down with a cold and grabbed the chlor-trimeton; however, it didn't do anything to help me, just made me drowsy and thickened my mucous. Apparently, by the time Mac began taking the chlor-trimeton his cold was dissipating. This was when I discovered that antihistamines were actually better used for a condition called hay fever due to their drying properties.

These drugs led pharmaceutical chemists to develop and explore antihistamines and they produced and studied many different compounds. In school, we were told there were as many as seventy-five antihistamines studied; however, they were very weak in antihistamine activity. One common effect was very little drowsiness. It was decided that due to the weak antihistamine effect, there was little future in marketing them to the public. In years to come this effect was utilized to produce a fantastic market for antihistamines that produce very little drowsiness.

Mimms Pharmacy was across the street from Westminster Presbyterian Church where Peter Marshall had preached. We opened at seven o'clock in the morning, closed at eleven o'clock at night for six days a week, and opened from eleven to eleven on Sunday. At the time, the boss was the only person working there with a pharmacy license. Obviously, sixteen hours a day was a long time. Quite often he would slip out of the store, go down to the theater two doors down, and rest in the back of the theater. When he did this, he would leave Mac, Gerald, and me to look after things. We were quite aware that Georgia law required that a licensed person be physically in charge of the prescription department and if anything came up we couldn't handle, we were to go to the theater and get him.

Mac's daddy, who lived in Columbus, either was serving or had just finished serving as a member of the Georgia State Board of Pharmacy. Sure enough, one late Friday afternoon, a well-dressed man came in and proceeded to enter the prescription department. I managed to intercept him and blocked his way, informing him that no one could go back there because it was closed. He assured me that he could and tried to get by me but I blocked him. Mac was sitting in the prescription department and when he realized what was going on he turned a little pale. The man then asked me what my name was and I told him. He asked who Mac was and Mac told him. He asked us what we thought we were doing, and I told him that we were told to allow no one in the prescription department and that was what we were doing. I then asked him who he thought he was.

In the meantime, Gerald, who was in the area of the soda fountain, realized what was going on and ran down to the theater to get Mr. Mimms. That man told me to get out of his way, and I told him again that he could not go back there. He then asked Mac if he knew who he was and Mac said yes sir. He told Mac to tell me who he was and Mac said, "Truman, this man is the chief drug inspector for the state of Georgia." So I asked him if this was true and he assured me that he was. I asked him if he had any identification, which he then proceeded to show me. I then told him that it was quite all right for him to go on back.

The inspector then proceeded to reprimand us for being in the prescription department and asked us if we realized what the law required in that regard. We assured him that we did. He then asked us if we wanted to finish pharmacy school and subsequently receive a pharmacy license. He told us that if he ever caught us in that situation again that would be all for us as far as a future in pharmacy was concerned. He asked Mac if he thought his dad would be pleased to hear of this episode, and Mac assured him that his dad wouldn't. By this time, Mr. Mimms had returned. Then it was his and Gerald's turn for a tongue-lashing.

The inspector finally told us that we had acted properly in refusing to allow anyone back there and asked me if I thought I would recognize him if he ever ran into me again. I assured him that I would and that I wouldn't block him from entering any prescription department again. He then told me that in the future as a pharmacist, I would have many instances where I would have to make decisions. Quite often people pressured pharmacists to do things that are illegal. He told me that if I always made sure that the welfare of the patient came first, not my interest or income, then I would be able to defend myself in court. As far as I know, he never told on us, either to the school or Mac's daddy. Eventually, after Mac and Gerald had gone on to other jobs and schooling, it became almost routine for Mr. Mimms to leave me in the store by myself, quite often for a whole day.

When I first started to work in a pharmacy, it was common to refer to pharmacy as count and pour, lick and stick, as it was a basic description of what we did. Paper labels had a gum back and after writing the instructions, the back was moistened so it would stick to the glass bottles. In fact, all the bottles were glass and most of them required cork stoppers. We dispensed a lot of tablets in cardboard boxes called slides. There was no such thing as plastic or scotch tape, so there was always a big ball of string on the wrapping counter. Pharmacies used white butcher paper to wrap packages and had developed a special wrapping process called the pharmacy wrap. This way of wrapping required no string to hold the package together. In fact, this technique was taught in the practical pharmacy class in school.

Down the street behind the pharmacy on Boulevard, which was later changed to Monroe Drive, were some old Victorian houses. The area was somewhat run down, and in a couple of these houses, some ladies of ill repute conducted thriving businesses. I finally figured out what was going on because one of them regularly purchased large quantities of prophylactics.

When Parke Davis Drug Company came out with a drug called Norlestrin, a precursor of birth control pills, these ladies' businesses got an automatic twenty-five percent increase in productivity. No longer did the ladies have to take off a week to go through menstruation. The madams were rather pleased.

One evening around nine o'clock the madam called me at the store and asked me what to do for one of her girls who had taken a handful of Nembutal and went to bed, leaving a note as to what she had done. She had taken the Nembutal about two hours before they found the note. They had roused the girl but couldn't get her fully awake. I suggested they take her to the hospital, but they ruled that out immediately and wanted me to give her something. I explained that I could not give her anything and that it was probably too late for a stomach pump to have much effect on her; however, in the hospital they could give her some stimulants to try to counteract the Nembutal. They asked what they could do, and I told them that the only thing they could do was not let her go to sleep for eight to ten hours, try to get some coffee in her and have two people just walk her around until she woke up, even if it took all night. I told them that they should be sure that if she quits breathing to get her to the hospital immediately because she would die if they didn't. They said they would do it because they didn't want to have to go to the hospital. When I got back to work the next day, I called to check on the girl and was told that she made it. I was also told that the girl was better off than the two who stayed up with her all night and had worked so hard to keep her awake.

It was about this time that a drug called Milltown hit the market. It was a new tranquilizer, Meprobamate, and it revolutionized medicine. Up until now, the most used drugs for this indication were phenobarbital, bromides, or opium derivatives. Soon after its debut, the same drug labeled Equanil hit the market. This drug was the precursor to a group of drugs released over the following years, which led to the book *The Valley of the Dolls*. The names of these drugs were, in order of the patents running out, Valium, Xanax, Ativan, Halcion, etc. Each of these drugs were in the same family and were developed by altering the chemical formula in order to produce the same effect, including me-toos. This changed the time for absorption or the half-life of the drug in the body. They were prescribed for nervousness, anxiety, insomnia, muscle relaxers, or sometimes for pure pleasure. Each change was granted a new patent by the government, which gave the manufacturer exclusive use of the drug for years. All of these drugs produced untold revenue for their manufacturers.

The drug Meprobamate was subsequently chemically altered to match the chemical produced by the first pass through the liver. This drug was called Soma (carisprodol) and prescribed as a muscle relaxer. It was granted a new patent. In order to further the use of Soma, the company combined it with aspirin and called it Soma Compound. The theory was that we had a muscle relaxer and pain reliever in one tablet.

We had an elderly woman named Zella who worked on the soda fountain and cooked short order foods. She made the best chili hot dogs I had ever eaten. One day a man came in and ordered two of them. He sat there and ate them and when it came time to pay he told my boss's wife, who was working the cash register, that they were the worst hot dogs that he had ever had and that he was not going to pay for them. When she informed him that he was going to pay for them, he got loud and started cursing. When he got loud, I immediately went to the front to find out what was going on. The man told me that he was not going to pay that b---- anything and that was it. When he said that, I hit him as hard as I could. He hit the floor and I told him that he was going to pay and that he was going to apologize to the lady. When he got up from the floor, he backed down the aisle, and using his hand, he knocked all the merchandise off the top row of shelves right onto the floor. All those glass bottles hitting that tile floor created a racket you could hear a block away. I grabbed him and shook him pretty hard and took his billfold out of his pocket and made him pay for the hot dogs and apologize to Mrs. Mimms, then I threw him out the front door.

I started cleaning up the mess he had made, picking up broken glass and getting ready to mop the mess up when Zella yelled out that he was coming back in. I immediately blocked the door so he couldn't get in. He started kicking the plate glass door. Mrs. Mimms yelled that he would break the plate glass, so I stepped outside with him and tried to hold him away from the door. He kicked me on the shin so I knocked him down again. A city bus stop was in front of the store and as luck would have it, one was stopped there at the time. When he hit the sidewalk, he rolled off under the bus right under the back dual wheels. The driver had been watching all the commotion and was ready to leave. He got out of the bus and dragged the man out from under it then got back in and drove off. Mrs. Mimms came to the door and said that she had called the police and they were on the way. The man then tried to get up and leave so I sat him down on the sidewalk and held him there with my foot until the police came and took him away. I still had a mess to clean up and have not wanted any more altercations in a store.

Rosalind discovered that the project we lived in had some nice floor-level apartments across the street and put in to an application to get one for us to live in. She was successful and we were allowed to move into one of the nicest places I had ever lived in. We had the living room and kitchen on the ground floor, two bedrooms and bathroom upstairs, and our own backyard that was fenced in. I even got some concrete blocks and a wire shelf out of an old refrigerator and made us an outdoor barbecue grill.

Laura and Karen were really growing now. We had some neighbors named Nations. Mrs. Nations had begun to feed a squirrel on our shared backyard fence and had almost made a pet out of him. He would walk the top of the fence between our backyards up to her door and she would feed him peanut butter out of a spoon. She named him Billy and would call him to come eat. From watching her, Karen came to understand that all squirrels were Billys and for a long time whenever she would see a squirrel she would exclaim, "There goes a Billy."

Paregoric, camphorated tincture of opium, is a common remedy and was in demand by anyone raising a child. It was very useful for teething pain and colic. Being a narcotic, it was also in demand by anyone who liked to get a kick. It was legal to sell anyone two ounces in forty-eight hours, and we had a book that all purchasers had to sign. In fact, there were quite a number of people who bought their allowance every two days. There were six drug stores between Peachtree Street and Plaza Drugstore on Ponce de Leon. Obviously, people could get quite a lot of paregoric just by going from store to store.

One of these men explained to me that he put the paregoric in the freezer and the camphor would precipitate to the bottom, then he would pour the liquid containing the opium in the alcohol off the top. He would then boil away the alcohol to get concentrated opium, which he would then inject directly into his veins with a glass medicine dropper. He showed me a silver teaspoon that he had filed down to a sharp point with which he could cut into the veins on the back of his hand in order to get the dropper into the vein.

What he told must have been true because many of these people's hands were swollen so bad that they could hardly hold a pencil to write their names in the narcotic exempt registry book. Some looked as if they had boxing gloves on. My bossman decided that if they bought paregoric, they must also purchase something else. He demanded that they make the purchases so that the narcotic sales would not be so obvious. The regulars caught on quick and would always make some little purchase in order to please him. He finally put up a little table of old merchandise marked down and began to get rid of a lot of dead merchandise. Most of them would pick up one of the items and nod in order to make the purchase. Some of these people were real con artists and would really put pressure on us to sell them more than the legal amount or to sell paregoric more often than the law allowed. Some of the tales and requests would almost make you cry.

One Friday evening around seven o'clock, two men came into the store while my boss and I were working and showed my boss some badges. They proceeded to arrest him on suspicion of selling exempt narcotics illegally. They took him and their car and left. They didn't allow him to call anybody, not even his wife. If I hadn't been there at the time no one would have known what had happened. That was when I found out that anyone could be arrested on suspicion and held for seventy-two hours before any charges had to be made against them. In the interim, you cannot contact anybody and nobody can contact you. The police department does not even have to verify that you are there. I called his wife and told her what had happened and she immediately called their lawyer. I went ahead and closed up that night and checked with her in the morning; she asked me to open the store and work until she could get him out of jail. Her lawyer had had no luck contacting him or even verifying that he was in jail. They held him until Monday morning when they charged him, then his lawyer got him out.

When he could talk about it, he told me that one of our special customers had convinced him to sell him an eight-ounce bottle of paregoric instead of the two-ounce size, and he promised not to come back for two weeks. Not only had he agreed to do it, he carried it to him at a service station in order not to have it sold in the store. This is directly against the advice given to me by the chief drug inspector regarding what you are doing and who will benefit. Apparently, the agents were watching the whole delivery and arrested the man immediately. They then came to the store and arrested my boss. The car he was driving was held for the six months that it took for the case to come up in court. The judge allowed a nolo contendere plea and dismissed the charges.

By the time he got his car back, he had given me another raise. Rosalind and I felt like I could go back to school full time. We also bought the car from him because his wife didn't want it anymore. It was a solid white 1957 Chrysler Windsor and had tail fins a mile long. We drove that car until I finished school.

My raise created a problem with the housing project because we were making too much money to stay there. We had to find another place to live. We still had big bills to pay, my tuition as well as the rent and other bills, but we had to go. Rosalind found us a house in Decatur on East Ponce de Leon Avenue. It was a nice little white frame house with lots of French doors and windows on the front and side porches and we could just afford it.

That fall I took off down to Southern College of Pharmacy to register and transfer my credits. I expected to finish up in two more years. We had then been in Atlanta four years. They informed me Mercer University had taken over operation of the school and that I could not transfer any credits at all. If I wanted to go to school there, I would have to start all over as a freshman in the first four-year class in the history of the school. Up to now, all students had to take a freshman year in another liberal arts school then go to Southern for three years in order to get a degree. My alternatives now were the same as when we started. Either go to the University of Georgia or Auburn University. In either place, I would not be able to get a job where I would be able to pay my own way. I felt like quitting school and getting a job, I told Rosalind that I could get a diploma in chemistry or psychology in a short time. Rosalind insisted that we were here to get a diploma in pharmacy because that is what I wanted. Even though the tuition was higher at Mercer, we really had no alternative but to accept what they offered so I registered and started school all over again.

Chapter 11:
The College Years, Again

I had been going to school for four years and had all the freshman courses as well as the sophomore courses and was having really no trouble with my studies. In fact, when we had to take algebra one I probably was better qualified to teach it than the pharmacy professor—whose job it became. The same was true for chemistry. Early in the quarter, when we had had a test in chemistry class, as I left the room, two fellow students (Wade Buchanan and Jerry Brooks), were waiting for me and asked me if they could study with me. I told them sure they could, but I didn't get off work until eleven at night and it took me thirty minutes to get home. That night both of them were at our house waiting for me. The next night there were four of them. From then on, throughout four years of school, we had three or four fellows at our house studying every night. When it became time for finals, we had as many as ten.

Rosalind always woke me up at six thirty every morning and sent me off to school. School started at eight, and I generally got out of school at three in the afternoon and went directly to the drug store where I worked until eleven. When I got home, I had at least one or two hours of studying to do before I could call it a day. Generally, on Saturdays, I worked for ten hours either opening at seven in the morning or going in at one o'clock. I worked every other Sunday from eleven in the morning to eleven at night. When it was averaged out, I was working more than fifty hours each week at the drug store. Therein was what later would turn out to be a problem at school, because they said we could not work more than twenty hours a week and go to school.

That winter was the first time we had had snow since we had been in Atlanta. One morning we woke up and everything was white. We had about six inches of snow. It was beautiful, but when I stepped out onto the porch to go to work I slipped down, slid off the porch, down the steps, onto the walkway, down another set of steps, and halfway across the street before I could stop. I managed to get up and get off to school. I didn't get to see Laura and Karen play in it, but Rosalind said they had a ball. That stuff began to melt then came a hard freeze. We had an icicle hanging off the back porch longer than our yardstick and as big around as a football.

That winter was one of the coldest I can remember. That little frame house was not insulated at all. It had a gas heater in the floor in the corner of the living room. The wind blew in by the windows and doors like a gale. One month we had paid the rent and my tuition and did not have enough money to pay the gas bill. Sure enough, they came out on Friday afternoon and cut the gas off. When I got home that night I took a hacksaw, cut the lock off the switch, and turned it back on. Monday when I got to work, I borrowed enough money from my boss to pay that bill—those people never did say anything about me sawing through the lock.

One day when I got home, I discovered the heater off and Rosalind trying to clean it out. She told me that Karen had put the plastic clothes hamper on the grill above the heater and she didn't find it until it was too late. The odor was terrible and it took some doing to get the melted plastic out of there and get it to where you could stay in the house with the smell.

Our deliveryman at the drug store normally delivered on a motorcycle. One time, when the motorcycle was in the shop, my boss let him drive his car. On Saturday morning at nine o'clock, he left for his first delivery. He didn't come back. Normally he would be back every hour or two and deliver some more packages. Around five in the afternoon, I called my boss and told him that the deliveryman was missing. He came in and began trying to find him. At ten thirty p.m., he found him in the emergency room at Grady Hospital. He had a wreck just before nine a.m. and was carried to the emergency room. The police towed the car downtown and had not notified anybody. When he got to him, he was still lying on a gurney in the hall. He had a broken arm and a concussion; at that time, a doctor had not examined him. My boss had a conversation with the hospital personnel and they got busy. He was admitted and in the hospital for five days. I know that it was a busy place, but I couldn't understand why that was allowed to happen, even if the man was black.

I got in trouble along here due to a customer using three or four doctors to get prescriptions for Empirin with codeine number three. I thought I was doing the right thing because Empirin number three was Borroughs and Welcome's brand of APC (aspirin phenacetin and caffeine) with 30mg of codeine in each tablet. He was obviously addicted to the codeine. I mentioned to his primary doctor that he was getting prescriptions for it from two more doctors. Apparently, his doctor accosted him and dismissed him as a patient. The patient in turn called my boss and raked him over the coals. My boss informed me that I shouldn't have told his doctor. He needed to retain all his customers; what they did was their business. I apologized even though I didn't think I had done wrong—I needed to keep my job.

In my new sophomore year at school, I joined a fraternity. Phi Delta Chi, a pharmaceutical fraternity, had a national convention in Minneapolis, Minnesota, and I was chosen to go and represent Mercer University. The fraternity paid for the trip. I was on a night flight from Atlanta to St. Paul and had never been on an airplane before. This particular plane was propeller driven and my seat was right behind the right wing. The exhaust pipes from the engine came right across the top of the wing right close to the back edge, and I could see it begin to glow when the pilot took off. He poured the gas to those engines and we began to climb.

I was busy looking at Atlanta's skyline at night and was enjoying the sights, until I looked down toward the wing and saw that exhaust pipe was white hot. It had changed from red to white. I didn't know anything about airplanes, but I had seen people welding and believed that if that thing got any hotter, the wing would melt right off. I mentioned it to the fellow sitting right beside me, and he raised up to look and told me that was normal. He had been in the Air Force, and they always did that. I breathed a little sigh of relief and relaxed some. I sure didn't like the thought of that wing falling off.

Wintertime in Minneapolis–St. Paul was quite an experience for me. The first thing that was obvious was I didn't own enough clothes to keep warm. Snow piled up head-high along the curbs with the sidewalks just clean enough to walk on. I couldn't even see the cars in the street until I came to a crosswalk. It was so cold I couldn't even walk a city block without having to step inside some building to warm up enough to try it again. I'm sure that some of those shopkeepers were quite surprised when I popped in and just stood there. I decided right then that I could not live that far north and would be glad to get back to Georgia.

Our return flight to Atlanta was a daytime flight with a stopover in Chicago. Once again, I was seated behind the right wing and could see that big jet engine hanging from the wing. When that plane took off, I felt like we were going straight up. I could see the heat coming from the engine. The countryside was absolutely white. Anywhere you looked, there was snow. The whole world looked like it was covered in a white blanket. We continued to climb and I enjoyed looking at the ground when suddenly the plane leveled off and I felt light in my seat. The plane actually bumped because I could feel it. I looked at the wing of that plane and realized that the engine I had been looking at was gone. I glanced around the plane and everyone was relaxed as if everything was normal. Could you believe I was the only one who knew we had lost an engine? As inconspicuously as I could, I called the stewardess over and told her we had lost an engine. She leaned over, looked, and assured me that we hadn't. I told her that I had watched that engine since I had gotten on the plane and now it was gone. She told me that what I had seen was the afterburner and that when the plane reached altitude the pilot retracted the thing for cruising. I felt a little foolish, but boy was I relieved. This country boy was getting an education.

One day, a long black Cadillac pulled up in front of the store and a nicely dressed man came in and introduced himself as a doctor and showed us identification, which proved that he was a doctor from California. He asked if he could write a prescription for his client for some blood pressure medicine, and we told him yes. He immediately issued a prescription for Cecil B. DeMille. Mr. DeMille was in town for an anniversary showing of *Gone with the Wind.* It was true that Mr. DeMille was in the car, because we went out to see. I think Mr. Mimms kept and framed that prescription.

While I worked at Mimms pharmacy, Eli Lilly Drug Company came out with a drug they called Darvon. The chemical name was propoxyphene. We were told that it was a chemical isomer of codeine; however, it was not habit forming. It was to produce the same pain relief as codeine, an opium derivative. This drug became a blockbuster revenue producer. Since codeine was used to reduce coughing, Lilly introduced what they called the reverse chemical structure of Darvon and labeled it Novrad. Novrad was promoted for cough. For some reason, it never seemed to catch on with the public—probably because it didn't produce the euphoria that codeine or Darvon did and didn't work as well for cough as codeine. Darvon seemed to produce more euphoria than pain relief and some people loved it. As the patent began to run out, Lilly combined the drug with aspirin and called it Darvon Compound. Finally, it did produce pain relief and was one of the biggest all time revenue producers for Lilly. As the patent ran out on Darvon Compound, in the future Lilly combined Darvon with acetaminophen (Tylenol). They called it Darvocet, which gave them another patent run and promoted it as a safe alternative to Darvon Compound because acetaminophen did not irritate the stomach or cause internal bleeding. The propoxyphene family of drugs produced revenue for Lilly for many years.

My boss owned a place on Lake Allatoona. Actually, it was a house that floated on the water and was tied to land by cables. It had a built in boat dock and he bought a Chris Craft cabin cruiser with twin gray marine engines. He would occasionally carry us up and entertain us, and that was really an experience. From riding on a piece of tin that was folded into a boat to a real cabin cruiser, I felt like I had arrived. He had a nickel slot machine in his cabin and it needed adjusting. It was set to pay forty to sixty and he wanted it to pay thirty to seventy. I told him I could do it and finally figured it out and reset it for him.

One block up Ponce de Leon Avenue at Park Avenue was McConnell's Pharmacy. Mr. McConnell called me one day and offered me a raise to come work for him. I mentioned it to Mr. Mimms but he couldn't match it, so I changed job sites by one block. Mr. McConnell was not a druggist but he owned the store. He had an older druggist named Jehu Beasley and a young one named Wendel, who started school with me and was now registered as a pharmacist. Mr. Jehu was a stately old gentleman and was a pleasure to work with. He was in his seventies and had seen a lot of changes in the practice of pharmacy. When he got his license, the pharmacist made ninety-five percent of all the medications that were dispensed. They made them in all dosage forms—tablets liquids, lozenges, suppositories, charts, lotions, and suspensions. At this time, we were mixing or making only thirty percent of all that were dispensed.

We had been living in the house in Decatur for about seven months when I received another raise, so Rosalind started looking for a better place to live. There was no way she wanted to go through another winter in that little frame house. She found one on Deerwood Drive, south of Decatur; in fact, it was located very close to Agnes Scott College. It was a small, brick two-bedroom house and was the nicest house we had ever lived in. We would live in this house until we moved from Atlanta.

I had always been told that Coca-Cola had cocaine as an ingredient until the Harrison Narcotic Act was enacted. It was not unusual at all for a person to walk up to the soda fountain at McConnell's Pharmacy and say, "Gimme a dope," a common term for a coke. We routinely dispensed doses of castor oil, ammonia cokes, and many other single doses of medicine to soda fountain customers.

We had one customer that I remember well. His name was Elie and he was a sixty-four-year-old dandy. Elie had retired from his job as a drummer. He sold men's clothing and had been on the job for thirty-two years. When he would come in to the soda fountain, he always asked for a dope. His legs gave him a lot of trouble. He had erysipelas, which left the skin on his legs scarred with open ulcers prone to bleeding. He had to keep his legs wrapped with gauze and covered with surgical support hosiery. I worked with him diligently and he improved visibly. He said that at night, they would often start bleeding and, when he woke up in the morning, the bed would be covered with blood.

Elie came in the store every morning around nine o'clock to have a cup of coffee and talk for a while. One morning, Elie didn't come in and by five in the afternoon we were wondering where he was. My bossman went to his apartment to check on him and discovered the police there. His landlord had gotten worried and called the police, who found Elie dead in bed. He had apparently bled to death in his sleep.

Our deliveryman at McConnell's Pharmacy was young and black. One Halloween he came in from a delivery and asked me to look at his arm. There was a small hole that went completely through the muscle on the underside of his upper arm. It was obviously a bullet hole. On questioning him, he said some black kids had thrown eggs at him when he rode by on the motorcycle. He circled the block and stopped to catch the kids and straighten them out when one of them began shooting. He said he ran back to the motorcycle and got out of there, but he felt his arm get hit and begin to sting.

I told him he had to go to the hospital emergency room and get it checked. He said he wasn't going because the police would get involved and couldn't I fix it up. I looked again and there was practically no bleeding. The bullet had missed the large arteries and veins, so I took a long cotton tipped swab, soaked it in Merthiolate, and pushed it through the hole and pulled it back out. I know that hurt, but he stood there and let me do it. I then put bandages over the two holes and told him that was all I could do. He was a little sore for a few days, but he recovered well and was normal in two weeks.

The next summer that same deliveryman got a bushel of peaches and cut them up and put them in a five gallon jug and added some sugar to it. He had decided to make himself some peach brandy. He then put the jug in the little back room where the water heater was located. One morning about two weeks later, my bossman went into the room for something and we heard a muffled explosion. We ran back there and he was standing in the door covered from head to toe with fermented peaches. He had moved the jug to see what was in it when it exploded. After he got through with that deliveryman I don't think he ever wanted any more peach brandy.

One day we filled a prescription for a lady for some vaginal suppositories. As it happened, I answered the phone by the soda fountain where three or four men and a woman were seated enjoying a break. The lady on the phone had a question about her prescription. She said the instructions were to insert one suppository into her vagina twice a day and she wanted to know what her vagina was. I asked her to repeat her question and she said wanted to know what a vagina was. Being a little surprised, I asked her if she was standing up and she said yes. I told her to bend over and place her hand between her knees. Then I told her to straighten up, keeping her hand between her legs and asked her if she had done so. She said yes. I then told her that was her vagina. She gasped and said, "But that's my privates." I assured her that her privates were indeed her vagina.

When I put down the phone and turned around, I realized that the customers at the soda fountain were transfixed on me. Then they all began to clap and laugh loudly. From then on if I had to answer a question on the phone, I made sure I answered it in the prescription department where we had some privacy.

As I mentioned earlier, Mr. McConnell was not a pharmacist. He worked in a drug store all his life, and when the opportunity came along, he bought this store. There was a strong feeling among the Georgia Pharmaceutical Association that no one should own a drug store unless he was a pharmacist. I think that set the stage for what happened shortly.

Lake Lanier was a new lake and had good bream and crappie fishing. One Monday morning Wendel, the pharmacist, and I went fishing early. When we got to the store to go to work at one that afternoon, there was something out of the ordinary going on. There were three men in there with business suits on and they had brought in a copy machine. They were going through prescription records and copying everything they could find. When we asked, they informed us that they were agents for the Georgia Drug Inspector's Office. They then sat us down and questioned us thoroughly on Mr. McConnell's work habits and responsibilities.

About three months before, a man had come into the store with two prescriptions. One was for penicillin with one refill marked on it and one was for Equanil with two refills marked on it. The man had been waited on by Mr. McConnell and chatted with him for a little while. He came back in a couple of weeks and refilled the penicillin prescription and chatted some more. In fact, he began to come in, visit, and spend time purchasing other merchandise. He came back and refilled the Equanil the two times that it was marked to refill it. Then one night he came in after the doctor's office was closed and talked Mr. McConnell into refilling the Equanil again. He then came in one Saturday afternoon and talked Boatwright into refilling. By the time he was through, he had the Equanil prescription refilled four times more that it had been authorized originally.

Those men charged Mr. McConnell and Wendel on the spot with selling dangerous drugs without a prescription. Mr. Jehu came out unscathed; he refused to refill the prescriptions. Since Mr. McConnell didn't have a pharmacist license, all they could do to him was fine him and place him on probation. They fined Wendel and suspended his pharmacist license for one year. I felt like those men were set up; it felt like entrapment.

Shortly after that episode, Mr. Mimms called me and asked me to come back to work for him. I hated to leave Mr. Jehu, for he was a fine man, but I didn't mind leaving Mr. McConnell so I went back down the street and went back to work for Mr. Mimms.

I had now made it to my junior year in pharmacy school. I had been in school for six years and actually finished the equivalent of four. Mama told me that one of my cousins was in the Atlanta area and was making over one hundred dollars a week. That seemed like an awful big salary to me, because now I was taking home around eighty dollars a week.

Mr. Mimms hired a young druggist fresh out of the University of Georgia named Jerry. He was very proud of himself and would answer the phone as doctor. One day the chief drug inspector called the store, and when he heard Jerry refer to himself as doctor, he hit the ceiling. He hung up the phone and came to the drug store to, as he put it, meet the doctor. When the inspector finished with him, I don't think he ever referred to himself as doctor again. The inspector informed him that his degree from the university was a bachelor's degree, not a PhD or MD. Jerry did not stay with us long.

About this time, a boy who started pharmacy school with me had graduated and actually purchased a store just off Peachtree Street. He began to advertise that if you purchased your prescriptions by the bottle of 100, you would get a lower price. This was apparently a no-no as far as the State Board of Pharmacy was concerned, and he was told to cease and desist immediately because the doctors had complete say as to how many pills a person could buy and to suggest that they buy more was not appropriate.

A druggist named Emory Connell came to work with us after that. He was in his sixties and had been in pharmacy for quite a while. His brother had been president of Mercer University in Macon up until he died. In fact, the new library building at Mercer University under construction was to be named the George Connell Library.

Mr. Mimms bought a nightclub up in Buckhead and enjoyed being a nightclub owner for a while. They served dinner and had a lounge with a piano player providing entertainment. Rosalind and I got to go one night. It didn't matter that he wanted me to do a little work while I was there. We had hit the bigtime.

He also bought a tract of land in north Buckhead and built a house. It was hard for me to imagine anybody building a house like the one he built. It was literally a mansion. It had five bedrooms in an L-shape with terrazzo floors in the great room and kitchen. The land was about seven acres and had a winding driveway to the house. The whole thing was hidden from the road. The crowning item was an Olympic-size (it seemed to me) swimming pool in the backyard. That year he and his wife entertained Jayne Mansfield and her husband, Mickey Hargitay, at their new home. It was probably her last trip to Atlanta.

Rosalind and I helped put on the Christmas party for underprivileged children wherein all the pharmacy students gave toys and candy to them. We even had a Santa Claus to pass out the favors. In the spring, we put on the sweetheart dance for all the students.

Sometime during the school year, I was called in by the dean and was told that I was not allowed to work more than twenty hours and go to school. He said that experience had shown him that a person could not keep up with his schoolwork and work more than twenty hours. I told him I knew I was not an A student, but I maintained passing grades and I had to work because I was paying my own way through school and had a wife and two children to support. He said that I should cut my working hours down to twenty hours and dismissed me.

With the steadily increasing tuition at school and growing children at home, there was no way that I could cut back and still meet our basic financial requirements.

Rosalind found a job through one of our neighbors and began working as a keypuncher with USF&G. The additional income was welcome; however, a big hunk went for someone to watch the children during the day.

That year a professor of pharmacy had taken a job with Mercer. He had a master's degree and was a little stuck on himself and his knowledge. He tried to be a stickler for accuracy and performance. However, he came across more like a spoiled child. The building the school was in was four stories high and, on the back end of the building, was a metal fire escape reaching all four floors. One day after a late biochemistry lab, one of my classmates said he stepped out on the third floor landing and heard a noise above him. When he looked up there were three senior students talking to this professor. Actually, he was talking to them, begging them to put him back on the landing. They were holding him upside down off the edge of the landing while talking to him about his grading habits. My classmate said he immediately sneaked back inside and left the building. He said he didn't want to know if they dropped him. Apparently, they didn't, for he was back in school the next morning; however, his demeanor had changed noticeably. Actually, he became a normal, fairly likeable professor. That was an attitude adjustment that worked.

At this time, Rexall and some other companies were producing generic products for sale at reduced prices. They marketed penicillin, phenobarbital, digitalis, and some other products for sale in place of some branded products produced by Lilly, Upjohn, and Merrell and others. The drug manufacturers were upset because these products were beginning to cut into their profits. Since these drug companies contributed a good portion of revenue to the pharmacy schools, they obviously didn't like the situation. The upshot of the situation was for the professors to teach us students that there was a problem with these generics, and they could not be depended on for reliability.

We had a professor named Sam who taught a course in retail pharmacy. One day in order to demonstrate to us the problem with these generics, he showed up for class dressed to a tee. He had on a nice tie and a new suit. He began by telling us that looks can be deceiving. These generic products looked real good on the outside but we could not depend on the inside being what they appear. To demonstrate, he tore off his coat and underneath he had on a shirt that was torn and had holes all in it. He said, see, what you saw as a dependable situation was not what you expected. You cannot depend on these drugs being what they are promoted as. It is illegal to substitute generics for brands and you should not promote the use of generics.

During late April of my junior year, I was elected president of the student body of Mercer University's School of Pharmacy for my senior year. Here I was back in politics. I felt an obligation to do a better job this time than when I was in grammar school.

Summertime came. We had finished seven years of school and needed only one more before we could embark on our career. About two weeks into the summer, Rosalind called me at the store one day and told me that I had a letter from the school. I told her to open it and read it to me. That letter was from the dean, and he informed me that I was out of school and wished me luck in my next chosen field of endeavor. To say we were floored is an understatement.

I was so upset that Emory Connell asked me what was wrong. When I told him, he got on the phone to Mercer University. When he got off the phone, he told me to bring in all my report cards and the letter and give them to him. He said that he was invited to Macon for the dedication of the George Connell building, and while there, he would try to straighten everything out. He told me not to worry.

Not worry! How could one not worry? That was the worst summer we ever spent. When Emory got back from Macon, all he could tell me was not to worry that he was sure everything would turn out all right. We didn't hear anything until three days before school started that fall when we got a letter from the dean telling me to be in school next week. There was no explanation or anything. That was all right with us because now we could finish school. Right there was a lesson we never forgot. Sometimes it is not what you know but who you know that can make a difference.

We had a neighbor down the street who worked for Decca Recording Company and we had become good friends. In fact, his wife told Rosalind about the house for rent that we had moved into. His name was Roger and his duty was to promote new records at radio stations and try to ensure playtime. When Decca recording artists came to Atlanta, it was his job to carry them around to these stations and promote them.

One time when Warner Mack, Mel Tillis, and Webb Pearce were in town to do a show, Roger invited me to come down when I got off at eleven o'clock to see the last of the show and meet the stars. I did so and we all wound up at their hotel room where Mel and Warner entertained us with some of their new songs. To say I was in hog heaven is an understatement, and it was rather late the next morning when I got home. I don't think Rosalind was too pleased. She found it hard to believe that we had played guitars all night. However, she forgave me.

One time Roger arranged for my brother-in-law, Bill Clark, and me to go backstage during a show featuring Loretta Lynn. We met her in her dressing room and she was very nice. She asked us to listen to the song she was recording to see what we thought. She then sang, "You ain't woman enough to take my man." Bill and I both told her we thought it would be a hit and she thanked us. She probably could have sung anything and we would have thought it was wonderful.

Mr. Mimms decided to take a vacation to Bermuda and would be gone for one week. He had just bought a new Cadillac and told me to keep it while he was gone. He didn't want to leave it at the airport. Boy was I in high cotton. I drove the gas out of that thing right quick. Then I filled it up with regular gas. That was a mistake. That high compression engine didn't like that gas at all and sounded like it was going to explode. It rattled, knocked, and jerked so bad that I siphoned the gas out and refilled it with high test gas. It finally settled down and was running normally the day before my boss came home. The morning I was supposed to pick him up at the airport, when I pulled out onto the street, the right A-frame broke in two. That car was incapacitated right there in the middle of the street. I had to call a wrecker to get the car. Then I picked him and his wife up in my car. I sure didn't want to have to tell him that I had broken his new car; however, he took it fairly well.

To this day, I do not like to borrow any other people's machinery. If I need or want something, I make arrangements to use or buy my own.

Our class had a senior trip to the Parke Davis plant in Detroit, then on to the Eli Lilly Company. We left Atlanta at night on a train. This was my first ride in a Pullman. It was very exciting to have your own little room with a lavatory and bed. The dining car was two cars up and the club car was next to it. We lived on that train for a week until we got back to Atlanta.

We had first class tours at Parke Davis and at Eli Lilly. Eli Lilly had a veterinary branch where they kept horses, dogs, and pigs. They showed us how they trapped the pregnant mare's urine from which they distilled and manufactured a drug called Premarin, an estrogen hormone. The pigs were kept there and they showed us how they extracted insulin from their pancreas for production of insulin for human use. The dogs were being used to test pain medication. Both of these manufacturing plants were exceptionally clean and they employed many people.

In the fall of 1962, the Cuban missile crisis hit the day we were having our fall seniors' party. The crisis caused several of our classmates to be called up, and this left us very saddened during our party. At least one of those called up was allowed to continue his education while in service, and when the crisis was over, he returned to school and graduated with the rest of us.

Laura was in first grade, I was in my final year and working, Rosalind was working, and Karen was within a year of first grade. We thought that we had our family complete. We found out that we were going to become parents again. What a surprise! Again in the following March we would have an addition to our family. USF&G

allowed Rosalind to work as long as she could. Sure enough in March, we had another little one. Travis (my father's name) came into our lives hale and hearty on March 16, 1963. He was just as precious as the girls.

Out of a clear blue sky one day, I received a call from a druggist that I had worked with in Moultrie at Crystal Pharmacy. He and a druggist had left Crystal Pharmacy after Mr. Ben died, and they bought a store in Cairo together. He told me that he was buying his partner out and that he wanted me to come to Cairo when I got out of school and work out some kind of partnership. I would be on a salary for a year then we would reach some kind of agreement on what we wanted to do.

Rosalind was not too keen on the idea of moving to Cairo, Georgia. I felt that I would prefer to raise our family in a smaller, rural community so she agreed. I notified the druggist that when I graduated, we would come on down and go to work. When I told Mr. Mimms that we would be moving he was not too happy, however, he wished us good luck.

Graduation day finally arrived. We had been put through the mill the last quarter of school. I think that they wanted to make sure that we were actually exposed to all we would need to know about pharmacy. We had to go to the main campus in Macon for the service. It was a great day for Rosalind and me. We had worked and scrimped for eight years looking forward to accomplishing this. We finally had done it. That piece of paper represented quite an accomplishment for us. Just seeing her out in the audience watching while I accepted the diploma made it all worthwhile.

The next step was passing the state pharmacy board exam for the license to practice pharmacy. The exam was given at Mercer's pharmacy school in Atlanta where we had been going for years. The exam was a three-day process with two days of written examinations and one day for the practical exam. At that time, pharmacists actually mixed and made a large quantity of the prescriptions that were dispensed and the practical portion of the exam demonstrated to the board members that we could actually compound and mix prescriptions properly. We filled prescriptions for suppositories, charts (powders), capsules, suspensions, solutions, eye drops, and eardrops. One of the board members was a Mr. Thomas from Thomas Drug Store in Thomasville, and I drew him to view and approve or disapprove my concoctions. After finishing the board examinations, we had to wait six weeks to discover whether we passed. What an agony the wait was. As luck would have it, he approved and I managed to pass the state board and subsequently received my license to practice pharmacy.

Usually during the practical exam, there was a question or problem that was a little tricky. The year before I took the exam the applicants were asked to prepare bottles of citrate of magnesia. The preparation of which requires a period of time before capping because the reaction produces gas. Some of the applicants capped their bottles before the mixture cured and within thirty minutes or so those bottles began to explode leaving quite a mess for us senior students to clean up before we could use the laboratory.

During our turn at the practical, we had to prepare a calamine suspension. The prescription we were filling resulted in a very thick suspension and required that the bottle method be used instead of the mortar and pestle. I was lucky and had put off filling that prescription until last and had observed that many of my compatriots were having a great deal of trouble trying to get the suspension in the bottle for dispensing. The prescription did not say to use the bottle method but it dawned on me that you had to use it in order to get it in the bottle. Many of them had to clean up a mess and start over in order to fill the prescription. At least during our turn at the practical there was not any broken glass flying around.

Chapter 12:
Life as a Pharmacist

We moved to Cairo and rented a wood frame house on River Road, or Fifth Street Southeast. I started working for Cairo Pharmacy for $125 per week. With a loan to pay off and rent, living costs, clothing, and groceries, we lived pretty close to the money.

I soon got into the groove of working as a pharmacist and realized very quickly that I was grossly overtrained and overeducated for what I was allowed to do in the retail field. The laws governing pharmacy had us so tied down that it was practically impossible to work a whole day without breaking some law. We could not make a single decision in regards to a patient. The only thing we did was read the prescription, fill it, deliver it to the patient, and we dare not discuss the medication, what it was for, or how it worked in the body. Any questions the patient had, we were to refer them to their doctor for answers. We had been drilled in school as to contraindications of drugs, what will mix with what, and what happens in the body when mixed.

The first time I called a doctor to report a contraindication, he told me that he had been prescribing that combination for some time and had never had a complaint. I informed him that if you give aspirin and Benemid at the same time they negate each other's benefit and often cause gout to be worse. He told me to dispense the combination and he would worry about their medical condition. I apparently had wasted years of education just to get a license to read, count, pour, lick and stick, and say thank you.

I decided right then that I would try to help my patients navigate their road to healthy living. I began to discuss their medications with them regardless of the wishes of the Georgia Pharmaceutical Association and the state board. The Association had actually produced a pharmacist code of ethics that discouraged pharmacists from discussing medications with patients. In fact, in school the last year, one of our professors told the tale of a preacher who had a prescription filled for penicillin, and when he asked the pharmacist what it was for, the pharmacist told him that it was for infections such as gonorrhea or syphilis. The preacher created big problems for the doctor, and the doctor in turn chewed the pharmacist out. The moral being that if the patient had questions, they should contact the doctor who had the proper knowledge to counsel the patient's problems properly.

Shortly thereafter, a young woman came in with a prescription for a vaginal infection and asked how much it cost. At this time, many of our prescriptions sold for $0.85 to $1.25, but this was an extremely expensive medication. I told her that it was $8.95 and she asked me if it would help stop the itch. I assured her that it would do so. She left and came back in a short while and said her husband wouldn't give her the money and asked if she could charge it. I told her that I could not because she didn't have an account with us. She left again, came back a little later, and said she wanted it filled. When I presented the prescription to her, she said her husband wouldn't give her the money but her boyfriend did.

A man lived in Cairo, and his primary job, as he saw it, was to look after all the older people who were on social security. He would be real busy on the first of each month. When their checks came from the government, he would drive them to the bank, then to all the stores they wanted to visit, and look after their money for them. Many of them could not read or count and he obviously took advantage of a lot of them; however, nobody would complain because they had no other way to get their business done.

He was a very obnoxious person and would insult you at the drop of a hat. One day he was in the drug store across the railroad tracks and apparently insulted the elderly druggist who was waiting on one of his passengers. When he did, the younger pharmacist reached around the older druggist and knocked him down in the floor. He told the man to get out and not to come back into the store. We all applauded the younger pharmacist's action; however, the man ignored the suggestion and went back to his normal routine as if nothing had ever happened.

That Christmas season I was still fairly new in Cairo when a man came in to do some Christmas shopping. He was interested in an eight-millimeter movie camera outfit that we had and I proceeded to demonstrate it. I asked the bookkeeper about him and discovered that he had a charge account in the store, so I proceeded with my sales pitch in order to sell him the outfit, which was quite expensive. He agreed to purchase it and left the store a happy man. When I returned to the prescription department, my boss informed me that the man's account was way past due and he doubted that we would ever get our money from him. I felt that he should have intervened rather than let the man get away with the camera outfit.

During the same season, a lady came in asking about the massager we had for sale. It was one like the barber used and wore on the back of his hand. I took it out of the box and showed her how to use it by plugging it in and massaging her lower leg. When I had finished and she had purchased it, my boss told me that I shouldn't have touched the lady, especially in the store. It so happened that the lady was the wife of one of our highly respected doctors. I told him that I had done nothing wrong and was proud that I had made the sale.

Cairo Pharmacy occupied the bottom floor of a two-story building and a dentist named Cheney was in the suite just above the drug store. Dr. Cheney was an older man who primarily pulled the teeth of people who had a toothache. He had a habit of pulling the tooth, showing it to the patient, then throwing it out his open window onto the parking lot at the side of the building. He had a little farm outside of Cairo and raised beagle hounds. He loved sitting on his back porch and listening to those hounds chase rabbits in the woods behind his house.

He was beginning to get a little forgetful, and one night he left the water running in the sink above the pharmacy department. The sink was stoppered and the water ran over, flooding the floor and our pharmacy department below. We had to mop up and dry out the next morning before going to work. I looked up and noticed that my Georgia pharmacist license hanging on the wall was sopping wet. I had worked so hard and long to get it and now it was desecrated. It survived the inundation, but was left with some of the signatures being blurred by running ink. A little over a year after I left Cairo Pharmacy, Dr. Cheney left his heater on one night and burned the entire building down. This destroyed a five and ten cent store, the pharmacy, his office, and the law office of Cain, Smith, and Porter above the dime store. I felt pretty lucky—at least my license wasn't burned up.

In order to augment my income, I talked to the hospital administrator and discovered they didn't have a pharmacist; he agreed to hire me on a part-time basis to run the pharmacy at Grady General Hospital. The pay was two hundred dollars a month and I could work at the hospital whenever it was convenient. I would spend my lunch hour there and dispense the medications needed by the twenty-eight-bed hospital. Most of the doctors made morning rounds and left orders, which I would fill when I got there. At first the nurses didn't care too much for me being in their midst and making changes; however, as time went on, they came to appreciate me and my work. I even began giving classes at night teaching pharmacology to them. Most of them gave up their time at home with no pay to come and learn about the drugs. This class went on for about eight years.

Teaching them about injections was a real challenge. There was a strong belief that the smaller the needle was for an injection the less pain involved. I explained to them that if you go into the backyard and turn on the water hose without a nozzle on it, the water just seemed to fall out of the end. If you then put a nozzle on the hose, the water would come out with enough force to actually tear up the lawn. The same principle applies to injections. The smaller the needle, the more damage is done to the muscle. It is possible to cut the muscle up to one half inch. Also, most of the pain receptors were close to the surface so the deeper you put the injection the less pain perceived by the patient. If you pinch the muscle you are using while rubbing it with alcohol then releasing it as you insert the needle, quite often, the patient does not even feel it.

I explained to the nurses that the cavity between the skin and muscle tissue is the subcutaneous area. I had noticed that they were teaching new diabetic patients how to give an injection of insulin using an orange. Following this procedure teaches that the insulin is to be injected straight in, often into the muscle tissue. I had seen some of their patients in the drug store who complained that they were having cysts formed in and around their injection sites. I told them that this was the result of injecting the insulin into the muscles. Insulin being protein-based would cause the body to encapsulate it. If given in muscle tissue, it then results in cysts. When this happens, the body is not receiving the proper dose of insulin, causing the doctor to increase the dose to get the proper blood sugar level. When the insulin is injected subcutaneously, the body can absorb all the insulin, resulting in a more constant blood sugar level. Therefore, you need to pinch up the skin and insert the needle on at least a forty-five-degree angle in order to avoid putting the insulin into the muscle tissue.

We discussed the different classes of drugs (antibiotics, blood pressure, pain relievers, stomach drugs, etc.). As they learned how the drugs worked in the body, they came to have a better respect for drugs.

I introduced a unit dose system in the hospital for the first time in history. It was a little crude by later standards; however, it was effective and cut down on expenses for the hospital due to unused doses of drugs having to be destroyed.

It was this year that the oral polio vaccine became available to the entire nation. Pharmacists, nurses, doctors, health departments, and hospitals were asked to participate in inoculating the entire nation in order to stop polio as an illness. Each pharmacist in Grady County was assigned a polling place or some community gathering place to administer the vaccine. My designated spot was the medical clinic in Calvary, a small town eighteen miles south of Cairo. We saw and inoculated ninety-eight percent of the population of Grady County that day. One family that I was involved with was a woman and her husband and her eighteen children, all living. I had never seen a family that large. The program was considered a nationwide success and eradicated polio as a threat to the United States population.

One day a man came in and introduced himself as Britt Worthy. We got into a conversation and he told me that he could locate anyone in the United States by using the telephone. When I questioned this, he said, "Let me show you. I flew the hump during the war, and I know General Jimmy Doolittle. I haven't seen or talked to him for a long time. I'll get the telephone people to locate him for me." With that, he picked up the phone and asked for directory assistance. He told the operator that he was trying to locate General Jimmy Doolittle but was not sure where he lived now. In about three minutes, the lady on the phone told him that Doolittle lived in California and that he was on the line. He told him who he was and asked him to speak to me and confirm that he knew him. With that, he handed me the phone. I had a short conversation with him; he confirmed who he was, and that yes, he knew Britt. He said he had flown with him during the war and had not heard from him in a long time and to please put him back on the line. My goodness, I had just talked to the man who was the first to bomb Japan during the war!

I looked up one morning to find a man standing at the counter with his hand over his left eye. When I asked him if I could help him, he just removed his hand and I could see a small nail stuck in his eye. He explained that he was doing some carpentry work and the nail had glanced up and hit him in the eye. It had penetrated the iris and the head of the nail was sticking out of his eyeball. He asked me to remove it and patch him up. I explained to him that he needed an ophthalmologist to remove it and to see if he could save his eyesight. I picked up the phone, called an ophthalmologist in Thomasville, asked them to see the man, and explained what was going on. They said to send him over immediately. The man did keep his vision in that eye; however, the iris was ruined and could not adjust to the light anymore, so he had to use glasses with a shade on that eye for the rest of his life.

By the time summer came around, it was obvious that I needed a raise in order to keep up with my growing family's needs, so I asked my boss for a raise. He told me that we had agreed that we would reach an agreement as to a partnership, and he had decided that he would sell me the entire store. I was to study the situation and get back to him as to what I felt would be a good price for both of us. I looked around and asked a bunch of friends in Atlanta and Moultrie about the situation. When I told him what I thought was a fair price he told me that he would consider the offer. Time went by and after a couple of months, I asked him about the situation. He said he was trying to come up with a solution because I had no money to put down. I told him that, in the meantime, I certainly needed a raise. He told me that I was receiving a good salary, and if I would keep a record of everything I spent for one month that he would show me where I could save money and still live off my salary. I told him that I had not gone to school for eight years and done without a lot of things so that when I got to this point in life I would have to tell my children that they couldn't have an ice cream cone when they wanted one. The end result of the situation was that I realized I would not be able to meet my boss's expectations as to the price of the store.

I had checked around and discovered that the going salary for a pharmacist was $150 per week and above in some places. Here I was still working for $125. I began looking around for a new place to work. I talked to the administrator of Archbold Hospital in Thomasville and was told that they needed a pharmacist; however, the starting pay would only be $110 per week. No store I checked within the surrounding area needed a pharmacist.

I met a pharmacist in Hogansville who said he was looking for a place to expand. He came to Cairo and looked around and said that he would finance me as a partner in opening a drug store I began looking around for a suitable building. Apparently, he had second thoughts because he later told me that Cairo was too far from Hogansville and he would have to back out of our agreement.

I discovered that a pharmacist, Bill, across the railroad track at Wight and Brown was leaving to start his own drug store in Cairo. As luck would have it, when Mr. Walter Williams who owned Wight and Brown Pharmacy found out that Bill was opening his own drug store, he told Bill he would sell him Wight and Brown. At the time, Wight and Brown was the largest Rexall store in Georgia. They sold more Rexall merchandise than any other store and were the third largest in the nation. Obviously, he was talking about a lot of money.

Bill managed to put together a group who subsequently bought Wight and Brown, with him in charge. Bill discovered that I was looking for a job, so he hired me for $175 per week. I didn't even have to move and I could continue my hospital work with an extra hour at lunch to do so. He said that Wight and Brown would pay my three-hundred-dollar fee to join the Cairo Country Club, and all I had to do was pay the monthly dues. I gave my boss my notice, and two weeks later I joined Wight and Brown as the sixth pharmacist working there. I was now a member of Cairo Country Club and could play golf there. I felt like I had really accomplished something.

That was a good time for my family and me, with good pay and good hours we were happy. We paid off our debts and, with the help of Mr. Hester at the bank, purchased our first home—three miles south of town and one mile off the highway down a dead end, dirt road in a community called Midway.

This house was a modern three bedroom/two bath home and we really enjoyed living there. It was on a six-acre lot and had an old tobacco barn with a small fenced in area. The house was not air-conditioned; however, we purchased a window unit and installed it in the large family room.

While living here I bought an old white mare from the people at the end of the road by the highway. Since we had some room, I felt that the kids would like to have a horse. The horse was very poor, but the man I bought her from told me she was pregnant. Looking at her, I couldn't believe it. I built her a stall by the tobacco barn and began feeding her well. The kids named her Gidget. She began to fill out and was a beautiful palomino. The kids enjoyed riding her, but one day while I was riding her, I felt movement in her sides and immediately got off. In a couple of weeks, she gave birth to a cute white colt. Suddenly, we had two horses. About a year later, Gidget dropped dead in her stall. The vet told me she had a heart attack. We later sold the colt and were out of the horse business.

I bought two yearling calves to fatten up. I planned on one for the freezer and one for sale. This would give us plenty of meat at little cost. The kids named them Bossy and Pet. When they got big enough I slaughtered Bossy and sold Pet. We had a hard time getting the kids to eat all of a sudden. They didn't like eating Bossy. I had bought some biddies and raised them to full-grown chickens and we had eggs aplenty. When I got a rooster, we had more little chickens. The kids didn't seem to mind eating the chickens as much as they minded eating Bossy.

We were on a party line with the telephone company with four other households, and many conversations were shared—quite often unknown. Being on call for emergency runs to the pharmacy, I asked the phone company for a private line and was told that I would be charged over four thousand dollars to run a private line to our house. We decided to remain on the party line.

That was the Christmas Rosalind surprised me with a brand-new Gibson guitar. I was very proud of that guitar and would not allow the children to play with it. One day when my sister Altis and her husband Bill came to visit, Bill picked up my guitar and began to play it. Travis was absolutely astounded and told Bill that was Baboo's hot tar, and he was not supposed to touch it. He couldn't speak well and couldn't say Truman so I was Baboo. I have been Baboo to our children and grandchildren ever since.

One of the pharmacists who worked at Wight and Brown was Hopson Blackman. Hopson had gone to pharmacy school and was licensed around 1918. When he stood for his pharmacy license there were three grades of pharmacists. Applicants scoring seventy to eighty were licensed by the state as druggists. Ones scoring eighty to ninety-five were pharmacists and ones scoring ninety-five and above were licensed as apothecaries.

Hopson's license stated that he was an apothecary.

Hopson had an astronomical knowledge of chemistry and pharmacy and spent most of his time compounding and making medications for many of our older customers. He made lozenges, carminatives, mouthwashes, earwax removers, sinus washes, eye waters, douche powders, suppositories, charts, etc.

We had problems at the cosmetic counter where ladies seemed to want to check the lipstick color. When they did so and put the lipstick tube back, it showed that it had been used. Hopson always checked the lipstick rack once a day, and the lipstick tubes that were harmed he would bring to the pharmacy. He would then place a methenamine tablet on top of a metal lid and light it. The methenamine would burn with a slow flame. He would then take the lipstick and rotate it in the flame, and when removed, it would look like new and you could not tell that it had been used.

He was raised in Grady County, knew almost everybody in town by their first name, and knew their parents as well. During the war, many of our patrons used him as their primary physician. I liked this man very much and learned a lot from him. He gave me the book of handwritten questions and answers that he used to study for his state board examination. I later donated that book to Mercer's pharmacy school for their collection.

Bob Wight was a customer at this store, and he was related to one of the founders of Wight and Brown. Due to this relationship, he took what I called liberties in the store. For instance, he would come in, crawl up on the counter, lie down, and demand his ears to be washed out with Peroxide. He was hard of hearing and thought this would help him.

He was an irascible old man and was known about town as one of the town characters. He drove an old Oldsmobile that was pretty much banged up due to him running into other people's cars. If someone parallel parked in front of him, he would almost always just push them out of the way instead of maneuvering around them. One day he ran into Clark Funeral Home's ambulance that Elmer Wilcox was driving. The police gave him a ticket and he went ballistic. His argument with Elmer ended by Elmer saying he agreed it was his fault because when he left the funeral home, he noticed that Bob's car was not in his garage so he should have known not to get on the street. Bob engaged a lawyer and proceeded to fight the traffic ticket in city court. He so aggravated the city court judge and lawyers that finally, after

Lauren Clark agreed to fix his own ambulance, the case was dismissed.

One of the pharmacists working here was Harry and we became friends. After one of my comments about fishing in the Okefenokee Swamp he asked me to carry him there on a fishing trip. We had a weekend off together and went to the Okefenokee. We put in the swamp at Lem Griffith's camp near Fargo and proceeded into the swamp to big water then started fishing our way back out through Minnie's Lake etc. We began to catch perch and catfish and were having a good time when I noticed that Harry was stringing his fish on a line and letting it trail in the water by the boat. I told him he shouldn't do that and to put them in the bucket we had brought along for that purpose. He said he wanted them to be kept alive as long as possible. About that time, we felt a tug on the boat and he realized that his fish were being stolen by a good-sized alligator. He grabbed an oar and began beating on the alligator but the alligator won and swam off with about thirty nice fish.

We felt lucky and kept fishing; however, he then put all his fish in the five-gallon bucket with mine. We had a grand time, and when we were through, we had a very nice string of fish consisting of about ninety. After making pictures of our string, we packed them on ice and carried them to Cairo. We had a good time giving our friends a nice mess of fish and telling everybody about our trip.

Roy was also one of the town characters. He was an elderly man who lived in a room at the Grady Hotel. Roy seemed to live off the street and just came and went anywhere and everywhere about town. He was small in stature, but always dressed as neat as could be expected for one of his status. I was told that he was a druggist and asked him about it one day. He went to his room and returned with his certificate from Tennessee stating that he was indeed a pharmacist.

When he came to Cairo, he worked in a drug store that was now closed, but he had never reciprocated his license from Tennessee to Georgia and never actually practiced as a pharmacist in Georgia.

I discovered that probably the reason he didn't practice pharmacy was because he was addicted to paregoric. Paregoric is camphorated tincture of opium. When he would come into the store, someone would have to watch him to ensure that he didn't get into the paregoric.

My boss never liked him, but seemed to tolerate him. One day I happened to be in the back of the store where I could see out the back door into the alley. I saw Roy leave the store and begin to cross the alley at the same time my boss was coming across the alley toward the store. As they met in the alley, I saw my boss hit Roy in the stomach as hard as he could. Roy went down to the ground in a coiled up position and my boss came on into the store. I went out to Roy and helped him up. He assured me that he was all right and not to worry about him. I discovered a week later that Roy was dead. He had died three days after that incident.

One day an old preacher came into the store. He said he had a sick mule and wanted to know if there was anything he could buy to help him. This man's name was Ulysses (Boy) George. He had worked for Mr. Legette who ran the Cairo Banking Company for years. Mr. Legette was dead now. Boy George said his mule had the lampus and asked if anyone knew what that was. I told him that I did. He said that mule was a gift from Mr. Legette and was the only thing Mr. Legette had ever given away. He didn't want anything to happen to that mule. Lampus was a colloquial term for inflammation or infection of the jaw—normally caused by the bit being too tight and rubbing it raw. I prepared him a paste of tetracycline and told him how to use it. I also told him not to use the bridle on that mule for ten days in order for it to heal. Two weeks later, Boy George came in and told me that his mule was a good as new. He became a customer of mine and traded with me until he died.

During my second year at Wight and Brown, some of Bill's partners became concerned because the money they had expected to earn was not coming to them. Apparently, Bill was keeping some of the money and not putting it in the bank. One of his partners was Elmer, who was a pharmacist also, and he became concerned enough to talk to me. He said a change was needed and asked me if I would run the store if they got rid of Bill. As it turned out, four of the doctors in town had gone into business with Bill and Elmer. In Georgia, this situation was frowned on by the state because the doctors could in essence control the drug business in town. Two of them asked to talk to me about the situation. Before I opened my mouth, I went to Elmer and discussed it with him. I told him that the situation was not any of my business. He assured me that I could and should talk to them and answer any of their questions.

Two doctors talked to me and asked many questions about the business and if I had seen any wrongdoing in regards to Bill. I told them that the business was as good as it was when I came to work there and I saw no reason for the profits to disappear. One of them told me that Bill told Elmer he had a cigar box full of money under his bed at home and it was drug store money. I told him I had not heard that and knew nothing about it. They told me that they were having a meeting that night and there was going to be a big change.

A banker was also one of the partners who had bought into the business. It was his duty to call the meeting. When he informed Bill about it, Bill called Elmer and they went up into the office and had a strong discussion that afternoon before the meeting. When they came out Elmer did not even look at me or speak to me.

There certainly was a big change, especially for me. The following morning when I went to work, Bill called me up into the office and informed me that I was fired immediately. Prior to the meeting, he had convinced Elmer that he would take care of business and that Elmer would receive his share of the money. I gathered up my license and tools and went home to tell Rosalind.

Here I was in Cairo, Georgia, which had two drug stores—one I had quit, and I had been fired from the other. I had my family here and a house payment to meet with no income. I went to Thomasville, looked for a job, and found none. I then went to Moultrie, and Mr. Minix at Minix Drugs hired me. I now had an income again, but I had to drive forty-five miles to and from work. I also received a bill from Cairo Country Club that showed I owed the three hundred dollar initiation fee. The statement showed that Wight and Brown had paid one hundred dollars on the fee but was erased, and now I owed the three hundred dollars. Apparently, they had a policy whereby a person could pay one hundred dollars a year for three years and be a full member. Bill had them refund his one hundred dollars. I began paying the fee in order to save face.

A doctor called me after a few days and apologized for what happened. He explained to me that there had been quite an argument at the meeting. The banker, Bill, Elmer, and one of the doctors had won. The upshot was that three doctors got out of the business. The other soon followed. The banker gave two of the doctors their money back. One doctor had not invested any money but put up bonds as security and had them returned to him.

Part IV:
Truman's Drugs, Inc.

Chapter 13:
Truman's Drugs, Inc.

We had been going to Eastside Baptist Church where Rosalind had become good friends with Emma. Emma was married to Clarence who owned a used car lot in partnership with his brother Leslie. This car lot was out by the high school on Fifth Street Southeast.

Clarence and Leslie had just purchased the Cairo Ford place and were moving their business down on Second Avenue. I approached Clarence and Leslie and asked them what they were going to do with their lot by the high school. They had not decided, so I suggested that we three go into business together and enlarge their building in order to operate a drug store.

I suggested they build the building and rent it to our drug store business. They were to put up five thousand dollars, as would I, and we would be equal partners in the drug store. I went to Citizens' Bank and asked for a five thousand dollar loan. The bank president told me that I didn't have enough collateral for the loan and would need a co-signer. I went to Leslie and convinced him to co-sign with me, and I received the loan.

This was 1966. Clarence and Leslie hired their brother-in-law, preacher L. Z., to enlarge the building according to my instructions. While the building was under construction, I filed corporate papers and Truman's Drugs, Inc. was born. One condition was that Leslie's two sons-in-law were to be included in their half of the business so in fact I now had four partners—Larry and Jimmy being the other two.

I began building gondolas and shelving to place in the store. We could not afford to hire it out with our limited capital. Rosalind painted the shelving and walls. Most of this work was done on our carport at home, then moved to the building when the roof was completed.

While working on shelving at the new store one day, the wife of my old boss's ex-business partner came by and asked me if I would take on her husband as a partner. She told me that when his ex-partner wanted out of their partnership, he didn't tell him directly. He left a note on the typewriter telling Bert to buy or sell. His partner had always been very frugal. He had saved all his life and had enough cash on hand to buy Bert out. Bert had not saved and was not in a position to buy him out. I talked to her and explained that I thought Bert was one of the best pharmacists I had ever worked with, but I could not take him on as a partner.

By now I had applied for and received my state, county, and city licenses authorizing me to legally operate a drug store. I then went to Valdosta Drug Company, a drug wholesaler, and talked to Len and told him what I was doing and asked him to sell me drugs. He told me that in his opinion I was wasting my time and money because Wight and Brown Drug Store and Cairo Pharmacy were two very established businesses and that a town and county the size of Cairo and Grady County would not support three drug stores. He did consent to establishing an account for me.

I then went to Columbia Drug Company, another wholesaler, and asked them to also sell me drugs. In South Georgia, it was necessary to have at least two wholesalers in order to get the merchandise needed.

I contacted Walgreens Drug Company and asked if I could buy a franchise from them. I felt like I could better compete with the Rexall store if I had a nationally recognized brand name also. They agreed and asked for my store plan for which they then sent me a layout of how to position my merchandise and sent me some prescription labels for when I opened. I was in business operating as Truman's Walgreens Drug Store.

I purposely built the prescription work counter wide open so customers could walk up to me and see me work. Most drug stores at the time had the prescription department sealed off and hidden in the back with a window for the druggist to look out of. Many of them had their floors elevated, and the druggist appeared to be looking down on the customers. At that time, most of the pills were counted out by pouring them into the druggist's hand. I had been given a pill tray for pill counting by Abbott Drug Company when I graduated, and I began using that instead of my hand. Occasionally when I would pour pills onto the pill counter, the exact amount would come out. This impressed many of my customers and assured them that I knew what I was doing.

The big day finally arrived. My merchandise had been delivered and most of it had been placed on the shelves. I opened the front door one morning and in came my first customer. Robert presented me with my first prescriptions. Robert became one of my most consistent customers. He traded with me for thirty-eight years.

Before the week was out, a big surprise! Walgreens suddenly quit selling franchises and had begun buying out those who had them. They had changed their business practice and decided that they would own and operate their own stores. I had to order new labels quickly and change my signs to Truman's Drugs.

After a few days, Dr. Hancock stopped by after making his morning rounds at the hospital and took a look around. He told me he was still very agitated with Bill and the banker and felt like they betrayed all the doctors. He told me he was going to send his patients to me. I thanked him profusely and promised to look after his patients. This was the beginning of a strong professional and personal relationship that lasted until his demise.

This caused my business to grow much faster than I had expected and I realized I was undercapitalized. I was very fortunate in that the drug wholesalers extended me additional credit. McKesson and Robbins wholesaler opened me a line of credit also and now I was dealing with three wholesalers. Eli Lilly, Upjohn, Abbott, Merck Sharp and Dohme, and Schering also issued me accounts so that I could get better prices by buying direct from the manufacturer.

I had been noticing that the grocery stores were taking a bigger portion of our front-end business by selling some desired items with a reduced price. Items like Maalox, alcohol, aspirin, etc. were a staple in the drug store, so I ordered a truckload of Maalox and priced it at cost plus five cents. This was a good move because it brought more customers into the store and gave the impression of low prices. I also ordered McKesson aspirin by the case and gave a one-hundred-count bottle with every prescription I filled.

Like the other drug stores in town, I began opening charge accounts for customers. One farmer in particular who I liked asked me to charge his medicine and I gladly agreed to do so. At the end of the month, I sent out statements, his included. In a day or two here came this farmer in and he was obviously mad. He asked me what I meant sending him a dun. I asked what he was talking about. He said that he had got this dun in the mail, shook it at me, and said he didn't like it one bit. I told him that that was not a dun but a statement showing what he had purchased that month. He said, "I have lived in this county all my life and have always paid my bills. I don't like getting duns." He told me that he always ran a bill with merchants in this town and when he sold his cotton and peanuts in the fall, he always came in and paid up. I finally assured him that he could do the same with me and that I would not send him a dun anymore. Sure enough, he made a very good customer; however, I only got paid by him once a year.

Up to this time, most cosmetics and medicinal products were introduced to the public through drug stores. I realized that grocery stores and department stores were becoming the primary source of introducing new products. Drug stores were getting out of the soda fountain business, which attracted a lot of customers. We were being told by our associations that we should concentrate on medical issues and prescriptions. Many young pharmacists were opening apothecaries with the pharmacy schools' blessings and leaving front-end merchandise to the grocery stores and department stores. Most of these apothecaries folded and went out of business very soon.

My feeling was that we were merchants. We deal in products. We offer a service; however, by law, there is no way we can charge for this service. The only people who can charge for services are the ones who can make a decision for the people seeking the service. Our drug laws over the years have been issued to protect the pharmacist. We have so many laws regarding our business that we can hardly go through a day's work without breaking some law. Most pharmacists are afraid they will be held responsible and be subject to lawsuits if they make a decision for a patient.

We had a weekly newspaper in Cairo called the *Cairo Messenger*. It was printed on Wednesday. I purchased a large supply and gave each customer a free newspaper. At one time, I was giving away in excess of four hundred papers each week. I continued giving away these newspapers until I sold the store. It always brought people into the store.

In a short while, another doctor came by and wished me luck. In the future, I would have a good relationship with him also.

Pretty soon Bill got wind of these relationships and came to see me one evening about closing time. He told me that I had better not cause him any more problems or he would see to it that I was eliminated. I assumed by this that he might cause me grief, and I made it a point not to irritate him or say anything against him in public, though I tried to let him know that he did not scare me. As it turned out, within a short time his banker bought Bill out in Cairo and gave him the store they had opened in Adel. Bill moved to Adel and eventually wound up losing his pharmacy license and going to federal prison for Medicaid fraud and for selling samples.

L. Z., who built the building for me, became one of my longtime customers. He spent many hours sitting on my settee talking to me. He was raised during the Depression and had in fact ridden the rails of freight trains as a hobo from Cairo to California. He told me that he carried his guitar and would play and sing for a bit to eat along the way at the hobo camps and in the small towns they passed through. The good part to me was that he tuned his guitar in the key of G and then only needed to bar chord it to go to the other keys in the song. He said that an old man had taught him to play and said that was the way it was done in New Orleans in the old days. He would also do any chores people needed in exchange for food. He said he was glad those days were over.

L. Z.'s son owned a bunch of rental houses in Cairo and L. Z. took care of them for him. He was a real good handyman. He told me that he also collected rent for his son. One of the renters got behind on his rent and wouldn't pay up. They couldn't evict them without renting another house and moving them into it. One day he went to the house and looked real hard at the front door and told the renters that he had to take the door down and take it in to repair a problem with it. This left them with no front door and no way to lock themselves inside. He said they were moved out by the next night.

Carroll Lee, a boy who was in pharmacy school at the University of Georgia, came and asked for a job. Things were going well so I hired him. He had worked some at Wight and Brown while I was there and we got along well. He told me that he had pretty much paid his way through pharmacy school by hauling whiskey to Athens and reselling it. Georgia was a dry state then, but Florida was not. We were about eighteen miles to the state line, where there was a liquor store. He said he would visit the line and fill up his car trunk before returning to school at Athens. This liquor store did a thriving business selling booze to the Georgians. Thomasville, Georgia, was as close to the line as Cairo, so they had a very good business. In fact, the Georgia State Patrol as well as the sheriff departments of Grady County and Thomas County thrived due to the fines collected from people caught bringing liquor into Georgia.

At this time, all pharmacy graduates had to submit a paper to the pharmacy board on something to do with health or pharmacy. This was required in order for the graduate to qualify for taking the board test and getting a license. Carroll was at an impasse and asked me what he could write about. I told him that I remembered a short line in one of my physiology books years ago indicating that the Negro race was susceptible to sickle-cell anemia and that the Caucasian race was not. Our professor had not discussed this with the class and it was passed over quickly. I suggested that he write about that illness. He asked me if I would write the article for him. I told him that I could not do that but that I would give him an outline so that he could write it himself. I don't know what happened, but in a couple of years there was a great amount of interest in sickle-cell anemia.

Leslie and Clarence's father was still alive, though getting old and a little senile. His wife had developed Alzheimer's and needed constant attention. The family would call the doctor often to come to the house to check on her. He asked me if I would go when they needed him. I agreed to do so and would check her blood pressure, give her a B-12 injection, and assure their father that she was doing as well as could be expected. If she developed a fever due to an infection, I would give her a round of antibiotics with her doctor's permission. She lived about two years after being confined to her bed and I went over there at least two times a month. After her demise, their father was despondent and was finally confined to bed also. I continued my trips to his house tending to him like I did his wife. This continued for about a year and a half until his demise.

Farmers in the area were having problems in the spring at planting time. Around almost every creek bed or woods when they planted corn, that night raccoons would come along and dig up and eat most of the seed planted. This mostly cost the farmer at least one or two acres of corn. Those raccoons especially liked the peanut seeds. Since almost every field was bordered by a creek or woods this was an awful financial loss. Up until now, we could sell arsenic or strychnine, which was used by most of the farmers to control this situation. The federal government had stopped the sale or use of these poisons and this left the farmers in a bad situation. After hearing the farmers complain I told my customers that we could supply them with a product that would not kill the raccoons but would stop them from wanting to eat the seed. I would sell them a pint of spirits of camphor and tell them to pour it over a gallon of the seed they would plant next to the creeks or woods. Allow the seed to get wet with the camphor then spread the seed out to dry. The alcohol would evaporate leaving a coat of camphor on each kernel. The raccoons would not eat this. It was not long until I was ordering spirits of camphor by the gallons.

A doctor's receptionist was a nice lady named Frances. One day she came into the store and told me she had a problem. She said that she had a rash in a very inconvenient place. When I asked her to describe it, she immediately dropped her pants and showed me her crotch area. She had a fungal infection, so I sold her some cream and told her that it would take seven to ten days to clear up entirely. If it appears to be gone in four to five days just keep applying the cream for the seven to ten days to make sure it is healed.

One day a man came in with a prescription for Gantrisin tablets for a kidney infection. Gantrisin tablets were made by Roche laboratories and were large and white with *Roche* imprinted on one side of the tablets. The man left with his prescription, and in a short time, he returned and asked me to come over to the side and asked me if I had given him roach tablets to take. He said that he didn't want to take roach poison even if it was good for kidney infections. I assured him that they were not roach tablets and got some from the front and showed him the difference in spelling and assured him that Roche Drug Company had made the tablets that I supplied him with and that they were for kidney infection.

A doctor called me one Sunday and asked if I had some tetanus vaccine on hand. When I told him that I did, he asked me if I would go to the store and give an injection to a patient he was sending there. I told him that I would and did so. That led to many more such episodes with tetanus, B-12, etc. It became more or less routine for me to treat his patients, especially on the weekends.

I was called by a doctor one day and asked if I knew what leukoplakia was. He had a patient who had a problem and asked me could I make some vitamin A lozenges, as he could not find any listed in his books. I assured him that I could. A Mrs. Edenfield showed up and insisted that I look in her mouth and confirm whether in fact she had this problem. Upon examination, I assured her that she did in fact have it and explained that this problem usually was a precursor to cancer. I told her that I did not know whether these vitamin A lozenges would cure her and that we could only use them for a while and see if they helped. They in fact did reduce the plaques drastically and she got along well for years. Later on when she was in the nursing home, she had her granddaughter bring her to the store for me to check and see if the plaques had returned. They had not. Apparently, she was only having trouble with her false teeth. They were not fitting properly and she asked me if I could adjust them for her. It was obvious from looking at her mouth where the problem was, so I carried them to the back and scraped them down at the point of irritation. When she put them back in it was obvious that I had fixed her problem. Her granddaughter became a customer of mine at that time and stayed with me until I quit the practice.

A Mr. Sam became a customer of mine due to his doctor sending him around. He was bailiff at the county courthouse and always came in and bought a bottled coke. I noticed that he always took a big swig from the bottle then would stroll over to a corner and turned his back to the rest of the store. I discovered what he was doing when one day he asked me for a two-ounce bottle. He explained that the top on the one he was using was worn and leaked in his pocket. He kept this two-ounce bottle full of bourbon in his pocket and would doctor his Coca-Cola with it. When asked, he admitted that he also used the same mixture in the courthouse while working. I don't think the judge ever discovered what he was doing. If he did, he didn't make it known.

I became friends with Lauren, who owned a funeral home. He operated an ambulance service in the county as well. I would quite often go with him on ambulance calls after hours. One day we picked up a man who had committed suicide by shooting himself in the mouth with a shotgun. Him being in the funeral business he prided himself by always preparing the body for viewing, if only by the family. He asked me if I had ever worked with plaster of Paris and I told him that I had. He asked me if I would help him rebuild this person's head so he could show him. We did so and well enough that the family could view the body and were satisfied with the results. This led to a long relationship, and I would often help him in the morgue when he had a problem.

One of the hardest ones I worked on with him was a friend of mine, a pharmacist I had known for years. He had a wreck on the Tallahassee Highway and was ejected. The car rolled over his head and crushed it. We put him back together well enough for his family to view him.

Lauren and I, along with a friend named Billy, bought a farm south of town consisting of about 120 acres. We planned to divide it up into mini estates and sell them as a new subdivision. We built two ponds on the property and designed roads. Suddenly, the oil crisis of the seventies hit along with runaway inflation and our plans died. We eventually sold the property and decided we were not cut out to be developers.

In 1969, a Mr. Lee, a customer who formed Lee Oil Company, purchased a lot at Mexico Beach, Florida, and had a mobile home placed on it. He came in one day and told me that his mother was not going to accept a mobile home anywhere and, since she was paying for a great portion of the place, he could not keep it. He offered to sell me the place on time for the amount owing on it and he would forget the down payments he had made.

I agreed and became the proud owner of a place at the beach. He had not hooked up the water, electricity, or sewage, so that became my problem. I purchased a service pole and had the electric company connect to it. They would not connect the line to the mobile home and said I should hire an electrician to do that. I looked at the pole and decided I could handle it and proceeded to hook it up. As soon as I flipped the switch on I realized something was wrong. Light bulbs began exploding and the refrigerator motor began racing. I had connected 220 volts instead of using the bastard line to reduce it to 110 volts. I flipped the switch off and decided to get an electrician to help me. Eventually everything was hooked up and ready to go. We enjoyed that place until the children got grown and quit going down there.

A Dr. Bill had a cabin on Alligator Point and had a twenty-four foot Lyman Lapstrake boat with two fifty-horsepower outboard motors on it. He decided he wanted a new boat and sold this boat to me. I joined a group in Thomasville who formed a boating club. One of the first trips planned after we joined was to put in at Chattahoochee and boat down the Apalachicola River to the coast at Apalachee for the seafood festival and the blessing of the fleet.

We were to spend the night then return the next day. On the trip, we invited a local veterinarian and his wife to join us as we had plenty of room on the boat for all. The trip down was uneventful and we enjoyed the scenery. There was only one place on the river where we could purchase gas. We could not carry enough to make the whole trip. Going down we had plenty. On the way back we realized that it took more gas going upriver that it did coming down, and that we would not quite be able to make it to Chattahoochee with what we had onboard. Sure enough we ran out of gas with about five miles to go. We were lucky enough to have one of the other boats agree to go on to Chattahoochee and fill our portable tanks and bring them back to us so we could get home. Shortly after that I traded the Lyman for an eighteen-foot cuddy cabin boat with a seventy-five-horsepower motor and used that boat both in the boating club and fishing at Mexico Beach.

A man called named Grouchy was a customer of mine. He got his nickname by always being against anything that the majority of people were for. He said that somebody should always be against whatever was proposed in order to make people think about what they were proposing. When he retired, he came into the store, sat down on the settee, and informed me that he would never die. He said he had just got on the government dole and people on the dole never die.

His wife was a heart patient and traded with me, and over the years we became good friends. She always consulted me on anything the doctors prescribed for her. After Grouchy died she became more dependent on me for almost all her decisions. Some of the medications being prescribed to her were not necessarily good for her and would make her feel worse. Quite often, I recommended that she not take them and depend on her heart doctor for advice. I continued to explain to her what was happening with her heart and she was better able to cope with her condition. When she was confined to the hospital in ICU for her last days, she begged her daughter-in-law to take her to Truman who would make her feel better. I only wish that I could have helped her more.

Mr. J. C. was a salesman for Eli Lilly Drug Company. One day he told me that he had a nephew graduating from pharmacy school and asked me to hire him so that he could finish his practical experience in order to take the state board. I grudgingly agreed because I thought that I would be saddled with someone who was spoiled and not a very good worker. As it turned out, he was a great asset. His name was Marx. After he had finished his practical experience and passed the board, he continued to work with me.

A doctor received notice he had to move his practice because the building he was in had been sold and was to be demolished by a new owner. He was seeing anywhere from sixty to eighty patients per day and didn't have time to find himself a new office. The chamber of commerce and the hospital authority had been trying to recruit new doctors and were offering free office space for one year, but they didn't seem to care about this doctor's situation.

He had been good to me by sending me a lot of customers, so I began looking for a building for him. I found a house by a service station that was empty. The service station was using it to store used tires, so I contacted the owner and negotiated a lease wherein I was to renovate the house for use by the doctor. It involved a new entrance midway down the side of the house with steps. The floor had to be tiled and the plumbing had to be installed so that water was available in his examination rooms. The house had to be rewired electrically to get it up to code. We finished the house just in time because the other side of his building was being torn down while he was still seeing patients on his side.

In the end, he had a much nicer place to practice medicine compared to his old office. We became good friends and enjoyed hunting, fishing, and playing golf together for the rest of his life. This doctor was a fine gentleman, and would tell his patients to go to Truman's and have them call him for their prescriptions. He normally would give a one or two week supply of medicine and then tell them come back when they ran out. That way they would not go back to Wright and Brown Drug Store.

Most of the time when the customers came in and we called, his telephone was either busy, or we had to wait for him to finish with his current patient. Quite often, he would have a young child in his office and would hand the child the telephone and tell him to talk to me. There I was trying to work and having to listen to the child jabber while waiting for the doctor to answer his phone. When I fussed about it, he just laughed and got worse doing it.

In the early seventies, we received a notice from the state of Georgia Medicaid program that they were going to decrease our fee for filling Medicaid prescriptions. The state paid pharmacies $1.95 for each prescription filled even though the pharmaceutical association had proved that it costs pharmacies an average of $3.90 to fill one. The physicians in the state were also informed that their fees would be reduced. Many physicians immediately opted out of the Medicaid program and quit treating Medicaid patients for the state.

There is a law that prohibits retailers from agreeing on prices for their products. It was called price fixing. I was upset so I called a meeting inviting all the pharmacists in southwest Georgia to Cairo in order to discuss the situation. The Georgia pharmaceutical association leaders got wind of the meeting and sent representatives. At the meeting, I explained to the pharmacists present that if we all accepted the reduced price, it would be detrimental to our business.

The state would be paying a set fee for each prescription filled regardless of the cost of the medication. If the average cost now of Medicaid prescriptions is $3.95 we might survive, but if costs go up, as they usually do, we will be paying much more for each prescription medication but locked in to very short markup. Whether we like or not, we are in the retail business and we must have a reasonable markup to meet expenses. If new medicines suddenly cost us sixty dollars and we only get $1.50 for filling it, there is no way we can be justified in accepting it.

The representatives from the pharmaceutical association took the floor and told us that we are professionals, and as such, must stick with a fee or the public would always view us as retailers. I told them that we were in fact merchants because we deal with a product. They then reminded us that we could not collectively agree on pricing policy. I told them that I wasn't calling for price fixing but asking each to consider what was happening to pharmacy. The government was effectively fixing our prices by locking in our markup. If we couldn't charge our own professional fees we would never be professionals. Chain drug stores were increasing their presence all over the state and would accept anything the state proposed just to gain volume. Up until then, the only way we had been able to stay in business was either increasing volume or decreasing employees. Where we each used to have eight or more employees the average was now four or five. I reminded them that many of the physicians had independently opted out of the system, and if we also independently demanded adequate payment, we might be able to produce a profit. I also suggested that if we decided to accept the situation at least we should demand a cost of living increase on the professional fee.

It seems that there was a strong feeling of competition among pharmacists and quite often they didn't seem to trust each other and would often undercut each other's prices. As we left the meeting, it was obvious to me that each was afraid that if he opted out, his competitors in town would stay in, causing him to lose business.

One day the manager of McKesson Robbins Wholesale Company's Albany office came by on the way to Tallahassee, Florida. He told me that he was on his way to close a store in Tallahassee due to the owners not being able to pay their bill with McKesson. Apparently, he had financed them and now had to foreclose. He asked me to go down with him and I agreed. On the way, he asked me to consider taking over the store and paying off the bill with McKesson. After looking at the store, I told him that I would consider it and that I had the man who could run it, but I would have to talk to him first.

I discussed the situation with Marx and asked him if he would agree to become a partner in the store and run it for us. He agreed and we continued to operate the store as X L Drugs. Marx moved his family to Tallahassee and was successful in operating the store. The problem was that the city of Tallahassee was planning to renovate South Adams Street where the store was, and we would have to move or close the store.

A pediatrician friend of mine informed me that he was planning a medical complex in Thomasville. This complex would be owned by MDs only; however, they would build a building on the corner and let me lease it to operate a drug store. This worked out pretty good for Marx and me, so we moved the store from Tallahassee to Thomasville and incorporated the business as Trumarx Drugs, Inc.

Chapter 14:
The Many Customers of Cairo

We had been in Cairo for a while and I contacted Roger who worked for Decca Recording Company. I asked if we could all go to the Grand Ole Opry in Nashville. He said that he could arrange it, and if he went with us, we could get passes to go backstage. We planned the trip and were looking forward to going, but when we got to Atlanta, we discovered that Roger had been in the hospital with a bleeding ulcer and had just been released. He said that he felt too weak to go. I told him that I could fix him an oral glucose solution that he could drink and it would do as good as the glucose they gave him in the hospital. He agreed to try it so I went to see Wendel, a pharmacist I worked with at McConnell's pharmacy. He now worked at a pharmacy in Avondale Estates. I bought a gallon jug, fixed a five percent sugar solution, and added some sodium chloride and some potassium chloride. I told him to drink six ounces every three hours and he would feel well enough to make the trip to Nashville.

He agreed and we went to Nashville to the Ryman Auditorium. With our passes, we were admitted to the stage area and stood on the stage with all the musicians. At that time, out on the stage was where all the musicians just stood around and waited for their turn. Then they would just step up to microphone and perform their act. There we stood with

Roy Acuff, Ernest Tubb, Oswald, Bobby Bare, Loretta Lynn, and others. We enjoyed talking to the musicians, who accepted our presence and just chatted with us. When Roy Acuff shook Rosalind's hand, he gripped it so hard that the ring on her finger hurt her very much. We had a good time and enjoyed the trip very much.

Roger said he got along real good. I heard about the University of Florida producing Gatorade a year later. I realized that I had done that the year before, but I didn't flavor it or realize that I could promote it. I was only interested in getting to Nashville and having Roger along. I apparently missed out on a great opportunity.

One of my customers was getting along in age and depended on me for information on his drugs. He lived about five miles out on the highway towards Pelham. He was more and more dependent on his cane and had difficulty getting around. His house was a very old country farmhouse with rooms on both sides of what is called a dogtrot. This is a large hall open on both ends running through the middle of the house. They had no running water and had to draw their water from a well situated at the end of the dogtrot. They still used a wood stove.

One day he told me that he was almost hit by a car on the highway, which he had to cross to reach his mailbox. I knew the postmaster and explained what had happened, asking him if the mailbox could be moved to his side of the road. He said he would talk to his mail carrier and see if he would do that. The next time my customer came into the store, he told me that they allowed him to move his mailbox and he thanked me profusely.

Another day he came in and was visibly upset. When I asked him what was wrong, he told me that he had been stopped by the state patrol. The officer had asked him for his driver's license and then informed him that his license was not valid. He told him sure it was. It was issued by the state of Georgia and said right on it that it was a permanent driver's license. He said the state patrolman told him that the law had been changed in the late forties or early fifties; nowadays, he had to renew his license every so often.

I assured him that the state patrolman was correct. I hated to confirm it, but I told him he would have to go to the license bureau and get a new license. He said he would refuse to do so because it said right on his license that it was a permanent license. I asked him if the patrolman gave him a ticket. He said, no, he only gave him a warning. I told him that if he were ever stopped again that he would have to pay a fine. He said, by golly, he would do that instead of giving up his permanent license.

One of my customers was a beautiful young woman who married into one of the best families in Cairo and had a voice like a nightingale. She told me one day that she had been asked to sing in church Sunday morning and was very nervous. She asked what she could do to calm her nerves. With her doctor's approval, I gave her a 200mg Meprobamate tablet and told her to take it one hour before church service and see if that would help. Apparently, it did because in the future when she was asked to sing she would come to see me and ask for a singing pill.

A close friend who was a veterinarian entered the race for state representative. He also came to me and told me that he was not used to public speaking and what could he do to calm his nerves because he had to begin speaking at all the civic clubs in town and in some of the churches. I told him he could take a 200mg Equanil tablet about one hour before he had to speak and that would do the job. After four or five speeches, he told me that he had gotten over his nervousness and wouldn't need any more pills. He went on to win the race and did a good job representing our area at the state level.

Our school system had a policy wherein a student who missed school due to sickness had to have an excuse signed by the family doctor. I noticed that at the end of the year a lot of the students who had had a bad cold and had come to me for advice were denied excuses for absence. I went to the school board and explained to them that a lot of people in Grady County could not afford to go to their doctor for a simple bad cold. Most of the times a cold remedy from the drug store did just as good a job and cost a lot less. These students did not need to be in school until they got over being contagious.

The school board agreed to accept excuses for sickness signed by me. This saved a lot of poorer families' money, and they came to me for most all their simple ailments. When I saw that they really were sick I sent them on to their doctor. The doctors in the county seemed to appreciate what I had done. They were no longer swamped during cold season with patients who only needed symptomatic relief and couldn't pay for their visit.

One of the families who traded with me had a daughter who was starting school. The school required the students to list their family doctor's name at the beginning of the year so that if anything happened and they needed help, the school new who to call. The girl put down Doctor Truman on the form. She had never been sick, and when she had a problem, her mother always brought her to me for treatment.

One day a lady brought her son in with a prescription she received from a doctor in Thomasville. The prescription was for an antifungal shampoo to treat her boy's head. It was a fairly new product and expensive. She asked me to look at him and see what I thought. I told her that her son had a condition called tetters. It is a fungal infection and causes the hair to come out in patches. As a result of the fungal infection, the head looks like the hair loss due to alopecia.

I told her that there used to be a preparation called Tetterine Salve that was used for this, and it was pretty good at curing the ailment. I told her that a good antifungal ointment would do a better job of curing him because a shampoo doesn't stay on the head long enough to kill the fungus. The shampoo also caused more problems for a black person's hair because it removes the natural oils and leaves the hair very stiff and unruly.

I sold her an inexpensive tube of the antifungal ointment and told her to apply it and rub it in well twice a day for at least ten days in order to kill the fungus. She came back two weeks later with the boy, his hair was growing back in the splotches, and she thanked me.

A gentleman named J. D. owned a used car lot and repair shop in Cairo. He told me he turned his repair business over to his sons and noticed every time he went by the place some of his expensive tools were left lying around outside. He would pick them up and put them under his bed in his house. After a while, the boys realized they were having to buy new expensive tools and told J. D. that somebody was stealing from them. He told them to just keep a closer eye on their tools.

J. D. was apparently the godfather of the little subdivision they lived in, and on Sundays all the neighbors gathered at his place and just sat around in the yard under a shade tree and enjoyed a lazy afternoon. One Friday afternoon J. D. had gone to his doctor for his checkup. They were longtime friends and hunted and fished together for years. When the doctor called in J. D.'s prescription to me, he said to tell him to take one tablet three times daily for singing in church.

J. D. didn't go to church very much. At that time, I didn't know that J. D. could not read and write, so I wrote that in the instructions. The next Sunday when they were all sitting around in a big circle under the tree, J. D. asked his wife to look at his prescription bottle and see if it was time for him to take his medicine. She didn't answer him; she just looked at the bottle and began laughing. She then passed the bottle around for everybody to see what she was laughing about. They eventually told him the medicine was for singing in church.

Monday morning, I looked up toward the front door and J. D. came marching in. His son was with him. He came up to me and told me that he was going to whip my ass. He was red in the face and as mad as anybody I had ever seen. His son was trying to hold him back while I asked him what in the world the problem was. He said that he had never been so humiliated in his life, that he would never trade with me again and would see to it that nobody in his neighborhood would either. I told him that I only put on the bottle what his friend, the doctor, told me to. I apologized profusely and promised that I would never do that again. He became one of my most loyal customers.

In the future, he went fishing with me and got mad at me again. We went out from Mexico Beach and began fishing off St. Joe Point. His doctor was with us, and before long, I looked back and J. D. was green in the face and had become very seasick. He began throwing up, then laid down in the bottom of the boat. He began to beg us to go in, but the doctor told him that we were here to fish, not to take him in.

J. D. looked over, saw the land at the tip of St. Joe Point, and demanded I put him off there. I told him I couldn't do that because it was forty miles around that point back to Port St. Joe and just try to relax, I was heading back to the marina. We were traveling parallel to the point, and he told me that he would buy this damn boat paying cash but he wanted off on that land right now. I told him that I couldn't do that and kept heading toward the marina. He informed me that if he ever got off that boat he was going to whip my a-- and he would never get on a boat again.

As soon as he got back on land, the seasickness left him and he settled down. He continued fishing at the marina while his doctor and I went back out fishing. When we got back, we had a good mess of king mackerel and J. D. caught some redfish. We had a good fish fry when we got back to our beach place and J. D. decided that he wouldn't whip me after all.

On this trip, I asked him to please tell his sons that he had all those expensive tools under his bed. This tickled his doctor and he had a good laugh at what J. D. had done to the boys. J. D. did eventually give them back those tools and told them they shouldn't leave them laying around outside the shop.

About a week later, J. D. came in with a prescription for insulin and was to inject fourteen units subcutaneously once a week. As I said, he could not read or write and asked me if I would give him his injection once a week. I agreed to do so. He would come to the store every Sunday and I would give him his injection. One Sunday I was out of town and a druggist who did part-time work was there and when J. D. came in for his shot, the druggist was shocked and told him that fourteen units per week was not going to do anything for him. J. D. asked for his bottle of insulin, and when he walked out the front door, he threw it across the street into the cemetery. Then he went and told his doctor what he thought of him.

One day I counted to see how many different brands of tetracycline we had on hand. I counted seventeen different brand names. At this time, the pharmacist was forbidden to substitute one brand for another and couldn't dispense a generic if the brand name was used on the prescription. I discovered that many of the companies were producing their brand of tetracycline and promoting their products to doctors using gifts or vacations—even stock in their company—for them if they would prescribe their brand. These prices ranged from $4.50 to $23.65 per one hundred. All of these brands were identical and I discovered that most of them were produced by one company and the only differences was the color of the capsules and the label was changed from week to week depending on the quantity purchased by individual companies. I began to distrust most of our drug manufactur-ers. It seemed to me they were making plenty of profit and were using laws regarding pharmacy to help them make more.

Ralph, a salesman for Valdosta Drug Company and a registered pharmacist, received his license the year before the Depression and worked in Macon, Georgia. He managed to save a little money in the bank in Macon. When he heard the banks were closed, he ran to the bank to see if he could get his money out and discovered he could not. He knew the banker and a few days later was told he could not get any money; however, there was a little dairy farm just outside of town the bank had foreclosed on and if he would take over the note and pay it off, he could have credit for his money.

Ralph accepted the offer, paid off the note, and became the owner of the farm. He kept it over the years and always paid the taxes, but he did nothing to keep the place up. It became a vacant piece of land when the buildings were removed.

He now lived in Valdosta where his wife was a beautician. They lived off his wife's income and saved Ralph's. He had savings accounts in every bank in Georgia, most of Alabama, part of Florida, and some in Tennessee. He was a very wealthy man. He kept his paychecks and commission checks in his pocket until he could find a new bank somewhere and deposit it when he could. Quite often, the Valdosta Drug Company bookkeeper would have to tell him to cash his checks. At the time, the federal government only guaranteed deposits up to five thousand dollars, so he had to look far and wide to find a place to put his money. He wouldn't allow any bank to hold more than the government guaranteed.

It so happened that two banks in Thomasville, Georgia, merged. As soon as Ralph heard about it he showed up and asked for his five thousand dollars that was not insured. The banker did his best to assure

Ralph that his money was safe in that bank, but Ralph would not budge. He told the man that he had lost money before when the banks failed and he would not go through that again. He got his money and began hunting another bank.

One day he was calling on me at Truman's Drugs when he got a call from his wife. She told him that the city of Macon sent him a bill for his part of building a road through his farm in Macon. The farm originally outside of Macon was now almost in the middle of Macon due to the city's growth. Over the years, people who lived in the area had established a path through Ralph's property, and the path through time had become a public pathway.

Ralph rushed up to Macon with his lawyer to protest the road construction; however, he lost his battle and now his property was in two distinct pieces. I asked him why wouldn't he sell the property and he told me that he didn't need the money and also due to the increased value, he would have to pay too much in taxes.

A man came in and told me that he was having a problem with his face and neck. Sure enough, his face and neck covered with pustules and little pockets of infection. The area involved was where a man usually shaves. I asked him if he used a safety razor and he said that he did. That was his problem. His hair was naturally flat but appeared kinky, when he shaved real close he actually cut the hair off at or below the skin surface. Subsequently, the hair tended to grow under the skin and cause infection pockets. I suggested he use Magic shaving powder to remove the hair instead of a razor. The shaving powder would not leave the hair sharp and it could grow out properly. I told him that his face should clear up within three weeks. This man became a customer and stayed with me until I sold the store.

I was working in the hospital one day and went into a room to visit a patient and discovered that he had a bottle of five percent sodium chloride being infused into his arm. I stopped the infusion, called the head nurse, and asked her why this man was being given this strength of sodium chloride. She immediately disconnected the IV and called the floor nurse. The patient had been prescribed sodium chloride for infusion and the nurse had inadvertently picked the wrong strength of sodium chloride. She was sure that if I hadn't noticed what was going on that the patient would not have survived. I recommended that the floor nurse be relieved of patient duties until she had been given a course in drugs and their effects on the body with emphasis on attention to detail.

The man who operated Chandlers Drive-In was a peculiar man, and when the restaurant became a popular hangout for most of the teenagers in town, he began carrying a pistol on his hip. He said he needed it in order to keep control of his business. Some of the teenagers had become rowdy at times.

This man, being a type-A personality, had over the years developed stomach ulcers and they became very bad. If fact, he wound up in the hospital with bleeding ulcers, and his doctor couldn't get the bleeding stopped. His doctor recommended that a surgeon be called in to operate, but the man refused saying that God's will should be done. His family was unable to convince the man to allow surgery, and when he became comatose, they would not override his decision and he bled to death.

One day a call came in from my brother-in-law, Altis's husband, telling me that she was in the hospital in Moultrie in serious condition. Rosalind and I rushed to Moultrie and discovered she was in surgery. A surgeon new to Moultrie established a practice and was performing the surgery. After five or six hours of surgery, he came out and told us she had eosinophilic granuloma of the intestine and he had removed a large portion of her small intestine.

When she woke up, her heart began to fibrillate. I felt like it was due to her receiving so much fluid during surgery that her electrolytes were out of balance. We were told that a new cardiac specialist was called to do a heart catheterization. This process was new to our part of the country, and I didn't like the thought of it being done. I felt that all she needed was to get her electrolytes back in balance and the problem would be solved. Rosalind tried to call her regular doctor and discovered he was playing tennis at the sports complex. Rosalind and I rushed to the tennis courts, called him to the fence, and asked him to call the hospital and tell them not to do the catheterization. After explaining the situation to him, he immediately called the hospital and stopped the procedure. He ordered some electrolytes, and her heart immediately settled down to a normal rhythm.

I was not familiar with eosinophilic granulation and there was very little information available in my books. I knew from the description that her eosinophils had infiltrated the intestinal lining including the muscles, rendering them useless and very brittle. This situation leads to peritonitis, which can be deadly.

Since I needed more information, I went to our library in Cairo and explained to our librarian that I wanted some information on eosinophilic granulation. Our librarian immediately researched and ordered me all the information available on the subject. She explained that it would take three to four weeks for subject matter to arrive.

She informed me that Florida State University had just installed a large computer, and it was possible I could get some information quicker if I went there and asked for help.

The computer operator at Florida State University was willing to help me and asked me to write down my questions because he had to key punch cards to feed into the computer in order for it to do the research.

After a couple of hours, the computer operator came out and handed me the answers to my questions. I had to pay the university twenty-five dollars for the time used on the computer.

Eosinophilic granulation is not a disease but a description of the results of a hookworm infestation. Since our part of the country was known as the hookworm belt of the United States, it made sense to me. My sister had almost died due to hookworms.

A young man came in and I noticed that he seemed to have trouble walking. He came up to the counter and asked me what he could do for hemorrhoids. He said he was in misery and needed some relief, but he was deathly afraid of surgery. He wanted to know if Preparation H would help him. I told him that I didn't think Preparation H would be much help. I asked him if he had ever tied a string or wrapped a rubber band around one of his fingers. He said he had and I asked him what happened. He said his finger began to hurt and sting, so he took the rubber band off. I then explained to him that his anus had two muscles approximately a quarter inch apart. These muscles are the only ones in his body that grip tight when the nerves tell them to relax. In effect, what happens is some of the intestines in the rectum get pushed through one or both of these muscles and gets trapped. This happens sometimes when you are constipated or have diarrhea. The result is tissue that is cordoned off by one or both of these muscles and begins to itch, swell, and hurt, just like his finger did with the rubber band around it.

I explained to him that the only way he could get relief was to get the tissue back on the proper side of the muscles or have a doctor do surgery to remove the tissue involved. I suggested he try to lie down in a bathtub of water and push the tissue back inside with his finger. He must lie down to get the weight of his intestines off his pelvis because that weight would make it very hard for the tissue to stay in place. He left and came back in about three hours and told me that he couldn't get it done. He said the tissue would not stay inside.

I drew him a picture of the two muscles with an explanation, suggested he take it to his doctor, and explain the situation to her. She could probably deaden the area and push the tissue back inside. He came back in two days later and told me she pushed the hemorrhoids back inside where they belonged. He had instant relief and no more trouble with them. I told him to be sure to eat plenty of fiber so as not to get constipated. This would help to prevent it from happening again.

Leslie, one of my partners, began to show signs of Alzheimer's and progressively got worse. He would get lost and someone would have to find him and bring him home. The Ford place assigned one of their employees to be his constant companion in order to keep tabs on him. His wife told me that he would get on his tractor and mow their large yard and pasture, and she was worried that he would fall off and hurt himself. He was headstrong and would not listen to her. I told her that the best thing that could happen is for him to get down where he couldn't walk. That way they would know what he was doing and where he was. The bad part about that was that he would be an invalid and require twenty-four-hour care. I explained to her that his situation would only get worse and that the caregiver is the one who suffers.

Sure enough, one day he fell and broke his hip. He was suddenly an invalid and required constant care. His wife began to call his doctor quite often and ask him to check on him. Because of my association with Leslie, his doctor asked me to check on him and if he really needed a doctor for me to call him. In the meantime, I was to give whatever assistance they needed and keep him informed. I began going to his house once a week and would check his blood pressure, listen to his chest and heart, and give him a B-12 shot on a regular basis. I advised his wife as to what and how to feed him in order to keep his weight up. This seemed to please his wife and reassured her that he was all right. That man got very good care and lived for seven years. He never developed bedsores or any of the typical problems that bedridden patients have.

A lady customer who had the misfortune of giving birth to a baby with severe spina bifida came in one day and asked me to look back and see if she had ever taken a drug named Bendectin. The baby did not live, and she had been through a depression for a couple of years. She had just heard that a drug given to women during pregnancy to control nausea had been connected to spina bifida births. At the time, we were filing prescriptions in files containing one thousand prescriptions stacked on each other. Each one had been stamped with a prescription number. I asked her if by any chance she had one of her bottles left around anywhere. We could not label the prescription with what was in it, but the number on the bottle would lead us directly to it.

She said that she didn't have any bottles left, but she could give me the approximate date she discovered she was expecting. I told her that would mean that someone would have to look through eight to ten thousand prescriptions to see if it could be found. She was very distressed, so I assured her that I would start looking and would call her if I found or did not find anything.

I started looking and in the meantime I researched what she had told me about the drug. Sure enough, some drug committee had suggested a connection between pyridoxine and spina bifida. Pyridoxine is an antihistamine that was an ingredient in the drug labeled Bendectin. There was no definite proof of the connection; however, a while later the drug was removed from the market. After a while looking, I found her prescription and it was for Bendectin. She was so proud to know that and she felt a sense of relief because now she had a reason for the situation, and it was not due to a default in her genes.

At this time, we sold a lot of valentine candy for Valentine's Day. We always ordered a big shipment and had one of our best days, business wise. One time we sold out at the last minute and I rented a plane, flew to the factory, and picked up another large order. I always told men not to leave the candy in their car, because in the heat, the candy will turn white due to the wax in the chocolate melting and forming on the top. This doesn't mean the candy is bad but it sure doesn't look good.

We had a salesman who worked for Geigy Pharmaceuticals. He was a very likeable detail man, and he would look through the prescription department to observe his company's drug movement. This was a common practice then. We got to know and like him. We discovered that his wife was a doctor in Alabama in his hometown.

One day when he had been in the store, I got a prescription for Percodan and when I reached for the bottle, it was gone. I knew that he had just been in and that the bottle had been there just a short while ago. I ran outside to catch him, but he was already gone. I immediately called the other drug stores in town and informed them as to what had just happened to me. He had just stolen a bottle of five hundred Percodan. I then called Geigy headquarters and reported what had happened. I also notified the Georgia Drug Enforcement Agency and filed a report. I never saw him again, but I heard that Geigy fired him. The drug enforcement officer said that they could not prove he stole the pills and there was nothing they could do.

I was working away one day when one of my customers, a preacher told me that he was in the concrete business and was becoming unable, health and money wise, to increase or continue his business—

he needed a partner. He was a heart patient and needed a cash infusion in his business to acquire some needed equipment. Also, if he had a partner, he would be able to ensure the business would continue in the event of his death.

He was making burial vaults and was very successful but needed to purchase a larger concrete mixer in order to keep up with the demand for them. He wouldn't want any cash for himself, but if I would finance a used concrete mixer truck, he would give me fifty percent interest in his business. I agreed and discovered I was now very involved in a business completely foreign to me.

We discussed how we could increase business and decided to make forms whereby we could make coping for cemeteries or walkways. They would also work for stops for autos in parking lots. We bought a form and began making birdbaths. We purchased a used concrete buffer machine whereby we could pour flooring for buildings and polish them so that the floor would be finished better than just screeding it.

One day he asked me if I thought we could pour the base for a business sign to be mounted upon. I assured him that we should be able to. He said that the Dairy Queen needed a modern sign and asked him if we could install it. We had to pour the base six feet into the ground and set six large bolts in the concrete so that the sign could be bolted down. It required a good, accurate measurement for the bolts to fit the sign. Another problem was the top of this sign was fairly large and had to clear the top of the building and still not extend over the state right of way for Highway 84. We were successful and were proud of that sign.

He informed me one day that he was leaving to be a preacher at a church in Live Oak, Florida. He had found someone to purchase his half of the business. We had hired a man to help him in the business and he agreed to purchase the preacher's interest by sending him so much money every month until he paid him off.

My new partner's name was Jimmy. He told me we should get into the swimming pool business and all we needed was a larger backhoe with a front-end loader that we could use in the concrete business as well. I went up to the tractor place and signed a note for the new backhoe and we were into building swimming pools as well.

About 1972, Rosalind told me that she was tired of us living in the country with her having to carry kids to after-school functions. Even though they rode the school bus, there was always somewhere they needed to be taken for a meeting or something. We sold the house in the country and bought a two-story house on Lullwater Circle. This house was perfect for raising kids. Each one had their own bedroom.

While we lived here, I built a gazebo for Rosalind in the side yard. While building it, a stray cat began to hang around me and soon became my overseer. He was a healthy looking Maine coon cat with good striping. He would stand there even when I began sawing with a Skil saw. He would climb the ladder with me, sit there, and watch me nail the roof on. Most cats in my memory did not like loud noises and would run when something like a saw turned on. I took a liking to that cat and we got along real well. I had a customer who came and groomed our dog occasionally. She had a son who was autistic, and one day her son saw my cat and fell in love with him. She asked if her son could have the cat and said her son got along better when he was with the cat. I hated losing that cat, but I was pleased her son and the cat got along so well together.

One of my employees at the drug store had a son, Joe, who needed a job and came to see me about hiring him in the concrete and pool business. I told him I would sell him my interest and he could pay me over time. He agreed and I was out of that business. I had not been able to keep any profits from it because we were always putting the profits back in the place.

Joe had an interest in flying and took lessons; in fact, he got his license and was learning to be a crop duster. He came to see me one day and asked me if I would co-sign a note for an airplane he could use in crop dusting. After much conversation, I agreed. He was very successful and paid the note off to my great relief. He managed to do so just before he crashed the plane while dusting a peanut field. He was not hurt in the crash, and the plane was insured so he came out all right.

A thirty-one-year-old man came in and presented three prescriptions from his doctor. Prednisone dospak, Aristocort cr. 1%, and Atarax 25mg. When I asked what he had gotten into, he said he had a fungus on his right hand and showed it to me. On inspection, I saw no sign of fungus infection. What I saw was some swelling and small clear blisters, which appeared to be closed sweat glands. He said it had been bothering him for about six weeks. I asked him if he had ever had an injury to his cervical area. I suspected he pinched a nerve in his cervical area or in his shoulder. He said he had been hurt about five years ago since I mentioned it and had no problems until starting to pitch softball about six weeks ago. He asked me what he should do and I recommended that he see a chiropractor or a physical therapist because all the medicine I had in the store would only give some symptomatic relief. He decided to fill the Aristocort cream, not the other two and said he would contact a chiropractor. He returned in a couple of weeks and showed me that the blisters had cleared and the swelling was just about gone.

A man called and asked me about his father who was a terminal cancer patient. We had discussed his condition before and that day the doctor was going to pull fluid from his lungs to help relieve some of his pain. The doctor told him this was a last ditch effort to help his father. He wanted to know how long his father would live. I told him that was anybody's guess, but the outcome was not going to be good. Some people hang on for two to three months, but others expire within three to four days. I told him that his doctor could give him a much better guess than I could. It all depended on his physical condition. He just wanted to ask questions that are not dumb. I told him there are no dumb questions when it comes to one's health. He thanked me for talking to him.

A lady came in and presented prescriptions for an antibiotic and Vicodin. The Vicodin had been crossed out and Darvocet-N 100 written in. She was bitten by a rattlesnake in her backyard close to her clothesline and spent the night in the hospital receiving antivenom and medications. The doctor had written for Vicodin, but she had told him that she could not swallow that pill and wanted something stronger like Darvocet. She came back in three days later and said she didn't feel well. She was swollen badly on the left side, hand, and leg. On inspection, I couldn't see any difference between her left and right side as to swelling. I told her the feeling must be nerve damage because the snake had bitten her on her left leg. I assured her that she would be all right it just feels like swelling. The nerves involved would repair themselves in a short while, just give it time.

The woman who ran a fertilizer plant called and asked me what saltpeter was. I told her it was potassium nitrate. What we have in the drug store was purified. A lady wanted some to put around her grapevines. I told her she didn't need the purified form, just go ahead and sell her some bulk. She said she had plenty, but wasn't sure what saltpeter was. She said thanks.

Chapter 15:
The Struggles of Health

One day one of my customers came in, sat down on my couch, and told me she wanted to talk to me. I sat down next to her and she said she just came from her doctor in Thomasville who told her she had terminal cancer and there was nothing they could do for her. She had been told to get her affairs in order because she probably only had six to eight weeks to live. She was eighty-six years old and had been a customer of mine for years. I noted she had not been taking any kind of chemotherapy and asked her what was going on. She said she had not been feeling well and began to lose weight. Upon having her physical, they discovered the cancer progressed to the point that it was untreatable.

She began crying and asked me why they would not try to treat her. She said, "Mr. Truman, old people want to live too." I explained to her that trying to treat her with the available medications would do more damage to her than helping her. The medications available to treat cancer kill good cells as well as cancer cells. Using the available treatments would only hasten her demise and cause her final days to be very painful.

I told her cancer cells were the bullies on the block in comparison to normal cells. They were larger and demanded more nutrition. When there is not enough nutrition available in the fluids around them they attack normal cells and take nutrition from them. I felt that one way to slow the cancer cells progress was to ensure they had as much nutrition available to them as we could. I told her that in my opinion the pain from cancer was in reality hunger pains due to most people feeling ill and not having an appetite. They then are in essence starving themselves to death. This in turn causes the cancer cells to become more aggressive. Hunger pain is one of the most intense and continuous pains man can have.

I told her that I would give her a diet for her to eat on a regular basis ensuring a good caloric intake with less carbohydrates and more fat so that she could slow down the cancer progress. She said she needed all the help she could get. I told her to take my diet and be sure to follow it and to come back to the store once a week for me to weigh her and for her to give me a report on how she was feeling.

She came back regularly every week and told me how she was feeling. I would weigh her and I kept a record of her weight so she could see how she was doing. She followed the diet and actually would add some more calories to it when she could. We had many conversations over the next three years until she died peacefully in her sleep at eighty-nine years old. She had almost retained her weight and had no cancer pain.

Her sixty-two-year-old son came in shortly after her funeral and told me that his mother wanted him to thank me for being kind to her and to apologize for crying in front of me.

Sometime after this, the librarian came to the store and said she was suffering from melanoma, which metastasized and established in her brain. She told me I apparently was interested in medicine and its processes due to my research on eosinophilic granuloma and would I see what I could find out about melanoma and explain the situation to her. She told me she had surgery for it some time back and it had already metastasized and she had subsequently been going to Dana Farber Cancer Institute every four to six weeks. It was established in her liver, gall bladder, and brain. On her last visit, she had been told there was nothing else they could do for her. Further radiation and chemotherapy was useless. She was advised to come home and get her affairs in order.

I had a good long conversation with her about cancer in general and explained my feelings about cancer pain being mostly due to hunger pains. Most people are depressed and when they undergo radiation and chemotherapy wind up nauseous. This leaves them unable to eat, thus leading to hunger pain. This is a real pain and most people assume that the pain is from cancer.

She asked me if I would suggest a diet for her and work with her through her illness. I agreed and gave her a suggested diet similar to the other cancer patient I had worked with. She was a petite lady and had very little body fat, so I felt she needed a good caloric intake that would come more from fat than carbohydrates. She never had a big appetite, and I explained she needed to force herself to eat. I also suggested she needed some B-12 injections in order to keep her energy level up. She called her doctor at Dana Farber and asked him for a prescription for B-12 injection, which he immediately forwarded to me.

She was in the process of remodeling and enlarging the library and told me she wanted to finish this project if she could. To her this would be the culmination of her lifelong dream.

She was a very private individual and asked me if I would come by her house after hours and administer the B-12 and talk about her diet. This way there would be little public awareness of her condition. I agreed, and once a week I would go to her house and she would show me the record of what she ingested. She kept minute details of her diet and insisted I keep the records at the drug store so I could monitor them closely.

I kept up this routine for almost a year until one day she told me her doctor at Dana Farber called to check on her. She told him she was feeling pretty good, so he asked her to return to Dana Farber for a check-up. They made x-rays and discovered the tumor had not grown and possibly decreased in size some. They suggested she keep up our regimen.

She was very pleased with her progress so we kept up our routine. After about nine months, her doctor wanted her to return for another checkup. She told me that her tumor actually shrunk and was definitely smaller than it had been. Her doctor wanted her to return in six weeks so they could irradiate the tumor again to help further reduce the size. I told her I personally would not agree to that; however, I am not a doctor and do not have the education they have.

She obviously wanted to live so she agreed to go for further radiation and treatment. When she returned to Cairo, she lost her appetite and could not force herself to eat. I continued my once weekly visits giving her the B-12 and encouraging her to try to eat. She began to lose weight and struggled to do her day's work at the library because of lack of energy.

Miss Wessie did not get to finish her work rebuilding and enlarging the library. She came very close, but she expired just a little over two and a half years after our first conversation about her condition.

At that time, we had Sunday hours at Truman's and Trumarx Drugs. Marx and I would swap Sundays. Truman's was open for three hours in the morning and Trumarx was open for three hours in the evening. Marx had a delivery boy in high school, and quite often, he would drop by on Sunday and visit with us. Rosalind always went with me to

Trumarx to help out, and one day when the delivery boy dropped by she saw him pick up a bottle and slip it into his pocket.

Upon confronting him, he admitted he had taken a bottle of Ritalin. We took the bottle from him and put it back on the shelf and immediately called Marx and informed him. I notified the local sheriff's office as to what had happened and they called in the drug enforcement agent. As it turned out, the boy lived close to Marx and Marx and the boy's daddy were friends.

A meeting was held between Marx, the boy, his dad, the drug enforcement agent, the sheriff's deputy, and me. The boy admitted he had been taking Ritalin from the store for quite a while and supplying it to his friends at school. Hundreds of bottles of Ritalin had been stolen.

The drug agent and the deputy apparently knew the boy's dad, so they suggested we accept restitution from the boy. This would have to begin after he finished school and got a job. He would also have to write a paper to Marx and me apologizing for what he had done. I got a phone call from him later and he apologized. I never heard anything else from him and he never paid anything.

Ulysses S. (Boy) George, the man who traded with me because of Mr. Legette's mule, came in one day. As he came in, a young man on his way out asked him, "How are you today, uncle?" Boy stopped and stared him down and informed him that he did not know him well enough to call him uncle and that he should be more respectful of his elders.

He told me that he just came back from Detroit where he was asked to preach a funeral. He said nowadays people just had no respect. The people in Detroit only wanted to put that person in the ground. He told them, they did not know how to funeralize a person. You should spend some time and show respect for the deceased not just put them in the ground with a few words over them. He had been a preacher for most of his life and didn't like what the world was coming to.

We had a good long conversation and when he was younger one of his jobs was to drive people around when they came to Thomasville during the winters. Thomasville was at one time the endpoint of railroads to the south and many of the nation's richest people bought land and established plantations there. They would spend the winter in Thomasville.

One of the visitors was Al Capone, and he always asked for Boy to be his driver when he was in Thomasville. Al knew some of the wealthy owners and was asked to visit them quite often. He said Al was always good to him and would give a good tip.

Boy also told me that when he was younger he quite often helped in a funeral home. One day they asked him to go to Panama City, Florida, and pick up a body and bring it to Cairo. He said that he got a late start home and as he approached Blountstown, Florida, it was getting dark. He said that there was a sign at the city limits of Blountstown that said, "N____r, don't let the sun go down on you in Blountstown." This was during segregation in the South. He said a policeman pulled him over and asked him what he was doing in Blountstown. He told him he was carrying a body back to Cairo, Georgia, and please let him go. He said the policeman told him he couldn't let him go because he was drinking and driving. Boy told him, "Bossman, I ain't drinking."

The policeman reached down in the floorboard of his patrol car and came out with a quart of moonshine. He told Boy to drink this. Boy told him that he didn't drink alcohol. The policeman pulled out his pistol, put it to Boy's head, and told him to drink, dammit. Boy said, "So I turned it up and drank some of it. The policeman said,

'See, I told you that you were drinking and driving so I've got to lock you up.'"

Boy said he did lock him up, but the worst part was that they put the body he was hauling in the cell with him. He said that was an awful night but in the morning they put the body back in his hearse and escorted him to the city limits and told him to leave and not come back to Blountstown. He had never been back and would drive many miles out of the way to avoid Blountstown.

He said, "Yes, many people were mistreated back then, but you always knew what the rules were and you could depend on people. Now you never know what to expect from people, black or white."

A customer in her fifties came in one day and told me that she didn't feel right. Upon questioning her, I felt she was having angina pain and recommended that she call her doctor. She said that her doctor was out of town and she would call him when he got back. I asked her to sit there on the sofa and insisted she take an aspirin. I called another doctor and asked him to check her out. He did so and immediately admitted her to the hospital and ordered cardiac tests, which confirmed she was having problems. He immediately sent her to Tallahassee Memorial Hospital where she was treated and kept for four days. The doctor assured me she probably would not have lived if she had gone home that day.

I discovered that the health department was handing our birth control pills and had no pharmacist involved. I went out and volunteered to dispense these pills. They set up one day a week for a birth control clinic and put me in charge. I counseled these women on the pills, and some of them were told they should use other types of birth control because they had problems. I didn't want them to have a stroke or a thrombotic occlusion.

I heard that two of my doctor friends had purchased an airplane. A Cessna 172 and it was a beauty. I expressed my interest and they told me I could use it to learn to fly, all I had to do was pay for the gas. I contacted a Mr. Black in Thomasville who was an instructor, and he agreed to come over to Cairo and give me lessons. I learned to fly in that plane and in a Cessna 150 that was for rent at the airport. I used it when the 172 was in use.

I did my solo in the 172, and when it came time to do my solo cross-country, I flew the Cessna 150. I chose as my route—Atlanta Municipal Airport, Montgomery, Alabama Airport, and then home. I had a radio but no transponder, which at the time was on most planes but not required.

I radioed the tower in Atlanta and asked permission to land and was told to keep my airspeed up and land behind an airliner that was approaching on final. I could not see the airliner even though I was on crosswind getting ready to approach final. As I turned on final, suddenly that big airplane swooped in front of me and I was told to get down as soon as possible and take the first exit to the hanger on the right. I landed in the busy Atlanta Municipal Airport and taxied to the nearest hanger to get my logbook signed. The manager signed my logbook and recommended I not come back into the Atlanta airport in a plane as little as the 150. I assured him that I would not.

I radioed the tower, asked permission to taxi out to leave, and was told to follow an airliner taxiing by me at the time, but to stay far enough behind that I wouldn't have to fight the propwash. I got in line and realized that there were six airliners ahead of me. By the time, I got in position to enter the runway my engine was getting mighty hot and I began to worry. After the airliner ahead of me took off, I thought I was ready but didn't get word to take off. I realized they were landing airliners on the same runway and I had to wait until I had clearance.

I finally got clearance to enter the runway and was told to take off, turn 180 degrees left at six hundred feet, and expedite. I assured the tower I was going as fast as I could and I would not be back. I kept that promise. The flight into Montgomery and on into Cairo was uneventful. Shortly after my solo flight, the Atlanta Municipal Airport made it a requirement that any plane coming in had to have a transponder. Later the airport was closed to recreational aircraft.

I enjoyed flying and took my mother on her only plane flight. She wanted to go to Fort Lauderdale to visit her sister, and I was pleased to oblige. When I carried my brother up and landed, he commented that he had taken off and flown many times but this was the first time he had landed in a plane. He had been a paratrooper in service and had never landed in a plane.

I proceeded to get my twin-engine certificate. I took the test flight in an old twin-engine Apache. The generator was not working properly and when I got into the plane with the instructor, the engines wouldn't start. I had to get out and prop the engine to get it started. I later flew this plane into LaGuardia in New York. When I left to come home after dark, the generator quit working and I had to fly almost all the way to Cairo without any lights. I used a flashlight to see my instruments. When I got to Cairo, I had just enough battery power left to see the runway and felt relieved. Rosalind was with me on this trip, and since she didn't like flying, this was not a good experience for her.

I flew into New Orleans, Key West, LaGuardia, Memphis, Little Rock, and many others before I realized that my reflexes were getting slow. I almost did a ground loop in Camilla flying a Stinson Tail Dragger. A short while later, I decided I needed to quit flying before I killed somebody I really liked.

In 1971, I realized I was performing many duties. I had taken on the job as chief pharmacist for the Royal Elaine nursing home that was 175 miles away from home in addition to chief pharmacist at the Grady County Health Department and chief pharmacist at Grady General Hospital.

I would fly to the Royal Elaine and spend four hours twice a week reviewing medical orders and overseeing drug dispensing to patients. Most of the prescriptions used there were filled by local pharmacists. I spent six hours a week at the health department ordering and dispensing medications to indigents and counseling patients on their medicine in addition to three hours a day at Grady General Hospital.

In early 1971, after reading an article in *Pharmacy Times*, a national magazine, I sent a letter to the editor outlining what I was doing in my community. Mr. Irving Ruben, the editor, asked me to submit an article, which he accepted and sent a photographer to Cairo to make pictures to accompany the article—titled "This Pharmacist Wears Five Hats." I started the article stating that the future of pharmacy lies in the ability to adapt to change and grow along with the medical field. Pharmacists must see to it that their profession does not become a "lost art" performed by technicians or clerks. Pharmacists can accomplish this by becoming professional providers of medical services and supplies. I had expanded my community pharmacy by also serving as chief pharmacist at Grady General Hospital, chief pharmacist at Royal Elaine nursing home, and chief pharmacist at Grady County health department. I was being paid for each of these services.

Upon reading the article, the dean of Mercer University's School of Pharmacy invited me to serve on their curriculum advisory board. I flew to Atlanta for the meetings and was received very well by the dean and his professors. Another result of my article was that I received a letter from the chief drug inspector informing me that my association with the Royal Elaine nursing home, which was over a hundred miles from Cairo, should stop. He said that the situation smelled of mail-order service, which was illegal in Georgia, and that I should stick to business in my own community. I felt like I wasn't doing anything wrong and I was not using mail service. I told him that even so, the VA was using mail order to deliver medicine to some of my patients. He told me that the VA was a federal situation that he had no control over, but he had control over me. The upshot was I decided to terminate my services to the Royal Elaine nursing home.

One elderly gentleman came into the store on a beautiful day and informed me that his pubic hair had grown too long and asked me what to do about it. I suggested that he get some scissors and trim it to the length he desired. He seemed shocked and told me he just couldn't do that. Two or three days later, he came in and informed me that he had just passed a stool over twelve inches long and what did I think about that. I assured him that it was normal and asked him to stop discussing his personal problems of that nature with me, I preferred health questions. For some reason, he never came back into the store.

We began having a problem with illicit drugs in the county. The University of Georgia presented a program teaching pharmacists how to test samples for marijuana, cocaine, heroin, and LSD. I attended this program at the university and came home with supplies to test these samples. I informed the police department and the sheriff's department that I could test for these drugs and give quick results. They began to use my services when they caught someone with something suspicious. I didn't charge for the service and told them my results could only give them reasonable cause for arrest. They would have to send the samples to the Georgia Crime Center for results to use in court. Both departments used my service for several years until field tests were available for them to use on site.

Chapter 16:
Battling the FDA

As I mentioned earlier, during the fifities, Benadryl was suddenly in great demand so Schering Drug Company developed an antihistamine called Chlor-trimeton and began promoting it heavily. It was expected to be the answer to the common cold. When I developed my first cold of the fall, I took Chlor-trimeton and realized that it had no effect on the cold, but made my congestion more pronounced. Then I remembered that during a lecture on antihistamines that there is a yin and yang in regards to smooth muscle reactions. Antihistamines constrict small blood vessels and decongestants dilate them. Anything that relaxes the muscles in the bronchial tube causes an increase of constriction of the muscles in the heart.

In effect, antihistamines produce a drying affect while decongestants cause a wetting effect on mucous in the respiratory tract. The professor also told us there had been over seventy-five antihistamines studied and the effects or benefits were directly related to drowsiness. In other words, the better the antihistamine, the more drowsiness. He also told us that antihistamines should be used for hay fever and not the common cold. In fact, in checking the drug use indications there was the statement that they are used for hay fever.

During the eighties, some drug companies began developing and promoting the non-drowsy formulations. There was plenty of money to be made due to the non-drowsy, long acting promotions. The hay fever indication had been removed from the drug information and the drug companies were promoting them for allergies. One of the problems that developed was the effect on the heart muscles and some people died as a result. The FDA recalled some of these preparations. We still have some of them being heavily promoted. Most of the companies began adding decongestants to the formula trying to make them more effective. It seems to me that is kind of like driving your car with the brakes on. You get to where you are going, only slower and with possible damage to the body.

I began explaining to customers who wanted something for a runny nose that their body was already producing antihistamines, which caused this, and they should be using a decongestant. Your respiratory tract includes the upper and lower tracts and it is one system. The upper tract produces approximately one gallon of normal saline every twenty-four hours, which is produced in the sinus cavities, nasal passages, Eustachian tubes, and bronchial tubes. When everything is normal, you don't realize what is going on. When your body is exposed to allergens or something it doesn't like the body begins producing antihistamines, which in effect thickens this drainage in order to protect the tissue from these allergens. Because the nose and eyes are not kept as wet as they should they begin to itch and you begin to sneeze. The throat is dry and begins to hurt.

I asked them if they had seen the movie *The Godfather*. If they had, I reminded them that the son who always had to use a handkerchief had hay fever, which resulted in over production of normal saline and results in a drippy nose. This is when you need an antihistamine. In the case of a runny nose, you need a decongestant, which will thin the mucous, and help your body get back to normal quicker.

A pharmacist from Jacksonville, Florida, stopped by to see me one day on the way home from Texas. He was promoting Prescription Compounding Centers of America (PCCA) and wanted to demonstrate some of the newer processes. When I saw what he had, I called Marx at Trumarx Drugs and asked him to meet us at Trumarx at six thirty and let him see what this man was promoting. Marx was interested, so we joined PCCA and began promoting our compounding capabilities. There is always a need for specially prepared medications because all of us are not the same weight. Most medications come in stepped doses to accommodate this; however, not everyone can swallow and needs different methods of taking medicines—for example, suppositories, wafers, lollipops, injections, etc. that are formulated in special strengths for the individual.

During the nineties, compounding was being promoted highly in pharmacy practice by PCCA and others, and pharmacists were trying to increase profits. Compounded prescriptions were not being paid for by insurance cards, so pharmacies could actually make better profits from them. I commented to them at a seminar that in the late fifties and early sixties, we had to compound many of our products extemporaneously. Upon hearing this, I was asked to come to Atlanta for their next seminar and present a program on compounding in the sixties. I did so and gave many of the formulas we used in the years past including suppositories and eye waters. I explained to them how to make a suppository without a suppository mold and told them if it is done in the hot summertime we had to work on a shelf in a refrigerator. I displayed prescriptions that had been filled in the fifties and early sixties wherein the doctor would send his formula and the pharmacist had to mix and make it. Some of these prescriptions had as many as eight different drugs in them. The druggist had to know how to mix them and in which order so that the therapeutic effect would be obtained.

Some pharmacists compounded excess quantities and sold their products to other pharmacists. This practice irritated some drug manufacturers and they called in the FDA. In some instances, pharmacists made errors and the FDA began to come down hard on compounding.

Schering Drug Company had put on the market an eye drop for allergies. They had some stability problems and pulled it from the market. The chemical involved was a common one and commercially available. Trumarx Drugs was in a complex with doctors' offices. Since we had been compounding special doses of medications for some of their patients, they asked us to prepare some for their patients when Schering pulled this product. Compounding eye drops was nothing new, so we agreed and prepared them for their patients.

One day the Schering representative was in the store, observed us compounding eye drops, and asked what we were doing. Marx told him and the conversation led to a letter from the FDA telling us to cease and desist compounding anything. At the time, any drug company representative was welcome in our pharmacy and we had a good relationship with many of them. Since this episode, we barred most all sales representatives from the pharmacy area. It seemed obvious to us that Schering had contacted the FDA and asked for action.

Marx informed the FDA that he would not cease because what we were doing was legal. The FDA immediately informed us that any compounded medication requires a new drug application before it could be dispensed. We were instructed to cease and desist immediately or face padlocks on the store and seizure of all our supplies and chemicals.

It so happened that the Georgia Pharmaceutical Association had a session on legal aspects of pharmacy planned in Atlanta and officials with the FDA were to appear and make some presentations.

I went to this meeting and carried my recorder in order to record the meeting for Marx. The meeting was to be all day with a break for lunch. After each speaker, there was a question and answer period. The question came up about the FDA's position on compounding and we were informed that all compounding is illegal and had been since 1938.

Our situation with the FDA had become common knowledge and one of the pharmacists asked the FDA official to comment on Trumarx's case. The official immediately informed the audience that the drug store involved was probably some old, decrepit, untidy place, that all compounding now requires a new drug application, and Trumarx would probably not be able to pass inspection.

Upon hearing this, I stood up and interrupted the man and informed him that our store was not decrepit or dirty and in fact had just been remodeled and was ultra-modern spic and span. Also, if his comment that all compounding was illegal was accurate, the letter we received forbade us from actuating amoxicillin suspension without a new drug application. If what he was saying was true since 1938, then I had a lawsuit against the State of Georgia, the State Board of Pharmacy in Georgia, Mercer University, and the University of Georgia. In order to pass the Georgia pharmacy board and get my license I had to demonstrate to them my capability in compounding. I had to prepare many different products for approval by the board members. I also was required to have on hand a class A balance and basic compounding equipment in order to acquire a license to operate a drug store. This stimulated a lot of conversation around the room and suddenly the lunch break was called. When lunch was over and we reconvened, we were informed that the FDA officials had to return to Washington and would not be back for the afternoon session.

Compounding by now had become a question nationwide, and in fact, there was a lawsuit in process in federal court in Houston, Texas. We were asked for a transcript of the meeting I taped in Atlanta, and Marx was asked to come to Houston to testify. The federal judge in the case enjoined the FDA from using Marx's testimony in any other case and Marx went to Houston and testified.

The result of the situation was that the FDA backed off on pharmacy and compounding protocols were instituted that the FDA accepted.

In my opinion, the attacks on pharmacy were encouraged by the drug manufacturers in order to protect their income from encroachment by pharmacists on their patented products. There had been an instance wherein a pharmaceutically compounded product had been the cause of eye infections leading to blindness. This had inflamed some in the FDA and pharmacy was attacked.

The drug manufacturers had been very successful in getting FDA approval for some of the drugs they put on the market. Some of these drugs had to be recalled shortly thereafter due to people being killed or maimed by these drugs. Apparently, there was some pharmacists who were compounding copies of patented products and dispensing them as the patented product. This practice in my opinion is illegal and should have been stopped; however, an all-out attack on pharmacy in general was not called for.

It occurred to me then that most of the medical education as well as continuing medical education was being funded by drug manufacturers. They even funded most of the continuing pharmacy education.

I also realized that the life expectancy in the United States was longer and many of the illnesses that were around when I was young were now gone. I hadn't seen a tar poultice in years. I couldn't remember the last mastoid operation I had heard of. No more granulated eyelids and very rarely impetigo. I hadn't seen char on a wound for years. Nobody had carbuncles anymore and risens were almost extinct. Erysipelas was not being diagnosed as such anymore. No more diagnoses of pleurisy. Vaccines virtually wiped out measles and there were no more quarantines. Tuberculosis hospitals with their iron lungs were a thing of the past. You didn't see goiters any more due to salt being iodized to prevent lumping in damp weather. The oral polio vaccine program had successfully eradicated polio. There was no more haemophilus influenza and nobody died of natural causes anymore. There was a medical cause for all deaths.

I remember the first penicillin we dispensed at Crystal Pharmacy in Moultrie was eighty-five-thousand units. Now it was customary to use five-hundred-thousand unit doses. Nowadays, we apparently have to use larger and larger doses of antibiotics to accomplish what it took forty years ago. Bacteria began developing resistance to antibiotics. It then occurred to me that the extended life expectancy in the States was probably due to increased sanitation and better eating habits as well as to some of the new drugs. It dawned on me that there were no more outhouses. Most all children wore shoes year round. People were leaving the farms and migrating to the cities where living conditions were better.

When Keflex came on the market, the FDA approved it for second line use when penicillin, tetracycline, or chloromycetin failed. It was not long before doctors began to use it as first line therapy. This was due to drug representatives touting it as the latest and strongest antibiotic available. Obviously, the more usage of a manufacturer's product the more money they made. Doctors wanted to use the drug in order to appear to be up on the latest developments in the drug field.

Part V:
Life Around the Pharmacy

Chapter 17:
The Community of Cairo

My partner Larry's wife was diagnosed with colon cancer and underwent surgery. The doctors called the surgery a success and said they got it all. She went back a few times for checkups and was treated with preventative chemotherapy. They then pronounced her cured. She came in and told me she had beat the big C and was very excited about it. After about a year, she began to have problems with her digestion and went back for a checkup. She came running into the store crying and told me that the cancer was back. The tests showed it was now inoperable and for her to get her affairs in order. She said there was nothing they could do for her. She lasted about six weeks and died one of the most horrible and painful deaths you could imagine. Her small intestines were completely blocked by the cancer, and she couldn't eat and suffered immensely.

In 1985, a drug called Tacrine (tetrahydroaminocrinine) was being tested in the treatment of Alzheimer's. It was reported to be helpful by a doctor in California who recorded good trials with the product. I had a patient whose father had just been diagnosed with Alzheimer's, and he came in and showed me wherein Tacrine was used with success and asked me if I could get some and fix a preparation for his father.

I subsequently received a prescription from his doctor for the Tacrine, so I purchased some from PCCA. I prepared oral doses in capsule form for him and sold a month's supply to him. After a couple of weeks, he told me his father improved and asked me to prepare another month's supply. When he picked it up, he said the price was very high and asked if I would sell him some at a lower price. I explained that the drug was expensive, and I could not supply it at a lower cost.

About three weeks later, he came in one day and asked me to check his arm. He had been shot coming back from Miami on Interstate 75 by a trucker. He had been involved in a road rage incident, and the trucker pulled out a pistol, shot him, and kept going. I told him he should go to his doctor or the emergency room for treatment. He said he would not do that because a gunshot wound had to be reported to the police and then he would be in trouble. He asked me again to treat him so I did. I cleaned the wound, cauterized it, and told him that if he developed a fever he was to go to the emergency room immediately.

He then volunteered that he had been on the Internet and located some Tacrine in Miami at a lower price and had driven down to purchase it. He got shot on the way home. He asked me what I would charge to encapsulate it so his father could take it. He accepted my price and I prepared it for him.

He came back into the store sometime later and informed me that his father had reverted drastically and did not even recognize him now. He had been duped by the person in Miami and had not received Tacrine but probably flour. He purchased some more Tacrine from me but to no avail. His father was too far gone for it to help him. He died a short time later.

One customer came in with a prescription for sixty grams of Topicort cream, and when I told how much it cost he asked me why. I tried to explain to him that this medication was still under patent and there was no substitute for it. The manufacturer spent millions of dollars to get approval from the FDA to market the product, and they had to recoup their investment. He told me that he had been going to his doctor every day for three days and was only getting worse. His doctor made him an appointment with a dermatologist in Thomasville for the next day.

He then asked me to take a look at his problem. We went into my office where he removed his shirt. I took one look and told him that all the cream in China was not going to help him because he had what was called Creeping Eruption (ground itch). The entire back of his upper torso was involved and had at least ninety worms. I told him that the only way to get rid of it was to kill the worms. Creeping Eruption is actually hookworms from a dog that have entered the wrong host and cannot penetrate the blood vessels in humans. They therefore crawl around under the skin searching for their host and will eventually die. This process takes about two to three weeks.

He asked me where do you get them, and I told him that he had been exposed to dog feces somewhere and had laid down in it. He remembered he had done some work on his trailer and had to lie on his back while fixing a leaky pipe. He asked me what to do to stop the infernal itching, and I told him that when it was on someone's foot we would normally freeze the worms with ethyl chloride. He asked me to do so, and I told him he had so many it would be very hard and very traumatic to him to freeze them. There was a preparation called mebendazole that he could take and that may help. He insisted I freeze them for him.

I told him that the only way I would attempt it would be with his doctor's permission, so he used my phone and called his doctor. I told his doctor what I thought, and the doctor was amazed and told me he had never been exposed to this situation in med school. I told him it used to be real common in the South, but was not as prevalent now because most everybody wore shoes the year round. He asked me what he should have done. I explained to him what I had told his patient. He told me to go ahead and treat him and let him know the outcome.

I warned the customer that it would be very painful but would be over within about twenty-four hours, so he told me to please do it. It took three bottles of ethyl chloride to kill most of the worms. Then I gave him a dose of the mebendazole to help finish the job. He paid me for the supplies that I used then he called and cancelled his appointment with the dermatologist. He came back in two days later and thanked me profusely, telling me he had gone back to his doctor and showed him the results and thanked him for allowing me to treat him.

By now, I was feeling pretty good about my abilities and felt like I knew a lot. One day my son began having trouble with itching on his hands and it was giving him a real problem. I treated him with OTC creams and lotions for itching but none even began to give him relief. I finally asked a doctor to take a look and he told me that my son's problem was scabies. A real common problem and I didn't pick up on it. This brought home to me that I was not so smart after all. One round of treatment with permethrin cream and he was cured.

Our pediatrician had retired from New York, moved to Georgia, and continued practicing pediatrics. He called me and asked if I knew how to irrigate a colostomy. I assured him I did and he told me he had a young boy in his office that needed help. He explained that the boy's mother had brought him in wrapped in a bed sheet, and he was in a mess. He had undergone surgery in Alabama and they sent him home in this condition. The mother said they told her to irrigate the colostomy and she didn't know what that meant. He asked me to come to his office and help him or show him what to do because he had never been exposed to a situation like this.

I gathered up some supplies and went to his office. This child was blistered and red all over his abdomen where his feces had ran out of the stoma. The first thing I did was clean him up. I asked the mother if they had fitted him with a bag. She said no that they wrapped a big towel around him and sent him home. I went to the store and got some Nupercainal ointment to ease the pain of the blistering. I used a Fleet enema to irrigate the colostomy, applied some paste around the stoma, and fitted him with a bag to collect his feces. I told her that she would need to come to the store and buy some more bags and supplies to deal with his problem. She told me that she didn't have any money and didn't know what she would do. From this, I assumed the hospital in Alabama discharged him quickly and sent him home because they would never get paid. I told her to check with the health department to see if they could recommend some help for her. I received no remuneration from her. The pediatrician thanked me and I never heard from the lady or the boy again.

A male preacher in his sixties came in and asked me to check his blood pressure. I did so and told him that his pressure was too high. It was 177/89. I asked him if he was taking his blood pressure medicines and he said no. He said that the Lord told him to just let Him take care him and that was what he was trying to do. Since he was overweight, I asked him if the Lord had told him to eat too much also. He said no, he just enjoyed his food. I asked him if he thought this was the way the Lord was steering him to heaven. He asked me what I meant. I told him that his overeating and lack of exercise was going to kill him.

Maybe this was the Lord's way of getting him to heaven in a hurry. He thought about it for a minute and told me to fill his blood pressure medicine; he was going to get back on it. I suggested he begin an exercise program and to watch his diet. I told him that the Lord had given us the knowledge to help people and I felt he needed to use this knowledge along with his spiritual beliefs.

A customer called me one morning and asked me what appendicitis felt like. I tried to explain to her the feeling and asked her why. She had a sharp pain in her right abdomen. She was very athletic and ran almost every day for exercise. She was leaving the next morning for Vail, Colorado, and didn't want to go if she might have a real problem. I told her to stand up on her left leg then pull her right knee up tight as she could against her stomach. She came back to the phone, and I asked her if it caused the pain to get worse. She said no, it eased off but came back when she released her leg. I assured her that I didn't feel she had appendicitis, but that she probably pulled a muscle in her abdomen from her exercising and it would go away soon. She left for Vail and apparently had no more problems with her pain.

A lady came in one day and asked me to transfer her prescription from one of my competitors. It was for her birth control pills. She handed me her empty case and inscribed on it was "For Clinical Use Only." It so happened that the drug inspector was there at the time, and he saw what was happening. I asked the lady what she paid for it and she said $2.50.

These packages were intended for sale to government agencies for distribution through local health departments. I knew this because I had been distributing them at our local health department. These pills were sold to the state for $0.17 whereas pharmacists were paying $1.97

each for them through their distributors. This competitor was obviously purchasing medications from people who were not on the up and up. The drug inspector immediately went to this pharmacist and explained to him what he was doing was illegal and that if he didn't stop immediately, he would pull his license. He confiscated all of my competitor's pills that had the inscription on them and left him with a warning citation.

My competitor called me and chewed me out for turning him in. He said he didn't think I would stoop so low. I informed him I didn't report him, but the inspector was standing right by me when the lady handed me her package. I informed him I should have turned him in if the inspector had not been there, because what he was doing was very much lower than my reporting him.

One of my elderly customers, a gentleman in his eighties, constantly came in and bought laxatives. When I told him he shouldn't be using that many laxatives, he said he had to have them. I explained that he was not taking enough fiber in his diet. I asked him if he was eating many vegetables. He said no, he was a meat and potatoes man. I told him his body was using up what he was eating and there was nothing left for him to expel. I suggested he get on a high fiber diet and that should help him. I told him to build up the fiber slowly so that he wouldn't gas up too bad. He said he would try it, but he was still going to take his laxatives.

In 1976, the medical staff at the hospital dwindled so low the hospital was in imminent danger of closing. The hospital board in the last few years had bought property and built offices in order to recruit doctors and had been successful for a short time. During this time, they decided the county needed a larger hospital, so they floated a twenty-year bond and added a wing on the north end. With practically no doctors, there was not enough money to operate and to pay the bonded indebtedness. The county was broke from over spending and not raising revenues and was not in a position to help the hospital.

I felt that the hospital board was not functioning properly and asked my friend who was on the county board of roads and bridges to appoint me to the hospital board. At my first meeting, I was informed that all decisions and recommendations from the board were always unanimous. I told the chairman the board had eight too many members then, because if only one opinion counted there was no need for nine people to be on it. That didn't make me very popular. I listened during the meeting, went back to the county commissioners, and asked for Bobby, a local car dealer, to be appointed to the board with me. They did so; Bobby and I began convincing the rest of the board that we needed to take action or the hospital would close.

The board then asked Archbold Hospital in Thomasville and Tallahassee Memorial Hospital in Tallahassee to make suggestions as to how we could improve the hospital. They both made us a proposition to take over the operation of the hospital for us. We decided to accept Tallahassee's proposal and entered into an agreement wherein they would lease our hospital and operate it for us. It was apparent to us that local board members did not have the knowhow, ability, or purchasing power to operate a hospital.

Tallahassee Memorial's lease was for four years with an optional four-year extension. They were successful in recruiting doctors and everything began to improve. After the third year, they informed us they would not be renewing the lease. There were problems involved with insurance due to them being in a separate state. Many state insurers would not recognize or accept bills from out of state. They asked us to explore transferring the lease to Archbold.

We contacted Archbold and were successful in negotiating a lease agreement with them for a fifteen-year period with options for five renewals. In essence, it was a seventy-five year agreement. This agreement turned out to be very successful and our hospital has since flourished.

Around this same time, I bought some property across from the hospital that the bank foreclosed on a while back. One day, the pediatrician from Thomasville came over and asked me to sell him a lot on it to open an office to practice pediatrics. I agreed to sell him a lot if he would agree to sell Marx and me the lot and building in Thomasville we were leasing. He agreed and it came about that Marx and I now owned the property and building in Thomasville.

A customer came in one day and asked me if I would give her some allergy shots. She had known about me giving B-12 shots and tetanus shots for some doctors. I told her I would be glad to help her if her doctor said it would be all right. She said it would save her a thirty-two mile trip to get her shots once a week. Her doctor agreed, so I began giving her once weekly shots. This led to more people wanting this service. I soon had five people coming in once a week to get their allergy shots.

I began to have conversations with these people and they all agreed that as soon as I gave them their allergy shots they felt better for a few days. I began to wonder what was in these shots. We were told in school that if you determine what people are allergic to, you could give them small doses over time to build up tolerance for the allergens. If this was true, then when they were injected with something they were allergic to they should feel worse for a day or two. I decided that they were either getting normal saline or they were real susceptible to the placebo effect. I finally decided that this didn't actually work, because it had been forty years since we were taught about this. If it did work, by now no one would have to suffer from allergies. I suspected that these people were actually reacting to their body producing antihistamines instead of having something like hay fever.

We always sold a lot of valentine candy on Valentine's Day. It was typical for most of the candy to be purchased by men almost always at the last minute. One year, this holiday was a good profitable business time for us.

We were a small town and downtown had a thriving shopping area. Many people came to town on Saturdays and spent the day shopping and visiting with friends and neighbors. It was soon disrupted when a small shopping center came to town and leased a large store to TG&Y. This store was a retail store larger than most five and dime stores and sold just about everything anybody could want. They made sure they were selling their products for less than most retailers in town. This pulled people away from the downtown area, leaving many of the small merchants with less business and smaller profits.

The year they opened and Valentine's Day came around, they stocked up on lots of valentine candy. Their managers had been schooled to make sure their seasonal merchandise moved out well. Obviously, they were not aware that the men in small rural communities waited until the last minute for their purchases.

About ten days before Valentine's Day TG&Y was not selling what they thought was enough candy so they reduced the price by thirty percent. Then five days before Valentine's Day, they reduced the price by fifty percent. This effectively killed our Valentine's Day candy business. There was no way I could compete with them and take the loss they were accepting.

A customer called and asked if I had a Glucometer II machine. She had a Glucometer III machine but wanted a Glucometer II machine so she can use strips her son gets from his insurance company. They send him more strips than he can use. She said she could buy a machine and use his extra strips cheaper than she could buy strips for her machine. I suggested she use his machine and his strips. She bought a Glucometer II machine and thanked me.

An elderly man came in and asked me if Dilantin was a depressant. I explained that it slows down the electrical impulses in the brain and anything that does that will interfere with normal brain activity. It is not a depressant like Librium, Valium, Xanax, or Ativan. He said after he took it in the morning, he would get sleepy an hour later. He said his doctor in Gainesville told him that he had a stroke, probably caused by overuse of his Albuterol asthma spray. He asked if his memory had been destroyed by the stroke and will he have to relearn everything. I told him his memory was still there but access to it had been interfered with by the stroke. Quite often, the brain will discover other access routes to his memory. Sometimes other associations will trigger the memory response. That explained to him what was going on. He said he used his toolbox for forty years, and when he came home from Gainesville, he didn't know where it was or what was in it. He said once he was told where it was he remembered all about it and had no more trouble with that instance. I suggested he give himself time and to be sure to follow his doctor's instructions.

A lady came in to refill her prescriptions for Ativan and Zantac. She asked me what the Zantac was for. I told her Zantac slowed acid production in the stomach to help prevent heartburn. She said she never had heartburn but the doctor told her it was for nervous stomach. She had been taking them for seven years. I explained that her stomach has to produce acid in order for food to digest. When you have a raw spot in the stomach wall, the acid will cause a burning sensation. She decided to leave the Zantac off because her doctor told her it was for nervous stomach. If it didn't help nervous stomach, she didn't want it.

I mentioned that she was taking too many Ativan tablets; she was supposed to take three a day if she needed them. She said she was taking four to five per day and thought that was all right. I cautioned her that Ativan was habit forming and could begin to cause nervousness when the effect wears off. I told her she needed to be careful or she would be taking more and more to achieve or maintain her state of euphoria. Over time they would make her weak and sap her energy, and pretty soon, she wouldn't feel like doing anything but sit around and worry about herself and not be able to function in a normal way.

She came back in about three weeks later and told me that she cut her Ativan down to two a day and was feeling pretty good. She appreciated me talking to her about her medicines and that she didn't miss taking the Zantac at all.

Chapter 18:
The Lastingers of Cairo

Rosalind had had abdominal pain over the years and had gotten to the point she needed relief. Her doctor diagnosed her as having endometriosis and began treating her with Progesterone. After a year or two with no relief, she went to a different doctor. After examining her, he felt she had an abscess on her right ovary. The pain had gotten so bad she agreed to have surgery.

The doctor had her sign a paper authorizing a hysterectomy along with the ovary if he felt she needed it. After the surgery, he told her he removed her uterus along with her right ovary. He also told her that while he was in there he removed her appendix to avoid the possibility she would have to have more surgery.

We felt like she would finally be out of her constant pain. And for a short while, it seemed like she would be all right. After a year or two, the pain returned. She put up with the pain for a few years, but it just got worse. About six years later, it got so bad she felt like she was dying.

I had an aunt in Fort Lauderdale who was dating a radiologist working at a large hospital. When my aunt heard about Rosalind's problem, she talked to the radiologist and asked him if he knew of a doctor who would examine her. He recommended a doctor who agreed to see her.

He asked for her medical records and we asked the surgeon in Thomasville to send them to him. The doctor in Fort Lauderdale said that he only wanted the records from the hospital, which had pathology tissue reports. He said that the doctor's records could have anything in them, but the lab reports would show what he really removed and what was wrong. The hospital in Thomasville did not want to release her records, but they finally agreed and sent them to the doctor in Fort Lauderdale.

She got in such bad shape that the doctor in Fort Lauderdale could not wait for these records and performed surgery. He informed us that upon removal of her appendix a few years earlier, the doctor inadvertently sewed her colon to her abdominal wall. This led to her having a lot of scar tissue and eventually her colon was growing into her abdominal wall. This had progressively gotten worse, and she was going into peritonitis when he operated on her.

During a follow-up visit, he said he received the lab reports from Thomasville and they showed that her ovary and uterus were normal. Her appendix was highly inflamed and infected. He said that she had chronic appendicitis, which was misdiagnosed then covered up by the doctor.

Since then I have been skeptical about some of the doctors I knew and their diagnoses. We were quite bitter about what Rosalind had gone through but thankful that this doctor had saved her life.

Clarence, another of my partners, began to show signs of Alzheimer's, and it developed quite fast. I did the same for him that I had done for his mother, father, and brother. I visited him every week checking on his blood pressure and giving B-12 shots. His wife did a good job, and he never developed bedsores or required hospitalization. His family's situation with Alzheimer's convinced me that the disease does tend to run in families.

One night just before closing, I looked up and a man was coming up to the counter. I asked him what I could do for him when he pulled out a pistol, pointed it at me, and said to give him all our money. The cash register was up front, and when I looked up there, I saw that another man had a pistol on my wife and was demanding money. I handed the man all the money I had in my pocket including the silver dollar I carried since I flipped it to decide whether to see a movie or go with Rosalind to a wiener roast (our first date).

In the meantime, the man holding a gun on Rosalind was walking her to the back of the store. I found out later he was telling her she was already dead, so just do what I say. As she walked by one of the counters, she slipped her rings off and dropped them where the man couldn't see what she was doing.

All this happened so fast that I couldn't reach the panic button on our burglar alarm. The alarm was set to call the police department, the sheriff's office, and then us at home.

They made us lie face down on the floor, and one of them told the other one to go ahead and shoot us. About that time, one said, "What is that?" He heard a noise outside and said there is someone out there. At that, they told us not to move, then they both ran to the front and out of the store. We immediately hit the alarm button. The police arrived shortly, but the robbers had gotten away even though the police tried to cut off the streets out of town. The sheriff's department did not respond until the next morning. They said they didn't get a call from the alarm company.

We thanked the police and went home still a little upset. When we got home our son Travis, who was about thirteen years old, was sitting in the den with his .410 shotgun across his lap. He was very anxious about us because he had answered the call at home from the alarm company and knew we had been held up. He was ready to help protect our home. We discussed the situation and believed that someone walked up to the front of the store to get a newspaper from the newspaper rack outside. We never did discover who had done so, or if anyone really had been outside.

We were asked to view some lineups of potential criminals and suspects to see if we could recognize the ones who had attacked us. It seemed that in each lineup there was at least one who looked vaguely familiar, but we really couldn't tell. About two weeks later, they asked us to look at a lineup again. This time there was no doubt in our mind that they had the ones who robbed us.

As it turned out, there were three involved. One was from Cairo and the other two were visiting from Jacksonville. The one from Cairo didn't come into the store but stayed outside to be their lookout. We were told that the three didn't try to get drugs from us because they only wanted money in order to buy some marijuana. The one who stayed outside thought that the other two didn't share all the money they had taken and was a little aggravated with the other two and when questioned by the detectives had told on the other two.

We spent some time in court before they all agreed to accept a plea bargain. The sheriff asked us if it was all right for them to plead robbery by force instead of armed robbery. This situation meant that we would not have to go through the trial. They pleaded guilty to robbery by force rather than armed robbery and were sentenced to seventeen years in jail.

After about six months, a lady came in and told us she was the local man's grandmother and asked us to please help her get her grandson out of jail. After what we had been through, we told her we were not interested in helping her get him out of jail. She kept coming back a few times, and Rosalind finally asked the sheriff to tell her to please stay away and leave us alone. He did so and she quit coming in. Every time she had come in it just brought back terrible memories. We felt very lucky to be alive. These men were released from jail after serving seven years. It didn't seem like enough to us. We were the ones who were told we were going to die that night.

We had lived in our house on Lullwater Circle for a while when we began to suspect something was wrong. One of Karen's girlfriends got to where she didn't want to come in the house and refused to spend any more nights there. She said the house was spooky. We considered her a little off until one of Rosalind's flat irons fell off a shelf in the middle of the night. The peculiar thing about that was the shelf it stayed on had a ridge along the edge and the iron had to be lifted up to get it off the shelf. Then one night I was preparing the coffee pot for use the next morning when I heard Rosalind walk behind me going to the laundry room. I spoke to her, and when she didn't answer, I turned around and she was not there. I raced upstairs and there she was in bed already. I told her what had happened, and we just looked at each other in disbelief.

Our daughter divorced and moved back in with us with her daughter Laura Rebecca. Every evening when I got home from work, she would run to the door to meet me. She always sat on my shoulder in the den to watch television and be with me. One night she was in the den with Rosalind when she and Rosalind heard the back door open. She came running to greet me; however, there was no one there. She went back to the den and told Rosalind that I was not there.

One night we had a party with about thirty people and cooked out. My Aunt Dottie and her husband came up from Fort Lauderdale to visit and spend the night. We had a grand time. We stayed up until midnight making music and singing on the carport. After we got into bed one of the toilets upstairs next to the bedroom where Aunt Dottie was sleeping began to make a terrible noise like air in the plumbing. It was loud enough to disturb everyone in the house. I went in and turned the water off, but the noise kept going. If anything, it got louder. The noise kept up for a good fifteen minutes and by that time we were all awake and began to laugh because we couldn't figure out where the noise was coming from. Suddenly, the noise just quit and we finally got some sleep.

We had a tiled walk-in shower that I generally used. It had a door that opened to the inside. This shower had a single switch that you pulled out to open the valve and could adjust the temperature by rotating the handle. One night I was taking a shower after being up kind of late and the water turned scalding hot. I immediately twisted the handle to cold, but nothing happened—the water stayed hot. I then pushed the handle in but the water didn't turn off. It stayed pouring out extremely hot. When I tried to open the door, it was stuck. I began to panic when finally the door opened. The minute I got out of the shower the water quit flowing. I had a plumber come out to check the system and he said nothing was wrong. When I told him what happened he just looked at me like I was crazy and said that was impossible. I never got into that shower again.

A twenty-seven-year-old woman with full-blown AIDS came in to get some front-end items. Her doctor called in her prescriptions, and she hadn't picked them up. Her prescriptions were on Medicaid and the rural HIV clinic's pay list and wouldn't cost her anything. I asked her if she wanted to pick up her medications and she said no. I asked her why and she said, "I am a dead woman anyway so there is no need for me to take that stuff." I tried to talk her into taking it, but she said that since she was going to die she was having herself a ball and enjoying everything she could. She said she would carry all the men in her neighborhood to the grave with her. They had given it to her, and she was going to make sure that any that would, she was going to accommodate. She left the store and I never saw her again. I called her doctor and informed him of the situation and he said thank you.

One day a gentleman, who was a customer at another store, came in and asked for some iodine swabs. He said his father had surgery and the doctor told him to clean the wound with iodine swabs. I told him those iodine swabs were normally sold by a medical supply company and most drug stores didn't carry them. He said his pharmacist already told him that. I suggested he just buy a bottle of iodine and some sterile swabs. They would be the same thing. He said the bottle might get contaminated if reused. I asked him why he thought that. I explained that the iodine would kill any germs introduced to the bottle and he shouldn't have any problem. He asked why his pharmacist had not explained this to him. I assured him I didn't know the answer to that. He left with the iodine and swabs. I don't remember him ever coming back to me for anything. Sometimes you just strike out.

Our next-door neighbor bought a lot on the eighth fairway at the country club and asked if we would like to buy the lot next to them. After what we had been experiencing, we felt a strong urge to do so. We agreed and purchased the lot and began designing our new house. We had purchased a two-bedroom house and moved our daughter into it. She subsequently married again and moved out. We placed our house on the market and moved into the two-bedroom house while our new one was being built. Our house sold quickly and we breathed a sigh of relief. We would not have to put up with those weird goings-on anymore.

Chapter 19: The Many More Customers of Cairo

I had a customer who had traded with me for years and one day he was in the store, and I asked him to sit down and visit for a while. He said no thank you. I asked why, and he said he noticed a lot of my customers who sat there died and he didn't want to take a chance. He never did sit down after that.

A veterans' administration patient came in and asked me to go over his medications with him and explain what they were for. He had some ibuprofen and lorazepam. After my explaining them, he said that nobody told him anything about his medicines. He wished he could still get his medicine from me like he used to do. The veterans' administration began to require all veterans to either pick them up or use mail order for their prescriptions. Mail-order pharmacy is illegal in Georgia, but the federal government can do as it pleases.

He said they only charged him two dollars for each prescription and he didn't mind paying them. He said they gave him $28.79 for his travel expenses to go get them. It appears to me that any savings they were making went to pay vets to go get their medicine.

A man came in with a prescription he wanted filled and charged to workers' compensation. He used to work at Mistletoe Plantation and got hurt on the job, but was no longer working there. I told him that I couldn't bill the insurance company unless they okayed the charge and told me where to send the bill. I explained I would be glad to work with them. I asked him to have his insurance company contact me. About an hour later, a lady called and said she was with Continental Insurance Company and asked about the prescription. I told her I needed an okay to charge it to her company. She said go ahead. I asked where I should send the bill and she said wait a minute. After a short time, she came back and told me to tell the patient to go to Walmart or Big B. I told him what she said and he left.

In about an hour, he returned and said neither Big B nor Walmart would fill the prescription because they could not contact the insurance company. I told him I would fill the prescription and let him pay for it, then I would give him a receipt and he could settle with the insurance company. I explained to him that Georgia has a freedom of choice law as to where he had to trade. I told him to contact his lawyer and get him explain it to the insurance company that he did not get his prescription filled.

Shortly the pharmacist with Big B called and said to send the customer to him. He had permission to fill and bill it to the insurance company. They would fill it for cost plus two dollars. I told him that Georgia Medicaid required all participants in their program to charge Medicaid the lowest amount they accepted from any payer. I asked him if this would void their contract with Georgia Medicaid. He said he didn't know about that. As long as they paid him his salary, it would be Big B's problem.

A customer came in to fill four prescriptions and asked me if he could take Delsym with them. I checked his profile and told him that he should have no problem, but why didn't he take an expectorant to loosen the phlegm and thus get rid of the cause of his cough. He said he just wanted to stop the cough. He bought the Delsym and left.

One of my customers ran a water softener business called Clearwater. Most of the water in South and Middle Georgia is called hard water. This means that there is a high amount of minerals in it. This calls for more soap in the laundry. Many people liked using soft water because you could lather up more readily when bathing.

He came in one day and said that he was getting too old to continue his business. He had a lot of customers in Cairo, but he also had many up in middle Georgia and over in Bainbridge. All these customers had to be serviced once a month. The service required tanks, which had to be brought in and recharged so they would remove the minerals. He would load up recharged tanks and make his rounds replacing the discharged tanks. His route kept him away from home two nights a month because he said he could not drive that far in one day.

He asked me if I knew anyone who would be interested in purchasing his business. He said he had to quit and needed someone to take it over so his customers would continue getting service. I told him I had a nephew I thought would do the work; however, he didn't have any money to invest. He told me he would sell me the business at a very low price and I could hire my nephew to run it.

I agreed and now I was in the water softener business. My nephew would come over every day and work. I would send out the bills and handle the business end. After a while, I began to receive notices from my customer that they were not getting soft water. I discovered that my nephew was not properly recharging the tanks as well as not replacing them on a regular schedule. These tanks were heavy and required a good deal of manual labor. I had to take over the work and spent a good deal of time away from the drug store.

One of my customers, who was an electrician, discovered what I was doing and asked if he could buy half of the business and help do the work. I agreed and told him that my son, who was now old enough, would do my part of the work.

The soft water business was being upgraded to automatic in-home systems, thus, requiring customers to recharge their own system. This situation looked to diminish the future of the way we were working. So when another party expressed interest in purchasing the business, my son and his partner agreed to sell out. This ended my foray into the soft water business.

A lady in her fifties came in and asked me to check her hands. She had a problem with the skin splitting open and cracking. They would also have blisters form on them. She had been seeing a dermatologist for a year and had no improvement in the condition. All the ointments and cortisones he prescribed for her cost a fortune and she was at her wit's end.

I told her I had customers in the past come in with splitting and cracking skin on their fingers. This happened mostly in the wintertime. These customers, I felt, had pinched nerves in their cervical vertebrae causing their problem. These people seemed to improve by using cervical traction and exercises. This was obviously not her situation because of the presence of blisters. I checked her profile and noticed she was taking female hormones. I suggested to her to go to her family doctor and ask him if she should change or discontinue the hormones. The hormones may be the source of her problem.

She came in about six weeks later and told me her hands had healed, and she was not having the problem anymore. I asked her if her doctor changed her hormones, and she said no, she just stopped taking them on her own. She said she would rather put up with her hot flashes than have the problem she had been having.

In January of 1993, I sent a comment to *Drug Topics* (a national pharmacy magazine) regarding an article they published about OBRA (the law requiring all pharmacists to counsel each patient they dispensed a prescription to). I told them I and probably most pharmacists out there already counseled patients when the need arose, and I didn't feel we needed a law compelling us to do what we recognized as our responsibility. I felt we already had enough laws controlling our business practices. They replied to my comment asking me to give them examples of what I wrote about.

In answer to their request, I sent them a sort of diary I kept over two days recording my interactions with my customers. My diary was accepted as an article and it became the cover story for the June 19, 1993, edition. They labeled the article "Pharmacy on the frontline: The way it really is!"

In her lead-in note, the editor at the time stated:

> Seldom has a manuscript sent in by a pharmacist seemed to define what the profession is all about as profoundly as that submitted by Georgia pharmacist Truman Lastinger, who operates a small drug store in the southern rural area of the state. Faced with the turmoil of trying to get computer updates that would meet all the OBRA 1990 counseling requirements, he decided to keep a diary of conversations with his patients over a randomly selected two-day period. We decided to present just one day's work. The conversations that follow, counseling by anybody's definition, are remarkable for what they reveal about the role this pharmacist plays in the health care system of the United States in 1993, and for what, we suspect, may be the role of many other pharmacists who deal with patients on the frontline of pharmaceutical care. In these conversations are the compassion, professionalism, practicality, and

honesty that lie at the core of good health care. They are a deeply moving look at a system, and at one part of that system, a pharmacist out there all alone doing the things he feels he has to do. Mister Lastinger made two points in the note he sent with the story. He said "I always considered myself adept in the practice of pharmacy as taught to me at the Mercer University's Southern College of Pharmacy, and I see my practice as going beyond the routine explanations of drugs and what they do in the body." His kind of counseling does indeed do that, and for that his patients should be eternally grateful.

I had a good many responses nationwide regarding the article. Most of them were affirmative and a lot of them were questions. I replied to every one of the comments I received. Needless to say, this all made me feel very important. But I went back to work trying to help my customers.

One of my customers, who had a kidney removed a good while ago, loved to walk for her exercise. She and a neighbor of hers walked every morning for at least two miles. One day she came in and told me her leg was hurting very badly and wanted to know what she could take for it. I checked her profile and saw that her doctor had prescribed some Cipro for a urinary tract infection. After talking to her, I told her that sometimes Cipro had a devastating effect on a person's Achilles tendon. I felt that she was having a reaction to the antibiotic she was taking. I explained to her that she was in jeopardy of having her Achilles tendon rupture and to stop taking the Cipro immediately and do not walk for a few days. And whatever you do, do not exercise or try to stretch your leg. I recommended that she not take anything for pain right now and let time heal the situation. It may take four to six weeks to return to normal where she can walk again without damage. And if she had to take something for pain to only take acetaminophen (Tylenol). I told her that she should never take one of those antibiotics again and that she should be extra careful what she takes for pain or infection because with only one kidney she could get into trouble.

About three months later, the phone rang and it was her calling from Aruba where she was on vacation. She had apparently caught another urinary tract infection and was calling from a doctor's office. She said the doctor wanted to give her an antibiotic, and she wouldn't allow it until the doctor talked to me. She said she had been in the hotel hot tub and felt like she got the infection there. She put the doctor on the line and I explained to the doctor what had happened with the Cipro and that I told her not to ever take that again. She asked what I would suggest, and I told her that I would recommend a cephalosporin. She thanked me and put my customer back on the line. We chatted for a few minutes, and before I signed off, I suggested she not get back into that hot tub. She laughed and assured me that she would not do so.

One night my burglar alarm went off, and when I got to the store, the police had already apprehended the burglars. There was a man and a woman in the patrol car with handcuffs on. They used a wrecking bar to tear the back door practically off the store, entered, and were leaving with Dilaudid and Percodan when the police caught them. I always used a silent alarm so that when a burglar entered the building he would not know that he triggered the alarm. This, in my mind, would allow the police to get there in time. This time it worked out perfectly.

I was allowed to visit the burglar at the jail. He was a middle-aged man and when I asked him why he tore the door up to get in when the air conditioner unit on the back wall was removed for repair, leaving a big hole he could easily get in through. He told me he was getting along in age and was not very athletic, and he preferred to just walk into the store. He admitted he was addicted to Dilaudid, and his doctor had been arrested, cutting off his supply, so he resorted to burglary. Besides, it was cheaper than getting it legitimately. He had come from Jacksonville and burglarized three stores on the way. When he saw mine was a little out of town on the highway, he felt that it was a good spot to hit.

After talking to him and the woman for little while, it dawned on me that not everyone who takes a narcotic for pain necessarily becomes addicted. In thinking about this, I also realized that not everyone who drinks alcohol becomes an alcoholic. I then began to believe that these people who become addicted must have a proclivity towards being addicted. The same can probably be said regarding amphetamines and marijuana. History has shown there has always been people addicted to something or other. Now we are seeing more people hooked on barbiturates, mood stimulants narcotics, and alcohol. Could it be only due to the increased population that we seem to see more of it? Or is it possible that doctors are prescribing them more often than they should in order to maintain a patient base?

At any rate, the people who are addicted need to hit absolute bottom in their addiction before they can kick the habit. At the bottom, some will do anything in order to get another dose. They will rob and steal even kill in order to get another fix. This seems to have become a national problem and the jails are being inundated with these people. However, there are a few who recover after hitting what they feel is the bottom. Most of these people are treated in rehab centers, but all who go to these centers do not recover. A good many relapse.

A female customer came in one day and asked me to look at her leg. She had a large ulcer on her calf. She was diabetic and quite often these ulcers are very hard to cure. She tried the sugar and milk of magnesia treatments recommended by her doctor and said they didn't help. I recommended she elevate her leg as much as possible and use compresses of Burow's solution then after drying to gently massage it with cold cream. I told her to alternate the process every two hours or so. She returned a couple of weeks later and showed me that the leg had healed with a new layer of skin on it. I bragged on her and told her she had done a good job. She was now having intermittent pain in the area and what should she do. I felt she was experiencing neuralgia and recommended that she hold an ice cube on the area for a couple of minutes when it was painful, then wait thirty minutes to an hour and apply warm compresses.

A male customer who had not been in the store for a couple of months came in with four bottles of pills he had received by mail order. His insurance company made him switch from me to mail orders; he wanted me to go over his medication with him. He had been employed in the pulpwood business and had had a log fall on him. His medications were paid for by his employer's insurance company. He had bottles of Tegretol and Motrin 800, which he had been on for some time. In addition, he now had Flexeril and Soma compound.

He said he drove to Columbus, about 120 miles, and when he got out of the car, he almost passed out. He asked if he should discontinue his medications or just cut down on them. I explained orthostatic hypotension to him and that his medications tend to aggravate the situation. I told him to stand up slowly and try to have something handy that he could brace himself on for a minute or two until his blood pressure equalized. I cautioned him that he should be very careful when getting up at night. He said he fell the other night but thought he just stumbled on something. I told him that if his situation was too exasperating for him to go back to his doctor and explain the situation to him.

Chapter 20: Pharmacy vs. Insurance and Manufacturers

The FDA was approving many new drugs and a lot of them were antidepressants. In looking at the insert that came with them, I saw wherein the patients were warned that the first few days or weeks they may feel peculiar or drunk. They may feel they can't tolerate the drug, but that they should stay on it and in due time they would be able to tolerate it and begin to feel better. It had always been my feeling that your medication should make you feel better and had told many people so over the years. I am not so sure whether many of these medications are in the best interest of the patient or if they are in the best interest of the drug manufacturer.

Being on the hospital authority demanded a lot of my time. Archbold, who was operating our hospital under a lease agreement, seemed to continually ask us to go to our county commissioners and ask for money for the operation of the hospital. Around 2006, we had a one-slice CT scanner housed in a mobile home out back of the hospital. To access the scanner, the patient had to walk outside the hospital for a short distance, and in bad weather, this was not a good thing. Archbold came to us and asked us to campaign for a SPLOST tax to be issued in order to raise money. They promised we would receive a new sixty-four-slice CT scanner, which was the latest in CT scanning. They also agreed to enlarge the hospital and place this scanner *inside* the hospital.

Since I was chairman of the hospital authority, I felt like I should bear the brunt of convincing the people of Grady County to agree and pass this tax. I began making speeches and promoting the SPLOST at all the civic clubs and to any group who needed a program and would have me. I explained to the public that a sixty-four-slice machine could detect many serious health problems before they got to the point of killing people. Having this knowledge would allow doctors to prevent rather than treat a patient after the fact. This could in fact save lives.

I felt that a new state of the art scanner inside the hospital would be a great thing for Grady County. A day or two before the SPLOST came up for a vote, which did pass, our administrator informed me Archbold was not going to get us a sixty-four-slice machine, but instead a sixteen-slice machine. I informed him we would get the sixty-four-slice machine, but he was adamant we wouldn't. I told him that we would cross that bridge when we got to it. In just a short time, the administrator gave his notice that he was quitting and was going to school to become a preacher. I hated to see him go and felt that he was leaving to avoid problems when it came time to build and install the new scanner.

I got a phone call from a customer who had a problem with rhinitis. I sold her some Dasin capsules, which stopped the water works but then she dried out too much and complained about sinusitis. I then switched her to Sudafed, but she began suffering from rhinitis again. She said she was going on a trip and didn't want to have to put up with the rhinitis while gone. I told her to get back on the Dasin, but stop taking it as soon as the dripping subsided. Taking it too long blocks the sinuses.

Many pharmacies and funeral homes loaned patients wheelchairs and hospital beds for years at no cost. The government and insurance companies began to pay for some of these services; however, the billing process was very strict and unyielding. Considering the time it took to deliver and set up the equipment as well as bill for the service, it was quite often unprofitable because you had to spend too much time away from your main business to tend to it. The alternative was to hire someone to do the work and to bill the insurance. Quite often, it was not profitable for a single drug store to pursue this avenue of income.

Around 1996, Marx and I called all the drug stores in a fifty-mile radius and proposed that we unite and form a corporation to handle this business for us. Any profits would be distributed according to the business each drug store sent the corporation. We agreed to do so and all of our equipment was turned over to the new corporation. We each put in a specified amount of cash to ensure a good start of the business. We hired a respiratory therapist to manage the corporation, which we named Care-all Health Services. We planned to extend our business into respiratory therapy and offer home IV products. Our manager bought a delivery truck and hired a secretary to do the billing.

We contracted with a drug company to produce a line of OTC drugs with the Care-all label, which we began to sell in our stores. We were off to a good start in our new endeavor when we began to realize that the local hospital had a direct impact on our business by inducing the doctors on their staff to refer all home health services to them. We tried to stop the practice even to the point of seeing a lawyer. There was nothing we could do to stop this practice, so we were left with only the business that showed up in our pharmacies.

After a short while, we needed another infusion of money because there was not enough money coming in to pay the help and continue business. We borrowed a sum of money from the bank to tide us over until the secretary could catch up with her billing. The situation got worse, and finally we discovered she had not completed many of the bills to the insurance companies or the government. A lot of them were too old now to submit. We replaced our manager then replaced the secretary. Eventually we had to admit that the business was doomed. We closed up shop and had to pay off the bank loan.

One day a Medicaid patient came in with five prescriptions for her child. The child already filled two prescriptions that month—the state at that time would only pay for five prescriptions a month. I explained to her that she could only get three of the prescriptions paid for by the state and she would have to pay for the other two. She elected to get the antibiotic, the cold medicine, and diaper rash medicine and leave off the eye drops and pain medications. I filled the prescriptions and as the lady left the store, she stopped to buy a carton of cigarettes. The carton of cigarettes cost her more than the two prescriptions would have. I guess people know what is important to them.

The burglar alarm went off one night, and when Rosalind and I got to the store, the police had two girls in the back seat of their patrol car. They broke the window out of the drive-through and crawled inside. They collected a good supply of narcotics and placed them by the back door. They were waiting for their boyfriends to come back to pick them up. The boys broke the window and helped the girls get inside. When the police got there, they told the girls to come out, and when they opened the back door, the policeman told them they had to go back out the way they got in. So they had to climb back out the drive-through window. We didn't lose any narcotics that night, but we had to clean up the broken glass and block the window until the glass man could come and replace it. I suppose this is one of the costs of doing business that most people don't realize.

The insurance companies really have the upper hand as regards compensation to drug stores. I had a customer injured on the job and the insurance company agreed to pay for his medications. One day he presented a new prescription and upon looking at the record, I discovered his insurance company had not paid their bill in over three months. I explained to him that his bill at the time was over two hundred dollars, and I didn't see how I could continue to give him his pills without assurances the bill would be paid either by him or his company's insurance carrier. He used my phone to get the insurance company and had a lively conversation with someone. He handed me the phone, and the person on the other end assured me I would receive a check shortly and please give him the medicine. I reluctantly did so. Then a week later, I received a check for $3.15. I called the company and discovered they only paid for one prescription, not all of them. When I asked which they paid for I discovered they reduced that bill from thirty-four dollars to that sum. The lady explained that was all they were allowed to pay for that medicine. I tried to tell her that I paid twenty-nine dollars for that medication, but she said there was nothing she could do about it. I lost that customer and the money I had invested in his treatment.

Another customer came in one day, presented a prescription, and asked me to charge it to his insurance company. He had been injured in a car wreck and the company was supposed to pay his bills. I called his insurance company in Florida to verify what he was telling me and was assured that yes, he was covered under his automobile insurance. I got the information as to whom I was talking to and where to send the bill. I then filled his prescriptions for a while until I realized I was not being paid. I then called the insurance company and asked for the person I had talked to previously and was told she was no longer employed. I explained my situation and asked why I was not being paid and was told that the limits on his policy had been reached and they were no longer obligated to pay his bills. I had lost out again.

An elderly gentleman came in and presented two prescriptions, one for Allopurinol 300mg and one for Motrin 800mg. He asked me how much they cost, and I told him about twenty dollars a month. He said he could not afford it. I suggested to him that possibly the welfare office or his church could help him with his medicine. He said he had already been there and they told him he didn't qualify. He asked me why doctors always prescribe so much medicine. I asked him if his gout was really hurting and he said no. He then asked me again why doctors prescribe so much medicine. I assured him that they were trying to help their patients. I told him that the only way to stop that was to stop going to the doctor and complaining. If he did this, the doctor would not prescribe him anything. I told him the more complaints he presented to the doctor, the more prescriptions he would receive.

An elderly lady came in and presented a prescription for her husband. He is eighty-six years old and is an Alzheimer's patient. She was looking after him at home. She asked what the prescription was for. I told her it is for Furosemide 40mg and that was to pull fluids from his body. She asked why the doctor prescribed him that, so I asked if his blood pressure was up or did he have any swelling. She said no to both. This was the first time she had used this doctor and wondered why he gave him this medicine. I asked her if she had her old prescription bottles and she went to the car and returned with them. She had two bottles, one was for Dipyridimole 50mg and the other was for Furosemide 40mg. Both bottles were six months old according to the date on the label. The Dipyridimole was for ninety tablets and to take one tablet three times daily. There were thirty-three tablets left in the bottle. The Furosemide was for sixty tablets with instructions to take one twice daily. There were three tablets left in it. She said the doctor told her to leave off the Dipyridimole, but she couldn't understand why he prescribed the Furosemide. I told her he did it because she told him that her husband was on it. She said to fill it then.

Then she said the doctor asked her if she wanted life support or CPR for husband when the time came and asked me what to do. I asked her if she was in his condition would she want to be kept alive on life support. She said no and she didn't think he would either.

She then presented another prescription. This one was for her and it was for Fenoprofen 600mg. She asked what that was for and I told her it was for pain or arthritis. She said she was not having that kind of problem and why did he give her that. I assured her I didn't know, but generally doctors prescribe medicine because she had a complaint. What did she tell the doctor? She told him that sometimes at night she had muscle spasms and took aspirin for it. She did not fill the prescription.

When I opened the store, it was right beside the high school on the town side. On the other side was a housing project primarily housing older people and retirees. It was a good neighborhood and I sold milk, bread, bacon, and other small necessities.

Most of the students arriving and leaving the high school had to walk. They came across the front of the store and for the first few years they were well behaved and caused no trouble. The only problem was when too many of them came into the store early in the morning to purchase candy and so forth for the day. They were apparently spending their lunch money. We had to have extra help every morning for an hour, then there was no need for the extra help. It became obvious that the profit made in that hour was not enough to pay for the extra help, so we started opening the store after school took in.

As time went on people became more affluent, and a majority of the students were being driven to school by their parents. This caused quite a traffic problem because they mostly used my parking lot to drop off the students in the morning and then to pick them up in the afternoon. In the morning, there was not so much a problem because the traffic kept moving with the cars stopping just long enough for the student to get out. In the afternoon, the cars would start arriving twenty minutes or so before school let out then they would sit there until their child got to the store. Sometimes the child was twenty to thirty minutes late getting to their car. This meant that some of the cars would block the entrance to the store so that regular customers could not get into the parking lot. This also meant that a lot of the students were left standing in front of the store waiting for their parents to be able to get in to pick them up.

Over time, the situation began to be a real problem due to the students beginning to use vulgar language and apparently having no respect for other people or their property. When asked to move along they wouldn't hesitate to curse you out and let you know they didn't have to mind or pay attention to anyone they didn't want to. Quite often customers able to get through the students were exposed to their vulgar language and bad attitudes. This situation obviously began to affect our business. No one wants to be exposed to situations like that.

By now, I had become a little skeptical of the drug manufacturers and their connection with the FDA. In order to support the finances for the FDA, Congress had made it mandatory for the drug manufacturers to contribute funding to the FDA for having their products studied and approved for use. It brings up the old maxim of he who pays plays.

I began to be aware that many of our new drugs were just offshoots or small changes in the formulation of old ones. These changes were not necessarily new drugs and quite often had very little or no advantage over the existing formulation. For instance, when a drug's patent was due to expire it became routine for the manufacturer to simply make a small change. They would add methocarbomol to lengthen the time it dissolved in the body and would label it CR, La, XL, etc. With the addition of the methocarbomol, they could get a new patent. This would extend their control over the drug. They could then establish a new wholesale price that was often much more than the previous one, and they did it under the guise that this one is newer and therefore better than the old one.

They explained to the FDA, government, and public that their research for a new drug was astronomical. New drugs are often discovered or developed by laboratories in schools. The costs of this is usually supplemented by grants from the government. The drug companies then spend much more money promoting the drug through ads and television directly to the public creating a huge demand for their new product.

Doctors wanted to be up to date in their practice and would routinely begin prescribing these forms. It also helped that the drug manufacturers were now hiring and using young, good-looking women to sell and promote their products. Now you almost never saw a man representing the companies. In the past, they always tried to hire pharmacists who knew something about these products. Now they hired these young women and would teach them just enough to sell their products.

Some of the things that transpired were quite amazing. As an example, Vibramycin had been on the market for many years and was now available in generic form. It had always been available in 100mg and 50mg doses. This offspring of tetracycline had quite often been used to treat acne and was pretty successful at it. Some manufacturers began to manufacture it in slightly different dosages and give it a new name like Oracea. They were successful in getting a patent for these new dosage strengths under these new names and sold these pills for as much as ten or more dollars a tablet while the older generic forms were selling for ten to fifteen cents per pill.

One company bought the trade name for Auralgan from Ayerst. They added a little acetic acid and got a new patent for the new formula. The old one had been on the market until the patent ran out and now the generic sold for ten to fifteen dollars. This new Auralgan sold for about two hundred dollars. Most doctors were very used to prescribing Auralgan and now the pharmacist could not substitute the old generic if the doctor wrote for Auralgan. In my mind, this is fleecing the public.

Doxycycline had been on the market as an antibiotic and the patent had run out. The generic form was available and was very inexpensive. The company decided to encapsulate the doxycycline in an enteric form, giving it a new name with a new patent and began to promote it for acne. This drug was priced at about three hundred dollars for a month's supply. In order to get the doctors to write for it they gave coupons to be handed out for three month's treatment that reduced the price to twenty-five dollars. Most acne treatments had to last much longer than three months, so after three months the drug went to the higher price. Any patient who had gotten visible benefits wanted to stay on this drug even though there was absolutely no advantage over the generic form.

The makers of Prozac saw their patent was to expire and began scrambling in order to keep their profits up. They developed a product called Sarafem. This product was exactly the same as Prozac except they sold it in a little paper package and promoted it for women with hot flashes. Then neighbors wouldn't see a bottle of Prozac in the medicine cabinets when they visited. It appeared that she was only treating hot flashes. The only problem was the public was being charged a lot more for Sarafem than the Prozac.

The salesmen's jobs were a lot easier because now the drug manufacturers could advertise these products directly to the public. They were required by law to also mention the side effects of these medicines; however, the side effects were not presented in such a way as to cause caution and warning about the use of these drugs to be noticed. These cautions came at the end of a long promotional effort and by then the patient was convinced that these drugs were the latest and best available and could now go to their doctor and demand these drugs. They felt like if the drugs were dangerous the government would not let them be promoted as they do.

It seemed to me that the doctors were being intimidated or paid by drug manufacturers to promote their drugs. In fact, there was a news article in London quoting GlaxoSmithKline saying they will stop paying doctors for promoting its drugs and will scrap prescription targets for its salesmen. They said they would stop paying doctors for attending medical conferences and said this practice appears to be a conflict of interest and puts commercial interests ahead of the best outcome for patients.

Chapter 21: Moving On

This environment as well as the increasing pressure from pharmacy benefit managers to accept lower fees for filling their prescriptions began to put extra pressure on our profits in the late nineties. It was quickly beginning to affect our bank account and it was obvious that the future didn't look too good. Two of my original partners died, and one got a divorce, leaving one partner at 25 percent and two at 12.5 percent each. We had a meeting and decided that we should sell out to a chain who seemed interested. The sale was consummated and I was asked to stay on in order to keep the business we had. The new owner began looking around for a new location for the store and purchased a lot further out on the highway close to the hospital.

We purchased a house in McDonough at Eagle's Landing Country Club because our children had migrated to Atlanta to live. When we visited them, it was simpler to have our own place to stay overnight. This house was on the golf course and we enjoyed our times there. It was especially fun when the LPGA Chick-Fil-A tournament was held there. We could walk the course and watch the LPGA players without having to buy tickets.

I thoroughly enjoyed working for the chain that bought me out. I was asked to substitute occasionally at some of the other stores. As I did so, I began to teach some of the pharmacists how to compound some of the preparations that I had been doing in the Cairo store. I suggested a list of products used in compounding that should be placed in these stores and showed them how to use them. They began to compound a lot of topical products and some suppositories. They also bought a capsule filling machine and began to use it. I gave them formulas to treat green fence posts to keep the wood from rotting, a product to toughen horse hooves, a formula for mildew prevention, and a poison ivy lotion. Welder's eye water was a popular formula, as well. I didn't give them all my formulas because I knew they would never use them.

In 2002, I was beginning to have some health problems, and the manager asked me to recommend a pharmacist to run the store. I was told they would use me as backup and relief pharmacist for the new location and I accepted. For a short while, as the new building was being constructed, I worked with the new pharmacist introducing him to our customers. I began to show him how to compound some of the specialty medications I prepared for our customers. I really looked forward to being a part-time pharmacist, but when we moved into the new location, I was told they did not want me in the store for at least three months so that the new pharmacist could take charge and the customers would not defer to me.

I was astounded at this turn of events and immediately turned in my key and my resignation. In short order, one of our good customers asked the new pharmacist for a refill of his compounded medication, so the pharmacist had to call me and ask me how to prepare it. I told him that I could not do so under the circumstances. I had tried to prepare him for these people and was told they didn't want me in the store for three months. I asked him to tell the customer to call me. I called one of my old competitors and asked him if I could use his store to meet and prepare special medications for some of my customers. He said yes and I told my customers to come to that store where I would prepare their prescriptions and administer their B-12 and allergy shots.

In a short time, the manager of the chain called me, apologized, and asked me to come back. I informed the manager I didn't want to work for anyone who wouldn't keep his word. Then the owner called and also apologized and asked me to come back. I told him no thanks, then told him same thing I had told his manager.

After getting my customers taken care of I realized I missed pharmacy very much. I then asked neighboring pharmacies if they needed part time help. K-Mart in Bainbridge offered me one day a week. Their relief pharmacist had a temporary health problem. I began working there and that was the only place I ever worked where the pharmacy was closed during lunch so that the pharmacist could eat lunch in peace. After a few weeks, their relief pharmacist was able to return so I was out of work again.

I then saw an ad in the GPHA journal looking for a relief pharmacist. The drug store was in Tifton, which was sixty miles from home. I really wanted to work, so I responded and was hired by Moon's Pharmacy.

Moon's Pharmacy was a thriving independent pharmacy. They also serviced a nursing home. At that time, people who serviced nursing homes could purchase drugs at a discount; however, the inventory had to be kept separate. The techs would switch from the retail pharmacy to the nursing home room as needed.

While working there, Moon's purchased a computer for dispensing pills. It would count the pills and place them in bottles with the label on them. They called the computer Phil. This cut down on the time techs had to count pills and label the bottles; however, they still had to monitor the level of pills in the machine. It just required a different job description. It never did cut down on the number of techs required to do the jobs.

While working here I also began to show the techs how to compound some products. They really liked doing this and talked the boss into building a clean room so they could do even more compounding. The clean room contained a hood so they could compound sterile products. I gave them some of my formulas also.

One day, my boss told me he had been diagnosed with a cancer in one of his eyes. In talking about it, I discovered he was seeing an ophthalmologist in Tallahassee I didn't think too highly of. He said the doctor told him he could cure the cancer with injections and save his eyesight. I recommended he see a doctor at Emory in Atlanta and possibly have the eyeball removed. This cancer was extremely hard to cure and the eyeball is too close to the brain. Any metastasizing would go straight to the brain with a very bad outcome. I told him he could live and see well with one eye, but he was playing with fire trying to treat it. He assured me he had faith in his doctor and began treatment.

In the meantime, his prior pharmacist came back to town and wanted his job back, so I was out of work again. I contacted Walgreens in Albany and discovered they needed some help. I started working there three days a week. I was still having to drive sixty miles to and from work.

I enjoyed working there. We had plenty of techs and we dispensed a lot of prescriptions each day. This was the first time I had seen assembly line pharmacy. They had an in-window where a tech entered the prescription into the computer. Then the pharmacist checked the entry on his computer and sent it to the scale and labeling tech. Then the filled prescription was returned to the pharmacist for verification. He would then bag the prescription for patient pick up. I spent a lot of time educating the techs and trying to improve their error rate. We opened at eight in the morning and closed at eleven at night, with each pharmacist working a ten-hour shift. So we had a good overlap of pharmacists on hand.

It was here that I first encountered using a scale to weigh the pills instead of counting them. The computer controlled the weight of pills and you just poured them into the container until the scale told you how many pills you had in the tray. I also discovered that the money was not counted at the end of the day. They used a scale to weigh each denomination and it gave you the total.

I was working away one day and looked up to see Maggie standing at the counter. She was waiting for her prescription, and when she saw me, she almost yelled out. This was the wife of the man I had made a bland Gatorade for years ago (before it was invented). We had a grand reunion and we recalled our trip to the Grand Ole Opry. She informed my co-workers about what had happened back then.

I worked here for about six months when I got a call telling me the owner of Moon's had passed away. I made it a point to go to his funeral, and it was a very sad time. He was very popular in his community, and the outpouring of love was very evident.

Our house in McDonough was very nice, but we were having problems keeping it up due to not being there very much. Our son Travis lived in Suwanee on the north side of Atlanta and told us if we sold it and bought a house near him that he would help keep it up.

In 2005, we put the Eagle's Landing house on the market and began looking for one near him. We couldn't find anything we liked right away, so we decided to build one in a neighborhood close by. The neighborhood was very close to him with practically no yards and the houses were very close together. After being used to our houses with nice yards, I felt hemmed in and was not very happy being that close to our neighbors.

We enjoyed being in the vicinity of Travis and decided to spend more time in the Atlanta area. I asked Walgreens to transfer me to North Atlanta so I could still work part-time. They agreed and I began working as a floater in Walgreens stores around North Atlanta. When I left the store in Albany, they gave me a bon voyage party and indicated they would miss me. They all signed a card expressing their love and appreciation for having worked with me. I hated to leave them.

One day while working at the store on Highway 141 at the intersection of Jay Bird Alley, a man came in late in the afternoon and asked me to check his blood pressure. I did so and asked him what was going on. He said he was feeling funny and his vision seemed fuzzy. He told me what drugs he was taking and asked me if I thought they were causing his problem. His blood pressure was in the normal range. I told him I felt he might be having transient ischemic attacks. He asked what that was and I told him they often preceded a stroke. I immediately had him take three aspirin tablets and told him to go straight home. I told him if he was not feeling normal in a short while to have his wife carry him to the emergency room. About two weeks later, he came in and thanked me for the information I had given him. He said that when he told his wife, she was concerned and carried him to the emergency room. He was admitted and spent a week in the hospital. His doctor told him that if he had not taken the aspirin and gone to the hospital he felt sure he would have had a severe stroke. He said he was feeling normal now.

One of my techs here asked me if I would cauterize a couple of skin tags for her. We didn't have any silver nitrate sticks or carbolic acid on hand, so I told her to bring in some fine sewing thread when she came to work the next day. She wanted to know what that was for. I told her I would tie the thread tightly at the base of the skin tags and in a couple of days they would fall off. She seemed skeptical, but she brought the thread and I tied them off. Sure enough on day three, the skin tags had fallen off and there was no sign they had ever been there. She said there had been no pain involved and thanked me.

I had begun to have some health problems and was not getting any satisfactory results from my doctor in Cairo. In 2007, Rosalind and Travis finally insisted I go to Travis's doctor in Duluth. After a preliminary examination and a CT scan, my new doctor made me an appointment with a urologist and cardiologist. He insisted I go to the urologist immediately. I told him I would as soon as I got back home from a funeral of a friend in Thomaston, Georgia. He insisted that I not go to the funeral, but go immediately to the urologist. Upon examining me, the urologist insisted I have a catheter inserted into my bladder. The results were astonishing. The constrictor muscles in my bladder had stopped working so I couldn't void properly and this had damaged my kidneys. He then sent me to a nephrologist where I was told that I was in stage three kidney failure.

I was not too happy having to use a catheter five to six times a day and the urologist told me that if I had prostate surgery it would solve that problem. I agreed to have the transurethral resection procedure. The procedure did not produce any benefits at all and I was stuck having to use a catheter.

The cardiologist ordered an echocardiogram and then cardiac catheterization. He told me he would call with the results shortly. When he called, he said I needed to see a cardiac surgeon and he was going to schedule an appointment. I told him that had to wait because I was going on a cruise to Alaska. I had always wanted to go and had made reservations. He told me I might have a heart attack while on the cruise, but I told him that could happen while waiting here. We went on the cruise and I really enjoyed it.

When we got home, the cardiologist called and informed me he scheduled me for a visit with a cardiac surgeon at Emory. The next thing I knew I was in the hospital recovering from open-heart surgery. I had had five bypasses. So now I am also a heart patient. I was out of work for three months and had to have a doctor's permission to return to work. This was the first time in my working career that I had been out of work due to sickness.

At this time, I had relinquished chairmanship of Grady General Hospital to a man who had been on the board almost as long as I had. I was not fully recovered from heart surgery and was unable to attend the June meeting. A couple of members informed me that Archbold Hospital had met with the board and told them the hospital would not be getting the sixty-four-slice CT scanner. They had brought some of our doctors to the meeting who agreed a sixteen-slice machine would be sufficient for their needs. Two members asked that a decision on the CT scanner be delayed until I could be there. The chairman then asked for a vote and the sixteen-slice machine was accepted.

I asked Rosalind to carry me to Cairo, and upon talking to the two members, we decided to ask for a special meeting of the board. Upon calling the chairman and asking him, he assured us that he was sure Archbold was going to purchase the sixteen-slice machine and that we needn't have a meeting. I explained to him that any three of us could call a meeting and that we were doing so. I took the floor at the called meeting. Archbold Hospital had many representatives there. I went through all the processes that the board and I had been through and reminded them that we had sold the county on accepting the SPLOST in order to purchase and install a sixty-four-slice machine.

I refuted all the points made to get the board to accept the sixteen-slice machine. The argument it shouldn't be used on pregnant women due to the excessive radiation was false because of the shorter time the patient was in the machine as compared to the sixteen-slice machine. They said that the machine now would cost in excess of eight hundred thousand dollars. I said that I could not believe that because four years ago when we passed the SPLOST the machine only cost five hundred thousand. In my experience, it was typical for equipment such as this to come down in price due to improvements and most products would cost less after a couple of years. The argument that all our scans would have to be redone at Archbold or Tallahassee Memorial was not valid because Archbold radiologists read all of our scans. The patients sent to Tallahassee would be rescanned for Archbold as well as for Grady General. I explained to the board that we had a good hospital and a good medical staff and that we should not accept anything but the best for their use. The sixteen-slice machine was now old hat and outmoded. I agreed that it would do a better job than the one we had been using, but if we were going to upgrade we needed to get the best available. After discussion, I explained we were not authorized to vote because the request for the meeting was for discussion only. I assured all the issue would come up at our next regularly scheduled meeting.

The day of our next meeting, I was called and asked to meet in Thomasville that morning with the powers that controlled everything. Since I could not yet drive, a member of the board agreed to carry me over and be in the meeting. The president and his subordinates as well as his lawyers were in attendance. They did all they could to get me to accept the sixteen-slice machine. I told them that I had spent many days telling the people of Grady County about the sixty-four-slice machine and what it could do. I had told them that Archbold's chief radiologist had assured us this machine could save as many as seven lives a year in Grady County. These assurances were what had helped pass the SPLOST.

Forcing us to accept the sixteen-slice machine would make me a liar in the minds of the people of Grady County. I had been in the county a long time and had a reputation that I would defend as strongly as I could. That when I died the only thing I could take to the grave with me would be my reputation. If they proceeded to only give us the sixteen-slice machine then I would go back to all these people and explain to them that Archbold was the one deceiving them not me. I would notify the newspapers and the radio station as to what was going on.

The board member then carried me home in order for me to rest up for the meeting that night. About three o'clock that afternoon I got a call asking me to meet with the president at the hospital an hour before the meeting. I agreed and was picked up and met with them. At this meeting, The president finally agreed they would place the sixty-four-slice machine in Grady General if I would agree to wait to get the cardiology portion for the machine until we could get a cardiologist. We went into our meeting and informed the board that we would be getting the sixty-four-slice machine.

Our current chairman had been on the board thirty years and in that position for three meetings. The September meeting was when three of our board members were either reappointed or replaced by the county commissioners. Since it was time for our chairman to be reappointed or replaced, the majority of our board members were successful in having the chairman replaced with a new member. He was very disappointed and tried to get the commissioners to not replace him; however, the board refused. If he had agreed to a called meeting when asked to do so his position on the board probably would have continued. The board members asked me to be chairman again, so I accepted even though my health situation was not good.

Walgreens allowed me to come back to work two days a week. They assigned me to the store in Cumming on Keith Bridge Road. This was a new store and the workload was not very heavy. We had a good staff of workers and within a couple of years we became one of Walgreens' busiest stores.

One day when I came into work, my manager handed me a message that she had received from one of our customers. I read the message and I quote, "Mr. Truman helped me when I came in with problems with my eyes. He explained to me what was probably going on that caused my problem and was heartfelt in taking care of me. Neither my optometrist nor my ophthalmologist had told me anything that I could understand. I left with a product he recommended. I feel much better now and can expect to get better or at least put up with my problem. Mr. Truman was truly a gentleman and the best person I have ever met. Please thank him for me." My manager thanked me and the store manager said this was the kind of message he enjoyed receiving.

On a Friday, a lady in her mid to late sixties appeared at the counter and asked me the price for sixty tablets of Pradaxa 75mg. I told her that it would be in the neighborhood of $250. She appeared distressed and told me she had been taking 150mg tablets and wanted to reduce her dose hoping that it would be less expensive. I asked her if she had insurance and she said no, but her doctor wanted her to take this expensive drug because she had had a light stroke approximately six years in the past. She said she had no problems and that the stroke had not impaired her.

She was very unhappy and said she had broken out in a rash and showed me her arms, which were covered with a rash and whelps. She said she had the rash on her chest and torso also. She thought it was caused by the Pradaxa, so she wanted to take less of it. I gave her a print out of the patient education report on Pradaxa and showed her where it stated that if you have an allergic reaction, such as she apparently had, to call your doctor. If you are allergic to something, taking less of it will not necessarily solve the problem.

She told me she was not real happy with her doctor and asked what other drugs she could possibly take instead of the Pradaxa. I told her Coumadin or aspirin each could be a possible alternative and that she should talk to her doctor. She asked what strength aspirin would work, and I told her that her doctor should be consulted. She asked what strengths aspirin was available and I told her that it came in 81mg and 325mg tablets. That like Pradaxa it would thin the blood to reduce clotting, which is what causes some types of stroke. She asked me to write down the names of Coumadin and aspirin on a card so she could remember them. She thanked me and left.

A few days later, I received a phone call at home from the pharmacist on duty who asked me if I had talked to this lady. I said yes and she asked me if I would talk to her now. The lady asked me again about the aspirin and Coumadin. She said she was going to get some aspirin and start taking it. She had discontinued the Pradaxa and her rash was much improved. She asked me if I thought the Pradaxa had caused her rash. I told her that if she had stopped taking it and the rash disappeared it was pretty strong evidence as to what caused it. I suggested once again that she talk to her doctor and reminded her I was not a doctor. She thanked me again and said she was going to buy some aspirin and begin taking it. That was the last I heard from her.

A short time after that I discovered that the maker of Pradaxa was fined four hundred million dollars by the FDA for misrepresenting Pradaxa in promotions. I also discovered that there were over one thousand lawsuits pending against the company.

In a first for the industry, I saw a news article wherein Pfizer will begin selling Viagra directly to the public. Drug manufacturers don't normally sell directly to the public. They sell in bulk to wholesalers who distribute the drugs to pharmacies, hospitals, and doctor's offices for sale to the public. In order to induce patients to use this service, Pfizer offers the first three tablets free and thirty percent off the second order. They still require a prescription.

Pfizer says they are using this procedure to counter the online pharmacies from selling fake pills. Since drug makers can't fill an individual's prescription, they have entered a contract with CVS drug stores to fill these prescriptions. This seems to me another nail in the coffin of typical drug stores. I wonder how long your neighborhood drug store will be able to stay in business. Many are holding on by offering compounding services, but the chains are now beginning to cut in on that process too.

Walgreens had to cut the tech's time due to the low reimbursements by the benefit managers, so we pharmacists had to work with a reduced staff. On top of that, Walgreens refused to accept a new contract with even lower rates offered by one of the largest insurance companies. I approved this situation because I had been thinking for years that we should not accept a payment lower than our operating costs demanded. This resulted in even more drastic cuts in help.

Grocery store pharmacies are expected to be loss leaders in order to get more people in the stores. While they are waiting for their prescriptions to be filled they are exposed to many impulse purchases. Suddenly all retail pharmacies are bombarded and accepting lower rates because everybody else is doing it.

A lady stepped up to the counter and asked for a refill for her husband's Viagra. Checking the computer, I told her that the prescription had no refills and we would have to have a new prescription. Since it was Friday night, I told her it would be Monday before her doctor would issue him a new prescription. She said, "Just sell me one tablet." I explained that I could not do that because of state and federal law. She said, "Well what in the hell will I do this weekend?" I assured her I did not know the answer to that. She left and returned in a little while and asked where the OTC Extenze male enhancement tablets were. She said, "I hope this works," and left the store.

Shortly after this I contracted pneumonia and wound up in the hospital for a week. When the doctor told me I had pneumonia I told him he must have misdiagnosed me because I had taken the pneumonia shot. He informed me there was more than one type of pneumonia and the shots didn't protect you from all of them. I probably should have known this because the flu shots the government insists the public take every year don't necessarily protect you from the flu. In some years, they are only twenty to thirty percent effective.

Reflections of a Pharmacist

My views on pharmacy have changed almost as much as the profession itself. I wish it could go back to the type of practice in the fifties.

Thinking about what I had witnessed in pharmacies, I realized that you cannot help someone unless they want help. Quite often, I observed someone treating a problem wrong or not sufficiently and suggested a change. Most often, when I initiated the conversation, the solution I offered was refused. You cannot help an alcoholic until he reaches the point of wanting help. This also applies to someone hooked on narcotics, sleeping pills, or tranquilizers. Generally, these people have to reach rock bottom before they accept the fact that that they need help. Then when they ask for help or advice, they sometimes would accept and quite often be thankful.

It dawned on me that I remembered a comment in school about an idiosyncratic reaction to a drug. This meant that after taking a drug a while your body gets used to it, and if you stop taking it, you begin having the symptoms that started you on the drug. This apparently is true of narcotics and sleeping or nerve pills. This is one reason why so many addicts or habitual users cannot successfully quit their habit.

I also began to understand that people who felt sick or bad always seemed to get better as soon the doctor put a name on their malady.

The doctors call this a diagnosis. In our area one season, a lot of young children began to break out in a rash. It seemed that it was an epidemic. The doctors could not figure out where it was coming from and what was causing it. They began to call the situation fifth disease. This really helped mamas because now they knew what was wrong with their child. The rashes would go away after two to three weeks and the family was proud of the doctors and the medications they had prescribed.

The doctors were beginning to see more and more people with aches and pains that did not have an apparent cause. These people's muscles hurt and they had aches all over. In order to give this situation a name they began to calling it fibromyalgia. This malady I felt was the result of depression. I noticed many people trapped in a bad marriage or deeply in debt would become depressed. Many times they did not know what was wrong, they just felt bad and ached all over. Many of them would not admit they were depressed or did not know they were. Doctors began treating them with pain medication. The drug companies then came out with special medication to treat this situation. Most of these medications were based on antidepressant drugs and prescribed for the pain. Once again, people were relieved they had a disease with a name and proudly blamed their feelings on fibromyalgia.

With the increased load of work at the pharmacy and my declining health, I realized that I must retire. When I told my co-workers in the pharmacy, they were very disappointed and expressed their reluctance to see me leave. I explained to them that my doctor told me it would be better to walk out rather than be carried out on a gurney. I gave my two weeks' notice to the regional pharmacy manager, who told me he hated to hear this, but he understood and wished me well in my retirement.

When I told my son Travis I was retiring, he asked me, "How many pills have you counted, Daddy?" On reflection, it must have been quite a few.

My co-workers surprised me at the end of my shift on my last day of work in April 2013 with a going away party. All of the people in the store crowded into the pharmacy department to say good-bye. I was presented with a very nice going away present and given a banner signed by all of them saying, "We will miss you." I sure hated to have to leave them.

My next hospital board meeting was in September, and I knew my health was getting worse, so I made the decision to inform the county commissioners I would retire after the September meeting and relinquish my place on the board. I met with them and gave them a report on the condition and a brief history of the hospital. I explained our hospital was ranked in the top one hundred rural hospitals in the United States, that we had the latest and best equipment installed, and were debt free. Our medical staff and supporting staff were among the best anywhere. The hospital created or supported more than three hundred jobs for the county and contributed over thirty-eight million dollars per year to Grady County's economy. The hospital was no longer referred to as a "Band-Aid station." The commissioners thanked me for the job that our board had done.

The next morning the *Cairo Messenger* published an article describing my retirement on the front page, and when I got to the editorial page, I discovered that the editor, in bold headlines, stated, "We need more citizens like Truman Lastinger."

During the September meeting of the board, I was interrupted and presented with a plaque from the board expressing their gratitude for my leadership in having a successful hospital. The hospital administrator presented me with a plaque honoring me for my thirty-seven years' service on the board. The board also informed me they commissioned a portrait to be painted of me to be placed in the hospital in recognition of my service. The Grady County Board of Commissioners also presented me with a proclamation thanking me for my service.

October 10, early in the morning, I suffered an acute myocardial infarction and spent the next eight days in the hospital. I was told they could not insert stents or do angioplasty because my bypasses precluded them reaching the area that needed help. The situation left me with atrial fibrillation. This is a condition I hadn't had. After working in pharmacy fifty-eight years and fifty as a registered pharmacist, apparently, I retired from my duties just in time.

About the Author

Truman Lastinger is a retired pharmacist of over fifty years. Born into a Georgia sharecropper family, Truman received his degree in pharmacy from Mercer University before establishing Truman's Drugs in Cairo, Georgia. Truman served as Grady County's Chairman of the Hospital Authority and is the author of numerous articles for the pharmacist journal *Drug Topics*.